Strategy and Diplomacy
1870–1945

Paul Kennedy has been Professor of History at Yale University since the autumn of 1983. After obtaining a first-class honours degree from the University of Newcastle in 1966, he studied for a D.Phil. at the University of Oxford. From 1970 until 1983 he was Lecturer, Reader, then Professor at the University of East Anglia. He has also been a Theodor Heuss Research Fellow, Oxford; Fellow of the Alexander von Humboldt Foundation, Bonn; and Visiting Fellow at the Institute for Advanced Study, Princeton.

Paul Kennedy's other books include *The Rise and Fall of British Naval Mastery* (1976), *The Rise of the Anglo-German Antagonism, 1860-1914* (1980) and *The Realities Behind Diplomacy: Background Influences on British External Policy, 1865-1980* (Fontana, 1981).

Paul Kennedy

Strategy and Diplomacy 1870–1945

Eight Studies

Fontana Paperbacks

First published in Great Britain by George Allen & Unwin 1983
First issued in Fontana Paperbacks 1984

Reproduced, printed and bound in Great Britain by
Hazell Watson and Viney Limited,
Member of the BPCC Group,
Aylesbury, Bucks.

IN MEMORIAM
Basil Liddell Hart
and Arthur Marder

Contents

Acknowledgements

I am grateful to the following for permission to reprint articles originally published elsewhere: to Professor Roy E. Jones, editor of the *Review of International Studies* (formerly *British Journal of International Studies*), and Messrs Longman, for essay 1; to the editors of the *Militärgeschichtliche Mitteilungen* for essay 2; to Professor Edward Ingram and the *International History Review*, for essay 3; to Professor Gerald Jordan, and Croom Helm, for essay 4; to the *Militärgeschichtliches Forschungsamt* and Droste Verlag, for essay 5; and to Barrie Pitt, editor of Purnell's *History of the Second World War*, for essay 7.

I should also like to acknowledge my continued debt to Helen Fraser at Fontana, and to my literary agent Bruce Hunter.

Norwich, January 1983

I

Britain's World Policy: the Larger Trends

1

The term 'appeasement', like 'imperialism', is one burdened with emotional and ideological overtones. Despite the widespread attention which A. J. P. Taylor's revisionist work *The Origins of the Second World War* (1961) has received in the press and elsewhere, today's politicians still use the word 'appeasement' in a pejorative sense, as meaning the cowardly surrender to the threat of force.

In the world of historical scholarship, however, the age of 'appeasement' has been studied with much less emotion and with a far greater understanding of the complex problems which faced British foreign-policy-makers in the 1930s. One obvious reason for this more sympathetic approach has been the opening of the relevant papers in the Public Record Office, which has allowed historians to trace the British government's consideration of the arguments advanced for and against the 'appeasement' of Germany, Italy and Japan.

The second historiographical trend has been the interest shown by scholars in analysing Britain's decline as a Great Power in *long-term perspective*, and in asking questions about the 'manner' in which successive British administrations sought to preserve their country's overextended global position in the post-Palmerstonian decades, when the economic and strategical tides were increasingly unfavourable to the British Empire. The essay which follows was an early attempt to see some *pattern* in British foreign policy and, in consequence, possesses the weaknesses as well as the merits of any historical attempt to simplify the past. It was first presented to the annual conference of the British International Studies Association in 1975, and later appeared in the October 1976 issue of the *British Journal of International Studies* (now the *Review of International Studies*).

The Tradition of Appeasement in British Foreign Policy, 1865–1939

If the policy of 'appeasement' is inextricably associated in the historical consciousness with the efforts of Neville Chamberlain's government to preserve peace with the dictators in the 1930s, its origins have been recognized by numerous writers as going back many years before the immediate crises concerning the Sudetenland, Prague and the Polish Corridor. Some have traced its roots to the failure to prevent Japanese aggression in 1931 or Italy's attack upon Abyssinia in 1935; others, with more sense of the positive side of 'appeasement', have focused upon the attitude of the British government and public towards Germany during and after the Versailles settlement; while Mr Gilbert, going a little further back in time, has argued that 'appeasement was born' at the moment of the British declaration of war in 1914.[1] Few, if any, commentators have suggested that one should seek the beginnings of 'appeasement' *before* that event, however.

It is the purpose of this paper, on the other hand, to argue that the real origins of the policy must be traced much further back, to the middle of the nineteenth century, and that the nature of British foreign policy did not greatly alter in its overall framework from that time until 1939; that there is, in fact, a British model of 'appeasement' whose operation is detectable for some seventy-five years or so before Munich, and that it was only after that particular crisis that this model finally broke down. To maintain such an argument a great deal depends, as it always has done, upon the meaning of the very word 'appeasement'. It may well be, as Professor Medlicott has urged, that the term is so contentious that it would be simpler to avoid its use altogether;[2] but the fact remains that, since it has proved impracticable to banish the expression, the only alternative open to us is to define its meaning as clearly as possible. Throughout this paper 'appeasement' will be held to mean *the policy of settling international (or, for that matter, domestic) quarrels by admitting and satisfying grievances through rational negotiation and compromise, thereby avoiding the resort to an armed conflict which would be expensive, bloody, and possibly very dangerous.* It is in essence a *positive* policy, based upon certain optimistic assumptions about man's inherent reasonableness, as was clearly the case when executed by Gladstone in the 1880s or Lloyd George in 1919, but it also contained that *negative* element, the fear and horror of conflict, which came increasingly to the fore in the 1930s and caused the word itself to take on a fully pejorative meaning. Indeed, until Munich or thereabouts, it may be said that the term 'appeasement' was a perfectly respectable one, and that the changed meaning of the word was concomitant with the final collapse of the original policy.

The Model

'Appeasement' in the above sense, it is worth arguing, has been a particularly British form of diplomacy since the middle of the nineteenth century, and was rooted in the following distinguishable, although often interconnected, motives:

Morality. The application of the concepts of 'justice' and 'morality' to politics has been prominent in British thought from the time of the evangelical movement onwards and, although receiving many a setback and much criticism from cynics, remained a strong feature among the formative political elements.[3] Reinforcing this idea of the fair and pacific settlement of disputes, and the disapproval of the use (and, often, the existence) of armed force, was the Cobdenite vision of the world being a harmonious community. International arbitration, the abjuration of war as an instrument of national policy except in cases of self-defence, the emphasis upon conciliation and compromise, combined to produce a climate in which it was necessary for statesmen, particularly those favouring action which might lead to hostilities, to justify their policy in moral terms.

16

Economics. As the so-called 'workshop of the world', mid-Victorian Britain was at the centre of a global economic system, importing raw materials and foodstuffs, exporting manufactured goods and coal, financing overseas developments, and providing services as a shipper, insurer and commodity-dealer. She had by this stage abandoned her previously successful mercantilist policy in favour of one based upon the calculation that Britain would gain the predominant share of an unlimited and ever-increasing world wealth through the free interchange of goods. While this had many economic advantages, it also meant that she was, more than most other countries, a 'hostage' to the international boom. Any disruption of trade, whether by a temporary slump or, worse still, war, affected her economy more than those of her more protectionist neighbours. This basic situation did not alter by the turn of the century, when such states as the USA and Germany were overtaking Britain industrially, for she still maintained her dominance in 'invisibles'; and this trade was even more vulnerable to the collapse of the world economy (as was shown in 1929–33) than that in 'visibles', many of which could be disposed of domestically behind tariff walls. Most British statesmen were well aware that war would inevitably mean a reduction in exports, an increase in imports, a decrease in invisible earnings, and losses of manpower, shipping, etc. The preservation of peace was, for an economy such as Britain's (but not, say, for that of Nazi Germany), a vital national interest.

Furthermore, the relative industrial decline of Britain from the 1870s onwards meant that she had an ever-harder task in adjusting ends to means: that is to say, her national wealth was increasing too slowly to pay both for expensive social and economic reforms at home *and* for the 'fire insurance' of large defence forces in an uncertain world. An expensive arms-race with some foreign power, in addition to increasing the risk of eventual hostilities, also exacerbated this dilemma. For such a budgetary reason alone, British governments could normally be relied upon to seek to end an arms-race by diplomatic means, and thus to reduce defence spending.

Global position. In contrast to the other Great Powers, Britain had interests in every part of the world. Even in the post-1815 period, when the Royal Navy's supremacy and the concentration of her rivals upon internal affairs made Britain more secure than ever before or since, this meant that her statesmen had to take into account their multifarious national obligations and could not devote all their attention or energies to one region. By the later nineteenth century, when other powers were challenging the Royal Navy's mastery of the seas, when land power (in the form of mass armies, strategical railways, etc.) was gaining ground in relation to sea power, and when many more dangers to Britain's imperial position were arising, the government was beginning to perceive with alarm the increasing gap between the country's strength and its commitments. The British Empire was becoming, to use Liddell Hart's later expression, the greatest example of strategical overextension in history. If all this tended to compel the government increasingly to consider which regions had priority and in which it might be necessary to give way gracefully, the simple existence of multifold dangers and obligations could occasionally 'paralyse' decision-making, for it was appreciated that if Britain concentrated too much in one region, she would have no strength to protect the others. Whether she clung on in all regions or escaped from some, her stretched global position was an enormously powerful reason for compromise with other states and for the pacific settlement of disputes with them – as, indeed, the government's defence and foreign policy advisers frequently pointed out.[4]

Domestic situation. The steady extension of the franchise from 1867 onwards made politicians increasingly aware of the factor of 'public opinion', whether expressed by mass-circulation papers and interest-groups or by electoral results; and although the public could be excited upon a point of national honour and moral wrong, it was generally recognized as disliking wars, especially expensive ones, and as being a brake upon a belligerent foreign policy. Moreover, the electorate was ever more reluctant to deny itself social and economic reforms in deference to a large defence budget. The declaration of war had, therefore, to be 'popular'. In addition, the continuous need to introduce constitutional, social and economic reforms to reflect the changing demands and balance within this ever-widening body politic was seen by most politicians as being their most vital task if they wished to stay in office. All but a few concentrated upon home affairs and regarded foreign complications as distractions which had to be settled as expeditiously and painlessly as possible.

To sum up, there were always such motives – moral, economic, strategical and domestic – operating in the public consciousness and prompting British governments from the mid-nineteenth century onwards to favour a foreign policy which was, with rare exceptions (e.g. 1878, 1911), pragmatic, conciliatory and reasonable. It was a policy predicated upon the assumption that, provided national interests were not too deleteriously affected, the peaceful settlement of disputes was much more to Britain's advantage than recourse to war. It was not merely in the 1930s, therefore, that 'Peace as National Interest' is a valid description of Britain's overall strategy.[5]

But precisely because this policy was pragmatic, a compromise, a peculiar mixture of morality and calculated national interest, it attracted criticism from two groups who, from their opposing points of view, advocated different conceptions of the bases upon which British foreign policy should be constructed. The first was the 'Left' or the 'Idealists', both inexact terms but used here to describe that strong 'dissenter' tradition in British foreign policy, i.e. the Cobdenite, 'Little Englander' or, later, neo-Marxist viewpoint, which disliked overseas wars and entanglements as immoral, a drain upon the economy, a diversion from social reforms and a devious way of propping up an obsolete aristocratic or capitalistic system.[6] Although in many ways this attitude was similar to that analysed in the 'model' above, it was more extreme and doctrinaire, and the Left was swift to criticize if it felt that the government was deviating from the straight and narrow paths: witness the Cobdenite isolationists' disapproval of *any* form of European entanglement even if it was advocated by Gladstone on behalf of the Concert of Europe; the criticism of Grey's foreign policy when it failed to secure reconciliation with Germany; and the disapproval of post-1919 administrations for not fully embracing the ideals of the League of Nations. The realities of power, the constraints upon statesmen in office, the natural impetus towards 'continuity' in foreign policy, and the need felt even by radical-Liberal and Labour administrations to balance what was ideal with what was practicable, was rarely a problem for this group.

On the other side of the political sprectrum was the 'Right' or the 'Realists', again an unsatisfactory term but used here to describe those who felt that the idea of a world living in permanent harmony was utopian, that might rather than right had usually had more influence upon international affairs, and that the government should not flinch from the use of armed force to defend national honour and interests.[7] This group rarely found the armed services adequate for all the country's obligations, was less prone to accept the assurances of foreign statesmen, regarded its own Left as being unrealistic or even traitorous, and expected to have most influence when a Conservative government was in office, although it was also willing to criticize its own party leaders for being too ready to compromise and conciliate.

The complete 'model', then, sees not only a basically pragmatic and reasonable tradition in British foreign policy since 1865, but also the existence of two non-governmental sentiments, one favouring more 'appeasement' and the other less. It is a crude outline, and in reality the pattern varies, at least in its emphases, from one period to the next; but a brief examination of the course of British foreign policy since that date suggests that it might indeed be graced with the title of a 'tradition'.

The Tradition Established, 1865–1914

The year 1865 is significant here, of course, because it was not until Palmerston's death – and as a reaction to his internal and external policies – that his successors were able to initiate the tradition described above. Under Gladstone in particular, they adopted, first, a strategy of internal 'appeasement', by which is meant that broad series of reforms in the structures of government so that they were more in line with the economic developments and social demands of the day; hence, following Disraeli's 1867 Reform Act came the sweeping changes in the army, education, civil service, Irish disestablishment, etc. instituted by the Liberals. Furthermore, they also executed a policy of external 'appeasement', both as a corollary to their domestic reforms and because the Schleswig-Holstein affair had exposed the limitations of Britain's ability to intervene on the continent. This disengagement did not mean pure isolationism, but it did increase the government's preference for rational and peaceful solutions to international problems, the best examples here being Clarendon's attempts to secure mutual armed force reductions in Europe, with arguments based upon morality and political economy; the endeavours to persuade both France and Prussia to respect Belgian neutrality; and the agreement to abide by the *Alabama* tribunal's findings (a decision which Bismarck, for one, thought a sign of weakness and decadence).[8]

As a consequence of the above, the government was criticized by the Left for getting entangled in European diplomacy, whereas the reaction from the Right was to display alarm at what it claimed was a policy of national weakness. Indeed, the pacific, cautious, mild-mannered handling of foreign affairs by Gladstone's first administration gave Disraeli the chance to secure for the Tories the patriotic 'card' which the Liberals had discarded after the death of Palmerston. In Disraeli's view, Britain should have had more say in the outcome of the Franco-Prussian War, should not have allowed Russia to abrogate unilaterally the Black Sea clauses of 1856, and should not have permitted the Dominions to sever their ties with the home-country.[9] When in office, therefore, he demonstrated that mixture of assertiveness and concern which permeated his Crystal Palace speech, and deliberately – one might say, artificially – sought to adopt a muscular, non-appeaser stance (in the Eastern Crisis, the defence of India, the purchase of Suez Canal shares, a forward policy in West Africa, Zululand/Transvaal and Afghanistan), all of which played into the hands of Gladstone in the latter's Midlothian campaign, the speeches of which, in their attitude to other states, were not far removed from those used by British statesmen in the 1920s and 1930s.

Gladstone's second administration represented, therefore, a deliberate attempt to return to what he believed was the traditional moral and pragmatic basis of British policy when it was not being 'debauched' by people like Palmerston and Disraeli. Encouragement was given to the concept of the 'Concert of Europe' (as opposed to the Bismarckian concept of power-blocs), and to the resolution of international problems through the friendly cooperation of the Great Powers; a retreat was made from Disraelian adventures in South Africa and Afghanistan; and this overall attitude of avoiding trouble and seeking a reasonable compromise with the demands of others could be seen in India (under Ripon's viceroyalty), in Ireland (the Land Act, Arrears Act and Liberal cooperation with Parnell) and at home (the third Reform Bill and other reforms designed to accommodate the aspirations of the working classes).

This policy of sweet reasonableness again ran into problems in a world still unconverted to Gladstonian principles, however, and the government felt itself compelled by events to occupy Egypt (to restore order), to extend the colonial empire (as a defensive measure against Franco-German annexations in 1884–5), and to take a harder line in Ireland (again, to restore order). But a detailed study of even these actions reveals men earnestly struggling to solve political problems on a rational and ethical basis. Predictably enough, their compromises were attacked on the one hand by the Radicals for not going far enough on the domestic side and for going too far over Egypt; and, on the other hand, by the Conservative opposition, the Whigs and the increasingly nervous middleclass intellectuals for going too far with internal reforms and not far enough in the defence of foreign and imperial interests and in the maintenance of maritime supremacy. 'Appeasement' in Ireland, i.e. Gladstone's conversion to Home Rule, brought much of this latter feeling to a head and led to the Liberal downfall.[10]

Even in the period 1886–1914 (which can be treated as one because of the emphasis given then to 'continuity' in British foreign policy), the tradition may still be said to have been maintained, despite such manifestations to the contrary as the Boer War, the reconquest of the Sudan and the Fashoda confrontation, naval races with France and Russia and later with Germany, and patriotic press agitations. For, when one examines the *broad trends* in British foreign policy in these three decades, and especially the workings of the 'Official Mind', there is a strong case for arguing that the basic pattern, although upset by displays of bellicosity and somewhat lacking in the moral aspect of 'appeasement', remained the same.

In particular, the background factors affecting the formulation of policy intensified in these years. Domestically, politicians were having to respond more and more to democracy's demand for reforms in education, the Poor Law, national insurance and pensions, and thus the question of 'guns or butter' was being increasingly posed by the rival parties. Moreover, with the steady rise of a Labour Party *per se*, both Liberals and Conservatives recognized that they would have to tilt their electoral appeals more than ever to the 'working man'. On occasion a patriotic appeal would work (e.g. the 1900 election) but that was a short-lived and risky platform (as the 1906 election showed), and it would be fair to say that the growth of democracy favoured the 'Left' unless Conservatives were flexible enough to modify their principles and to make themselves attractive electorally to more than the middle classes. But all this meant that extreme caution had to be exercised over questions involving peace or war, and that the pressure upon financial resources intensified, defence budgets especially being a source of continual political controversy.[11] Worse still, it was in these years that Britain's relative world position openly showed a decline occurring in industrial, commercial, colonial, naval and military terms. By the turn of the century, with such acute problems arising as those in South Africa, the Western Hemisphere, the Mediterranean and Near East, the approaches to India, and in China, with Britain eclipsed by newer states in steel, chemical and electrical production, with defence expenditures at new heights (despite the navy proposing to abandon the Two Power Standard and the army's deficiencies exposed by the Boer War), there was a great deal of truth in Joseph Chamberlain's description of the 'weary Titan, staggering under the too vast orb of his own fate'.[12]

Secondly, the long-term pattern of foreign policy in this period was to solve problems by 'appeasing'. Faced with all these difficulties, British policy was bound to incline towards a reduction of commitments, the elimination of antagonisms, and the avoidance of confrontations which might lead to war, especially with a Great Power. Relations with the expanding United States furnish the best example here.[13] War with such a fellow Anglo-Saxon country was regarded as particularly immoral and 'unnatural'; it would also be a disaster economically; it would give Britain's other rivals their opportunity elsewhere in the world; and the defence advisers were pessimistic as to its eventual outcome for the British Empire. Whether one emphasized the negative or the positive motives, everything pointed to a policy of 'appeasement', which was in fact carried out. Washington's right to interfere in the Venezuela/ British Guiana dispute was recognized; Britain abandoned her half 'share' in the future isthmian canal; Canada was given little support over the Alaskan boundary quarrel once London felt that Roosevelt was serious in his threats of action; and British naval and military forces were withdrawn from the Western Hemisphere, which became incontestably an American sphere of influence.

Even the intractable question of Anglo-German relations after 1906 was not attended without frequent attempts at reconciliation which bear comparison with those of the 1930s. Hopes were placed in international agreements (Hague conferences) to reduce the burden of armaments. When this failed, proposals were made for bilateral arms reductions, such as Churchill's 'naval holiday' idea. Colonial concessions in the Middle East and Africa were suggested to Germany, in recognition for her claim for a fairer share of the world's raw materials. Binding military guarantees to France were avoided, lest this provoke controversy. Haldane's mission to Berlin in 1912 was a forerunner of frequent journeys by British statesmen there in the 1930s. And Anglo-German friendship societies, stressing common cultural and political ties, were set up and flourished. The size of the German fleet, and the prospect of a German defeat of France and the Low Countries, could never be ignored by London and ruled out any declaration of disinterest in what Berlin did; yet the natural response of the British government was to try to solve matters of dispute by compromise, rational discussion and mutual understanding, thereby avoiding the dreadful toll in men and material which the outbreak of a great war would bring. Between 1912 and 1914, the years of the so-called *detente* in Anglo-German relations, it appeared that this policy was paying off.[14]

Once again, too, the policy of pragmatic compromise attracted criticism from the Left and the Right. To the former, the British government's diplomacy still involved the country far too heavily in the game of power-politics, it diverted attention and funds from domestic affairs, and it encouraged the jingos. When relations with France or the United States or Russia were poor, a settlement of differences (usually at Britain's expense, despite the emphasis upon mutual goodwill and tolerance) was favoured; when Germany was the problem, it was urged that concessions should be made to her, the navy budget should be cut as a gesture of good faith, and no entangling commitments should be made with Germany's foes. The ideals of 'Peace, Retrenchment, Reform' made the Left unalterably opposed to foreign commitments and impatient when Liberal governments displayed too much caution and reserve in executing foreign policy along the lines of these high-minded principles.[15]

For the Right, visibly alarmed not only at domestic developments but at the obvious signs of Britain's steady decline as a world power, the exact opposite was true. What they sought was an end to this policy of retreat, an indication that Britain would no longer be 'pushed around', a rejection of left-wing policies which led to the disintegration and decay of the Empire, the United Kingdom and British society itself, and a thoroughgoing plan to counter all this by the regeneration of the whole body politic.[16] And if Liberal administrations were most frequently the target, this did not mean that Conservative governments escaped unscathed: the Salisbury/Balfour administration of 1895–1905 was criticized, for example, for failing to protect British interests in China, for being too 'soft' towards France over Fashoda, for neglecting the maintenance of British naval supremacy, for the pathetic performance of the army during the Boer War, and for cooperating with Germany over Venezuela and Baghdad Railway matters.

The Tradition Continued, 1919–38

In view of the above, is it not valid to argue that the now infamous 'appeasement' of the unsatisfied nations (especially Germany) in the interwar years was to a very large extent a revival of older habits, the differences being ones of degree and not kind? Only in the very late stages of this era, it seems, does the pattern break down and the policy of 'appeasement' come to be regarded as something shameful.

The *moral* overtones which permeated post-1919 attitudes towards international affairs, for example, were pure Gladstonism, reinforced rather than diluted through their recent articulation by an American statesman, Woodrow Wilson, himself a life-long admirer of Gladstone.[17] The entire League of Nations idea was mid-nineteenth-century internationalism writ large, and it is therefore quite predictable that, of all the Great Powers, Britain should have been the most enthusiastic about the ideals of Geneva. The pacific settlement of all disputes, the rule of law rather than the rule of force, the condemnation of those old-fashioned and dangerous patriotic sentiments, the turning of swords into ploughshares and, above all, the belief in the sanctity and efficacy of an international 'public opinion', which would deter aggressors by moral suasion alone, were parts of this tradition, now raised to new heights by the Union of Democratic Control, the League of Nations Union, the Liberal and Labour parties, the National Peace Council, the Peace Pledge Union and all the smaller groups which grew up and flourished in the interwar years.[18] Equally 'Gladstonian', and of particular importance in the 'appeasement' of Germany, was the concept of national self-determination; what was claimed for the Saarland, the Rhineland, Austria and the Sudetenland in the 1930s, the right of the majority to decide their own political future, was similar to that which the Grand Old Man had claimed for the Italians, the Boers, the Afghans and the Bulgars in the 1850s and 1870s. The disastrous course of the Great War, which had exposed the consequences of international jealousies, arms-races, secret diplomacy, imperialism and the like, had made the British public more receptive than ever before to the politics of moral enthusiasm and international amity, and the general intellectual climate (at least, if measured by the anti-war literature of Graves, Owen, Blunden and others, the 'revisionist' histories on the War Guilt question, the creation of the Left Book Club) mirrored and increased this awareness.[19]

The *economic* motives for 'appeasement' were, if anything, even more compelling, compared with Gladstone's time, than the moral ones. The traditional Victorian economy, as Hobsbawm puts it, 'crashed into ruins between the two world wars'; it not only ceased to grow, it actually contracted for a while.[20] The worldwide slump after 1929 caused many already struggling industries to collapse, unemployment to rise alarmingly, investment to shrink, protectionism to flourish, Britain's invisible earnings to contract even more rapidly than her trade in visibles, and (in 1933) the beginnings of a balance-of-payments problem. It did not, however, alter the economic orthodoxy of the Treasury, which insisted upon reductions in public expenditure as the first step to counter the crisis. Given the contemporary political and ideological scenario, defence spending was the obvious victim – a decision which, however justifiable in the harmonious atmosphere of Locarno, appeared more questionable in the threatening circumstances of the 1930s. Yet, even when the Ten Year Rule was abandoned in 1932 and the Empire's many defence deficiencies were being catalogued, it was simply not possible for Britain to rearm as quickly as the military experts wished. A whole host of recent studies has illustrated the dreadful dilemma in which the British government found itself after 1935; between a heavy rearmament programme which might possibly give security but which would ruin the economy (the 'fourth arm of defence', as Inskip put it); and a less ambitious programme which, while avoiding financial ruin, left Britain appallingly weak in military terms. It was a dilemma not solved until 1941 (if then) by the creation of lend-lease, but throughout the 1930s it provided one of the most powerful arguments for the pacific settlement of overseas disputes.[21]

The same could be said of the *global/strategic* motive for 'appeasement', which is clearly related with the economic one. As a Foreign Office memorandum of 1926, listing all of Britain's obligations, put it: 'We have got all that we want – perhaps more. Our sole object is to keep what we have and to live in peace.'[22] But this was easier said than done when there were so many others in the world who sought a change in the *status quo*. In the post-1919 years a weakened Britain already faced problems in attempting to 'appease' the demands of Irish, Indian, Egyptian and Palestine nationalists on the one hand, and the desire by the Dominions for greater autonomy on the other; but the almost simultaneous rise of threats from Japan, Italy and Germany – and all this at a time when the United States was in an isolationist mood, many of the Dominions desirous of following suit, Russia an unpredictable and possibly malevolent factor, and France ridden by an unattractive mixture of obstinacy and fear – created an impossible gulf between Britain's global obligations and her capacity to fulfil them.[23] Hence the warning – one of many – of the Chiefs of Staff in December 1937:

> We cannot foresee the time when our defence forces will be strong enough to safeguard our trade, territory and vital interests against Germany, Italy and Japan at the same time. . . . We cannot exaggerate the importance from the point of view of Imperial Defence of any political or international action which could be taken to reduce the number of our potential enemies and to gain the support of potential allies.[24]

As Michael Howard has observed, the Chiefs of Staff were in effect asking for a repetition of Lansdowne's post-1900 feat of settling Britain's defence problems in the Far East, Western Hemisphere, Mediterranean, Africa and India; that is, 'to extricate the country, by diplomatic manoeuvre, from the prospect of a conflict against a combination of adversaries which in their professional judgement could not be sustained'.[25] Nevertheless, it might also be added that, as the crisis in British world policy developed throughout the 1930s, so correspondingly did the alarm at the country's manifest defence weaknesses and the dread at the losses and horrors which war would bring slowly begin to dominate the consciousness of both Neville Chamberlain's government and the people at large. The much publicized expansion of the *Luftwaffe*, and the dawning realization that British cities were no longer invulnerable to the direct effects of war, introduced a factor which had never existed in the days of the *Pax Britannica*. In other words, the *negative* rather than *positive* motives for 'appeasement' were coming to the fore – and thereby encouraging the notion that the policy was a craven surrender to threats rather than the wise and rational application of moral principles. It is doubtful, however, whether this was the general view of 'appeasement' before the Munich crisis.

If the strategical grounds for 'appeasement' were enhanced in the interwar years, so, too, were the *domestic political* reasons. As I have argued elsewhere,

> the 1920s mark the real *end* of that long era in which Britain's policies were decided by a select group of aristocrats, country squires and men of commerce, who argued without much concern for the views of the masses about the 'national interest' and who usually displayed a wish to preserve that interest energetically, if need be by armed force; and the real *beginning* of the period when the attitude of the majority of the population in regard to improved social services – pensions, insurance, health, education, etc. – was to be the most influential factor of all in the success or failure of governments.[26]

Nor was the 'impact of Labour' as the central feature in British politics confined to the early 1920s alone.[27] With this uncertain domestic scene, and with a public opinion psychologically scarred by the First World War, sympathetic to the internationalist/pacifist ideals propagated by the League of Nations Union and other anti-militarist groups, and quite failing to see the need for large defence forces or a vigorous foreign policy when the 'war to end all wars' had just finished, governments, even those with traditional sympathies for the preservation of British power abroad, had to respond in order to survive electorally. As Baldwin (then Chancellor of the Exchequer) put it in 1923, defence expenditure *had* to be cut, otherwise

> the inevitable result will be the stabilization of taxation at something very near to its present level (5/- in the £1), the consequence of which may easily be the substitution for the present Government of one whose regard for the defence Services is not particularly marked.[28]

And the same awareness of public opinion, especially when the latter was articulated so constantly by 'Idealists' such as Cecil, Angell, Murray and others between the early 1920s and 1936,[29] made it impossible for the British government to contemplate, say, intervention in the Far East, or guarantees to East European states, even had other factors not ruled such measures out of order in the first place. Only when the public was swayed by moral arguments, such as in the Abyssinian affair, did an opportunity arise for abandoning passivity in foreign policy; but even there confusion existed over such crucial points as the institution of sanctions, while the economic and global/strategical factors further suggested a policy of caution. In any case, with the Labour Party and the trade unions making known their opposition to a 'capitalists' war' – a conflict which only they had the privilege of defining – the policy of 'appeasement' appeared to be the only feasible one until the domestic political scene altered.

It was, then, a combination of all the above factors – moral earnestness and a desire to avoid war, belief in an international harmony between peoples, awareness of Britain's weak economic position and her particular dependence upon world peace, concern about her global obligations and the inability of her defence forces to fulfil them, and sensitivity to an electorate which disliked foreign entanglements, power-politics and expensive wars – which provides the explanation for Britain's 'appeasement' policy. Whether we examine policy towards Japan;[30] or Italy;[31] or Germany itself,[32] we can never travel far without encountering these familiar features. All that this paper has done is to suggest that, far from being a peculiar condition of British foreign policy in the interwar years, the structures of 'appeasement' have had a far longer heritage. It was, after all, the natural policy of a Britain steadily losing her dominant role in world affairs, steadily becoming democratized, and steadily recognizing that, for a mixture of ethical and pragmatic reasons, the conciliatory approach in diplomacy was of greater advantage to the country than the resort to threats or even to the use of force.

It was perhaps equally inevitable that the reappearance in heightened form of this tradition after 1919 should again provoke criticism from the Left and the Right. The constant pressure from 'Idealist' circles has been alluded to above, has been covered in many studies, and need not be repeated in detail here. It is sufficient to recall that their major complaint was that the government never went far enough in its reduction of armaments, avoidance of foreign entanglements, extirpation of the methods of the 'Old Diplomacy', support for the ideals of the League of Nations, and conversion of the rest of the world to their own enlightened habits of mind. The Right has been less well covered,[33] perhaps justifiably in a period when its concepts about foreign affairs suffered such an eclipse. Occasionally it lifted its head – from major items such as the size of the navy's cruiser fleets to minor ones such as Kipling's blast against the Labour government for seeking to abandon Remembrance Day in 1930[34] – but for many years it appeared as a voice in the wilderness, to be heard only among service personnel, the Foreign Office, backbenchers in the Tory Party and a few editors. Even when, by the mid-1930s, their arguments in favour of increased defences began to elicit more sympathy in governmental circles, differences of opinion – as to which of the armed services should have priority, or which foreign power was the most dangerous – reduced their overall impact; indeed, the more, say, someone like Amery emphasized the German threat, the more he was willing to see a compromise effected with Italy.[35]

Even in this two-sided criticism of 'appeasement', where the Left cried 'too little' and the Right 'too much', therefore, we seem to find confirmation of the pattern. Yet this time, peculiarly enough, the tradition was not going to remain unchanged. By 1938, if not earlier, familiar features were being replaced by an unprecedented situation which brought the policy of 'appeasement' to an end and contributed to the widespread execration of that concept in the popular mind ever since. The pattern was breaking up.

The Model Breaks

During all the previous periods that an 'appeasement' policy was being implemented by the British government, the criticism from Left and Right had tended to cancel each other out; and a Foreign

Secretary such as Grey could at least console himself with the thought that if his actions were being denounced by a radical like Sir John Brunner on the one hand and an arch-patriot like Leo Maxse on the other, then they were probably the moderate, judicious and sensible policies which the country needed, and he should not therefore bother to modify them substantially! All foreign policy being a compromise between national ideals and the reality of world affairs, the only differences occurred between times (e.g. *circa* 1930) when the pacific aspect was more prominent in public sentiment, and those (e.g. *circa* 1900) when a more vigorous attitude prevailed. For most of the interwar years, the policy of 'appeasement' had received the broad support of the Left (even if disappointed at governmental caution), and encountered only the muted suspicions and criticism of the Right. By the later 1930s, and especially by 1938-9, however, certain changes were occurring.

In the first place, the Right had become much more outspoken and self-confident in its criticisms, and was beginning to make inroads into the parliamentary Conservative Party. Secondly, the Left was now abandoning its support for 'appeasement' and joining in the attacks upon the government's foreign policy, not from the opposite (and therefore counterbalancing) viewpoint as the Right, but from the same (and therefore reinforcing) viewpoint. Moreover, a newer group of Conservative MPs, crystallizing around Eden, which supported the internationalist ideals of the League of Nations abroad and was not so hostile to the Labour Party at home, was becoming increasingly uneasy at Chamberlain's unwillingness to oppose the demands of the dictators. No doubt the ideological bases for the attacks from these various groups were fundamentally different, but for once their attitude was the same: namely, that the 'appeasement' of the dictators, especially Hitler, was a false and dangerous policy. *For the first time*, 'Idealists' and 'Realists' were exerting pressure in the same direction and no longer neutralizing each other's impact upon the government. This combination, although naturally taking some time to become effective, was ultimately fatal for the policy of 'appeasement'.

The revival of the criticism of the Right was not in itself a new phenomenon: it had also occurred in 1870-2, 1884-6 and 1903-14.

The reason for the reoccurrence of this phenomenon in the late 1930s is an obvious one. The 'Realists' had suppressed their feelings, or had at least not being able to ventilate them with any marked effect, in a period when public belief in Gladstonian/ Wilsonian ideals of international amity and the pacific settlement of disputes was so strong. When, however, it could be argued that aggression and militarism and nationalism were still rampant in the world, that the sentiments of the League of Nations Union clearly had little place in the *Weltanschauung* of the Nazis or the Japanese military, that right was an inadequate instrument for settling problems unless ultimately supported by might, and that the British Empire itself was now perilously exposed to danger unless it showed that it was determined to defend itself and its allies, the position of the Right no longer looked so old-fashioned. This is not to say that Chamberlain was in much danger from this development before Munich, perhaps before Prague; he dominated his own Cabinet, had an immense hold upon the Conservative Party, and a large majority in the Commons. Nevertheless, the rather desultory 'anti-appeaser' voices of Churchill, Amery, Lloyd, Keyes, Spears, were already receiving reinforcements in the course of 1938, especially with the exit of Eden and Duff Cooper; and when Prague revealed that their predictions had been 'right' all along, their influence increased enormously among Tory backbenchers and such important journalists as Garvin. Still, this was not a large grouping, nor was it coherent while Eden kept his more 'idealist' and middle-of-the-road Tories at a distance from Churchill;[36] and the obvious countermove for a government under attack from the Right was to lean towards the Left in the expectation of getting at least tactical support from that quarter. By the time of Munich, however, support for 'appeasement' from the Left was no longer as forthcoming as hitherto, and shortly afterwards it was to disappear altogether. This was the most remarkable and important change of all.

Traditionally, the Left had advocated conciliation, compromise, a disavowal of overseas commitments, an abjuration of power-politics and military actions; but this did not mean that it favoured 'appeasement' *to all peoples all of the time*. Admittedly, much of the anti-war sentiment of the 1920s and 1930s came from Quaker and

Christian-pacifist circles, which opposed the use of arms under any circumstances; but there were also those Socialists who argued that, while support for a 'capitalists' war' was wrong, a struggle on behalf of the working classes of Europe was perfectly justified. There were others who, like Cecil and Davies, had recognized that world affairs still required an 'armed policeman' to preserve order but felt that this should be carried out, not by the nation-states, but by an international force. Finally, there was that large, assorted, liberal-ethical sentiment which, although disapproving of the resort to force, also came to see that the weak needed to be protected from the strong. The road to this conversion was long and arduous, accompanied by much soul-searching, and attended by an early disbelief in other countries not being actuated by internationalist principles, by a conviction that the British government must in some way be responsible for the grievances of foreigners, and by the assumption that all such complaints could be rationally and fairly settled around a conference-table without any resort to war. At most other times in recent history, such beliefs might have been preserved, if occasionally shaken; but in the brutal and cynical world of Fascist dictatorships, this was not possible. What Japanese, Italian and especially German policy did was to undermine and discredit the previous arguments of the Left in favour of 'appeasement', and to turn it against a British government which still pursued that course of action. The moral basis of 'appeasement' was bound to collapse when a foreign policy of inaction and/or acquiescence meant that high ideals were being flouted, international guarantees and territorial boundaries ignored, and civil liberties and democratic rights brutally suppressed; under such circumstances, a pro-German policy was tantamount to 'aiding and abetting' Fascism. 'Appeasement' became, not a positive, progressive policy, but a negative, detestable one.

Thus, the Left's commitment to the Republican cause in the Spanish Civil War, the trade unions' reaction to the suppression of their German opposite numbers, the decision to cease voting against the defence estimates, the advocacy of alliances with anti-Fascist states in Europe, were all indications of such a trend, although to describe it as such is to play down how confused and equivocal it was. The slow, halting conversion of the Left from an attitude of pro-'appeasement' and non-entanglement to one of opposition to Neville Chamberlain's policies has been well covered.[37] What is significant for our purposes is the way it broke the pattern of 'appeasement', because it meant that the pressure from dissenting Conservatives and the Labour opposition was, in this matter at least, identical. It is no doubt true, as Maurice Cowling has shown,[38] that foreign policy events in the 1930s could be used by Chamberlain to bolster his domestic political position, and by his critics to undermine it; but it was not until the latter had found a common cause of complaint that the Prime Minister's strong situation was likely to be seriously affected. The 'model' that had been working since 1865 without much basic alteration in structure (except, of course, 1914–18) was now breaking down, partly because Hitler's own actions were discrediting 'appeasement', and partly because of the unholy alliance which was being formed among Chamberlain's critics.

At Munich both sides were still launching separate attacks upon the government, although, during the Commons debate which followed, the Conservative anti-'appeasers' were in touch with Dalton to see if they could coordinate their tactics. In the next few months, the signs grew more obvious: under which other circumstances would the left-wing papers have praised Duff Cooper, Churchill and Nicolson, or renowned anti-Communists suggested an alliance with Stalin?[39] Moreover, although it can be argued that a full-blooded cooperation remained impossible while all these politicians did not wish to commit themselves fully to their strange new bedfellows, there is no doubt that, after the spring of 1939 at least, Chamberlain was on the defensive and backing away from the rapidly growing force of anti-'appeasement' feeling. In this, he found himself in an ever-deteriorating situation, for the economic and global/strategical reasons for avoiding war had not altered – if anything, they had increased; and Hitler, by all his post-Munich actions, was steadily undermining the 'peace with honour' claims of Chamberlain and indicating that more would be demanded in the future. Yet the Prime Minister knew (or it was soon made known to him) that more could not be given. The year 1939 represents the period when the external pressures exerted by Hitler, and the internal pressures exerted by the anti-'appeasers', overwhelmed the Downing Street strategy of keeping Britain out of a European war.

The change of tone by the government in the two days following the German seizure of Prague – from the complacent statements of Simon, Halifax and Chamberlain himself on 15 March to the latter's sterner warnings of the 17th[40] – was symptomatic of what one might term the new 'pattern' of events: one characterized by the efforts of Chamberlain and his close associates to maintain their previous policy of securing a general and lasting agreement with Hitler, and by a reluctant retreat from this position because so many shades of British opinion refused any longer to tolerate it. Discussion with the Germans might continue in secret throughout the spring and summer of 1939; but in public the government now had to show that it was being firm rather than conciliatory, that it recognized the need to back up right with might, that the European balance of power was not an anachronism but a vital British interest, that military guarantees should be given to European countries which desired them, and – the hardest pill of all to swallow – that it was willing to approach the 'pariah' state of Russia with a view to an alliance. In other words, Chamberlain was still hoping that a policy of 'appeasement' would work, although at the same time taking measures in case it did not.[41] It was not, in the eyes of his critics and of the public at large, a particularly convincing performance.

All that the late summer crisis over Poland did, therefore, was to produce the final example of the new 'pattern' of actions and reactions. Hitler had presented the British and French governments with yet another violent *fait accompli*; and their immediate – and, one suspects, most deeply felt – response was to prevent this problem from involving their countries in war if at all possible.[42] But this was not to be. The two days of public pressure put upon Chamberlain, far greater than that of March 1939, forced him reluctantly to go to war. The Left insisted upon it, the dissenting Tories clamoured for it, the Conservative backbenchers now also wanted it, and even a Cabinet which had probably been the most docile this century to its Prime Minister's wishes, felt that it could no longer be avoided. By the evening of 2 September 1939, Chamberlain was virtually isolated, his supporters falling away on all sides, and the Left and the Right combining openly in their Commons speeches against him.

And yet, his policy, now so widely execrated, was the continuation of a tradition established three-quarters of a century earlier; was the one which formerly had been so popular in the public mind; was the 'middle ground', so secure against the impracticalities of Left and Right; and was the means by which Chamberlain was planning to bolster up his domestic position and to carry out Britain's financial recovery and political stabilization. By 1939, far from the middle ground being safe, it was being undermined and sinking fast, with everyone seeking to get away from it. It still remains surprising that Chamberlain, by all accounts a skilful political tactician, allowed this to happen. Partly it was because of his genuine loathing of war, and his desire not to inflict upon Britain any repetition of the horrors of 1914–18; partly because he had been aloof, had dominated his Cabinet, and had therefore rarely encountered anyone with the intellectual equipment and force of personality to challenge his ideas in the central decision-making body; partly – and this emerges more and more clearly from the private letters to his sisters – because he was somewhat vain, intolerant of criticism and convinced that he alone possessed the correct qualities to steer Britain through this difficult period: he was, therefore, unwilling to admit that his policy was mistaken until war was actually declared, and he never repented of his actions at Munich.

Finally, it is worth arguing that Chamberlain never perceived that 'appeasement' in itself was *not* a political absolute. Normally, it was true, considerations of morality, economy, global strategy and domestic affairs made a foreign policy of reasonableness and compromise appear to be the logical form of British diplomacy. Under special conditions, however, these considerations could also work against 'appeasement'. The moral sentiment against Britain's involvement in war and international struggles could be outweighed by that against wanton aggression, the flouting of international treaties, the destruction of small states, and the suppression of civil liberties; apprehension about the deleterious economic consequences of rearmament and war could be matched by an equally acute fear of what the *matériel* (and other) results of losing that war could be; awareness of Britain's many commitments elsewhere in the world, which had prevented any firm commitment to Europe for almost twenty years after 1919, could eventually be discounted when the vital significance for national security of preserving the continental balance of power reasserted itself;[43] and public opinion, in its slow and perhaps confused way, could begin to feel that the grounds for a cheap, pacific, non-interventionist foreign policy might under certain circumstances be rendered invalid. In this aspect, as in the others, Chamberlain seemed to be standing still while the people changed their views and then became critical of his failure to move with them.

Conclusion

It has been argued in this paper that a 'tradition' of 'appeasement' can be detected in British foreign policy from the mid-nineteenth century onwards, and that this was, in a sense, the 'natural' policy for a small island state gradually losing its place in world affairs, shouldering military and economic burdens which were increasingly too great for it, and developing internally from an oligarchic to a more democratic form of political constitution in which sentiments in favour of a pacific and rational settlement of disputes were widely propagated. It was also a policy which to some critics in the country displayed too great a proclivity towards surrender, whereas to others it revealed, in its execution at least, too little respect for the principles which they felt should animate international relations. The 'appeasement' policy of the interwar years was, in this respect, the continuation in a heightened form of traditions established earlier; but this pattern broke when Hitler's aggressions undermined the credibility of the bases upon which 'appeasement' rested, and when the criticism of the Left and the Right, supported by an increasing proportion of the British public, insisted that the policy could no longer be maintained. This left Neville Chamberlain, as heir to and chief advocate of 'appeasement', with the dilemma of either abandoning the tradition or of making desperate efforts to ensure its prolongation by securing a lasting peace with Hitler. When this stratagem failed, Chamberlain was exposed to the full blast of contemporary (and later) criticism for having executed a diplomacy which now satisfied neither the moral nor the practical requirements of British policy.

The final consequence of this abandonment of the tradition of 'appeasement' in 1939 was, not surprisingly, a semantic one. When Gladstone sought to accede to the reasonable demands of other classes or nations, his appeal was based upon high principles as well as practical arguments; when Lloyd George urged concessions to Germany in the Fontainebleau Memorandum, his motives were not scorned by the French or the Tory backbenchers even if his conclusions were disputed; and when C. P. Scott first wrote in the *Manchester Guardian* of the desire for a 'peace of appeasement', everyone understood this to be a constructive, positive, honourable concept. After Munich, and especially by the time of Prague, this had completely changed: even such prominent advocates of the former policy as Clifford Allen, Conwell-Evans, Lord Lothian, Robert Cecil and Norman Angell had come to protest at any further toleration of Hitler's demands by then.[44] And as their estimation of 'appeasement' changed, so the meaning of the word altered as well – as dictionaries produced before and after this period demonstrate.[45] 'Appeasement' became a word of shame, not of pride; a word useful in the discrediting of one's rivals; conversely, as Eden clearly felt at the time of Suez, a word which had never to be applied to one's own policy if one could possibly help it. It was a sad end for an expression which, in its original form, encapsulated many of the finer aspects of the British political tradition. Even today, while a foreign policy rooted in those traditional elements of morality, economy and prudence may be – indeed, probably is being – carried out, the last thing its executioners would desire would be to have the word 'appeasement' attached to it.

2

Among the multitude of naval historians past and present, no name is better known than that of Alfred Thayer Mahan (1840–1914). Not only did he write an impressive array of maritime studies but – and this was his real claim to fame – his well-presented theories upon 'the influence of sea power upon history' won great acclaim from admirals, strategists and politicians across the globe. Successive generations of officers were brought up, by lessons at their naval academies, upon the 'principles' adumbrated by Mahan; and large numbers of later historians have devoted their time to demonstrating the 'influence of sea power' upon this or that campaign, and this or that nation's history. With very few exceptions, little intellectual effort was made to scrutinize Mahan's general claims or to set his ideas within the specific historical context of late nineteenth-century navalism and imperialism. Only *after* the Second World War, when the awesome nature of the clash between Nazi Germany and the Soviet Union for the 'Heartland' of Eurasia was being slowly understood, and when British naval mastery had clearly gone, could historians in the West reassess the relative influences of sea power and land power (and, for that matter, air power).

This article was written when the author was struggling with such a reassessment, which later appeared in book form as *The Rise and Fall of British Naval Mastery* (London, 1976). Its generalizing nature, and the counterposing of the ideas of 'the evangelist of sea power' with those of Halford J. Mackinder, 'the prophet of land power', attracted the editors of the German military history journal *Militärgeschichtliche Mitteilungen*, which published it in 1974.

Mahan *versus* Mackinder: Two Interpretations of British Sea Power

'It is an interesting commentary on human affairs that Mahan's exposition of the influence of sea power on the course of European and American expansion should have occurred at the very time when new instruments of the Industrial Revolution were beginning to erode principles and theories upon which his doctrines were based.'

G. S. Graham, *The Politics of Naval Supremacy* (Cambridge, 1965), p.124

To begin this paper by claiming that the writings of Alfred Thayer Mahan upon sea power in general, and British sea power in particular, have been of the utmost significance to students of naval history, would be to come close to offering a truism. The reception accorded to such books of his as *The Influence of Sea Power Upon History 1660–1783* (1890), both at the time of publication and in the decades following, reflected the importance which his message was seen to have for all modern states which bordered the seas. In his own land of the United States, prominent statesmen such as Theodore Roosevelt were to accept his advice and doctrines wholeheartedly; in Britain he was fêted and revered, the more especially since he had openly expressed his admiration for the Royal Navy and had brought intellectual support to the 'Blue Water' school of strategists; in Germany, Kaiser Wilhelm II ordered a copy of Mahan's book to be placed on board every warship, while Admiral Tirpitz's strategy was much influenced by it; and from Japan to Latin America this scholarly captain's ideas became accepted as a gospel by maritime men.

So widespread did Mahan's general views become that it is possible to present only a brief synopsis here. He claimed that 'the key to much of history as well as of the policy of nations bordering upon the sea' would be found by a study of the naval conflicts of the seventeenth and eighteenth centuries, and he proceeded to illustrate by historical examples how certain immutable conditions (the geographical position and physical conformation of a country; the extent of national territory to be defended or extended; the size and character of its population; and the nature and wisdom of its government) were the real reasons for the steady rise to world power of the British Empire at that time and for the relative decline of those states such as Spain, the Netherlands and France which had opposed this. As such, his writings were regarded as a tool with which to unlock an understanding of developments in international power-politics over the preceding centuries. More important still – and this was the true ground for Mahan's immense influence at the official level in the two decades before 1914 – he also appeared to offer important lessons and predictions to all those states which wished to maintain or to extend their influence in the world *in the future*. It was not strictly as an historian, but as a prophet, that Mahan was respected at this time.[1]

This being the case, it is worthwhile to examine some of the political and military implications for the future which emerged from his works, or were in some cases read into them by his enthusiastic but one-sided followers: that large battlefleets, and a concentration of force, decided control of the oceans, whereas a *guerre de course* strategy was always ineffectual; that the blockade was a very effective weapon which would sooner or later bring an enemy to its knees; that the possession of select bases on islands or continental peripheries was more valuable than control of large land-masses; that overseas colonies were vital for a nation's prosperity, and that colonial trade was the most treasured commerce of all; that 'travel and traffic by water have always been easier and cheaper than by land'; that an island nation, resting secure upon its naval might, could with impunity ignore the struggles of land powers and adopt if necessary an isolationist policy; and that the rise of a country to world greatness without sea power was almost unthinkable. Taken altogether, they formed the basic tenets of the pre-1914 navalist philosophy, much of which endured well past that particular epoch; it centred upon the belief that sea power had been more influential than land power in the past and always would be so. Finally, Mahan, while urging the need for a strong American fleet, fully expected and firmly hoped that Britain's naval predominance would remain unassailed in the future. He certainly neither contemplated nor wished for a decline of that British Empire whose foremost naval scholar he had become.

It may be doubted in retrospect whether the importance which Mahan and his disciples attributed to the influence of sea power upon the political struggles of the European Great Powers between the seventeenth and nineteenth centuries was fully justified in fact. Admiral Fisher, usually a convinced Mahanite, was at one time honest enough to admit that the battle of Trafalgar, glorious though it was, had done nothing to check Napoleon's continental aggrandizement: Austerlitz, a few months later, was of greater significance there.[2] However, to attempt a modification of Mahan's interpretation of the past is beyond the scope of this paper, and even the most sceptical would admit that his work was very illuminating and that no scholar since his day could write about the rise of the British Empire without acknowledgement to the role of sea power. What certainly deserves greater questioning – and it is the intention of the present essay to do this – was the presumption in Mahan's writings that what had happened in the past was going to occur in the future as well. In point of fact, his mind was too rooted in previous events to be much of a success in the field of prophecy. As his biographer has admitted,

> In activity and by disposition Mahan largely looked to the past; he gained his lessons from a study of the past and used the past for analogies. There can be no doubt that Mahan was so absorbed with the past that he often failed to appreciate future trends in naval warfare. He was not sufficiently alive to the fact that history frequently does not repeat itself and that the shape of things to come may not always follow the pattern of the past.[3]

Nor should this conclusion be at all surprising to fellow scholars in this discipline. However skilled historians may be in tracing themes in the past, they have rarely achieved much success in predicting the future. The variables of history – the accident, the role of individuals, the changes caused by technological break-throughs and unforeseen events – and the sheer complexity of world society usually permit us to identify the significant historical trends of a period only in retrospect.

Ironically enough, it was while Mahan's popularity as a pundit was at its height in Europe and the United States that a much more perceptive – though less well known – prophecy of future world politics was being elaborated. On 25 January 1904, the geopolitician Halford Mackinder read a paper to the Royal Geographical Society entitled 'The Geographical Pivot of History'.[4] In it he suggested that there had been what he called a Columbian epoch – about four centuries of overseas exploration and conquest by the European powers – which was now coming to an end and that another, far different, age was about to begin. With very little of the world left to conquer, 'every explosion of social forces' would take place in a much more enclosed environment and would no longer be dissipated into unknown regions; efficiency and internal development would replace expansionism as the main aim of modern states; and for the first time in history there would be 'a correlation between the larger geographical and the larger historical generalizations', that is, size and numbers would be more accurately reflected in the sphere of international developments. This being the case, Mackinder continued, it was important to consider what the future would bring to the great strategical 'pivot area' of the world – central Russia. That vast region, once the source of the many invading armies which had for centuries poured into Europe and the Middle East, had been outflanked, neutralized and much reduced in importance by the mariners of the Columbian era, who had opened most of the rest of the world to Western influence. For four hundred years the world's trade had developed on the sea, its population had on the whole lived near to the sea, political and military influences had been primarily influenced by sea power. Now, with industrialization, with railways, with investment, with new agricultural and mining techniques, central Asia was poised to regain its previous importance:

46

The spaces within the Russian Empire and Mongolia are so vast, and their potentialities in population, wheat, cotton, fuel and metals so incalculably great, that it is inevitable that a vast economic world, more or less apart, will there develop inaccessible to oceanic commerce.[5]

Mackinder's stress upon the importance of the 'Heartland', later taken up by Haushofer and other Nazi geopoliticians and somewhat discredited as a consequence, is probably too simple, one-sided and deterministic to be accepted in its entirety today; but the broad outlines of his argument were prescient and compel the closest attention. Certainly, his audience at the Royal Geographical Society was impressed by this unusually wide-ranging paper. One of them, Leo Amery, ventured to go further and, while not laying stress so specifically upon central Asia, elaborated one aspect of Mackinder's message in even clearer power-political terms:

sea power alone, if it is not based on great industry, and has a great industry behind it, is too weak for offence to really maintain itself in the world struggle . . . both the sea and the railway are going in the future . . . to be supplemented by the air as a means of locomotion, and when we come to that . . . *the successful powers will be those who have the greatest industrial base. It will not matter whether they are in the centre of a continent or on an island; those people who have the industrial power and the power of invention and science will be able to defeat all others.*[6]

These predictions, of the rise of certain superpowers with massive populations and industrial strength, was not new to political thinking – as early as 1825 de Tocqueville had forecast the inevitable rise of the USA and Russia – but they were now being expressed in a much more definite form. Some twenty years before Mackinder, moreover, Sir John Seeley had pointed to the immense developments which 'steam and electricity' were bringing to those great continental states, against whose consolidated resources and manpower the widely scattered British Empire would find it impossible to compete unless drastic changes occurred in its own structure. 'Russia and the United States will surpass in power the

47

states now called great as much as the great country-states of the sixteenth century surpassed Florence.'[7] Yet if Seeley still placed hopes upon the transformation of the Empire into a much more centralized organic unit, Mackinder could not be so sanguine. Britain would continue to maintain its strategical and maritime advantages *vis-à-vis* Europe, but these would count for little against the rising superpowers. Already in his book *Britain and the British Seas*, published in 1902, Mackinder had insisted:

> In the presence of vast Powers, broad-based upon the resources of half continents, Britain could not again become mistress of the seas. Much depends on the maintenance of a lead won under earlier conditions. Should the sources of wealth and vigour upon which the navy was founded run dry, the imperial security of Britain will be lost. From the early history of Britain herself it is evident that mere insularity gives no indefeasible right to maritime sovereignty.[8]

If it were possible to express Mackinder's novel and rather isolated views with the utmost simplicity, one might say that a decline in Britain's relative world position was being at least hinted at, if not forecast, because of two closely linked developments:

1. Britain's naval power, rooted in her economic strength, would no longer remain supreme when other nations with greater resources and manpower overhauled her previous industrial lead, and
2. Sea power itself was waning in relation to land power.

The first of these developments was undoubtedly true and in it, clearly, lay the chief cause of Britain's long-term decline.[9] In a certain sense, this had always been quite probable, for Britain's economic domination of the world after 1815 had rested upon a unique concatenation of very favourable circumstances. It was not to be expected that she would remain eternally either the only or even the greatest industrialized nation; when others took the same path, a relative decline was inevitable. It was more perturbing, though, to learn that weaknesses in the British system were accelerating this long-term trend: scattered and small-scale industrial plant; a reluctance to invest in new techniques or in the industries (chemicals, electricity, etc.) of the future; inadequate technical education in the nation at large; the lack of competitiveness and poor salesmanship in foreign markets; the unwillingness of the ruling élites, through social inclination and a devotion to *laissez-faire*, to take much of an interest in matters of trade and industry. Many people proclaimed their alarm when German and American steel production overtook Britain's, or when their country's share of the world's manufacturing capacity dropped steadily from 31·8 per cent in 1870 to 14·7 per cent in 1906–10, but no one could produce a solution to the problem. Comfort was taken from the fact that British trade could still be directed into her vast 'formal' and 'informal' empire after losing out in more competitive markets, and that her role as the world's leading financier, insurer, commodity dealer and shipper actually increased in response to the international demand for these services; but this did not ease the fears of those who perceived that Britain's unique commercial and industrial lead, upon which Pitt, Canning and Palmerston had been able to find the ultimate support for their foreign and naval policies, was gone. In view of all this, would it be possible for her to stay the pace in the power-political struggles of the twentieth century also?

It would be some time before the answer to that question was clear; but even at the turn of the century it was obvious that the spread of industrialization was altering the world's international balance in many ways. Nations long dormant, though potentially powerful because of their populations and resources, had been galvanized by the Unbound Prometheus – the impact of technology and organization – and these revolutions were already having strategical consequences. In the Western Hemisphere the United States was assuming a more and more dominating position, its economic activities and political influence permeating the Caribbean and Latin America. In the same way, Japan was pulling ahead of its neighbours in the Far East and extending its control there. The newly united German Empire, boosted by an amazingly swift industrial and commercial expansion, was steadily changing the old balance of power in Europe. Finally, industrialization was not only allowing Russia to take the first real steps to develop its immense resources but was giving it, through strategic railways, a means of direct military pressure upon China and India. All of these changes implied at least a consequent diminution of Britain's influence in the areas concerned, and some a distinct restriction upon her hitherto almost unchallenged predominance and freedom of action. The same was true for the other great political development of the later nineteenth century – the colonial expansion of the Great Powers. Before this, the British had usually had to contend with the spasmodic challenges of the French but now many others entered the fray, with the result that Britain's 'informal empire' had either to be annexed or it was lost to new rivals. No doubt the British secured a larger share of the colonial spoils than anyone else – with their head-start, this was scarcely surprising – but again their position had relatively declined. Strategical supremacy was also affected by the acquisition by foreign powers of important bases along the world's shipping routes, for instance Bizerta, Dakar, Diego Suarez, Port Arthur, Manila and Hawaii.

These changes bewildered many Britons, even though their feelings were often concealed by a display of national pride and bravado which mid-Victorians would have considered both unnecessary and distasteful, Palmerston always excepted. The British public of the 1880s and 1890s would have been more upset still had the second aspect of Mackinder's thesis been better known to them: *that sea power was itself waning in relation to land power*. This, too, was a very long-term trend, in which the changes were to be measurable only over decades and in which the consequences were to be perceived only in the next century; but once again it is worthwhile to examine briefly its general characteristics in Mackinder's time.

Perhaps the real villain of the piece was the railway, ironically a British invention and one which had greatly benefited the British economy and people. Nevertheless, the transformation it wrought upon such areas as central Europe, the 'Heartland' of Russia and the mid-west of the United States was far more decisive; the industrialization of these three regions, despite the assertions of certain economists in recent years, was scarcely feasible without the railway. The transport of goods, which had for centuries been cheaper and faster by water, now became easier by land, a tendency which was to increase with the introduction of motorized transport in the twentieth century. And not only was industry stimulated but commerce, which had long been difficult, now flourished under the new conditions: the opening of the Mont Cenis (1871) and St Gotthard (1882) tunnels greatly increased the northward flow of Mediterranean fruits and vegetables, for example. The Columbian epoch of which Mackinder spoke, when most trade and populations had remained close to the sea, was slowly ending as continental countries were freed from this physical restriction. With the improvement of land communications, a nation without much seaboard but with a large population and extensive territories could now exploit its resources, and the peculiar advantages of small, predominantly naval/commercial countries such as Holland and Britain were being gradually lost.

People, too, could be transported across land much faster, a fact which not only affected shipping companies adversely but also had direct military implications. The body which appears to have appreciated this first was the Prussian General Staff, whose efficient planners turned railway timetabling into a work of art. In 1866 it had been able to put 400,000 into the field in a very short time for the campaign against Austria; and 'it mastered the problems of mass organization and movement so brilliantly that in 1870 1,183,000 men passed through the barracks into the army in eighteen days, and 462,000 were transported to the French frontier in the same time.'[10] The traditional British strategy against one power or a coalition dominating Europe, of despatching expeditions to the peripheries, be it in the Baltic or to the Portuguese or Italian coast, would now be a much more risky proposition if the enemy could swiftly rush a far greater force to the threatened point by rail instead of having to rely upon forced marches along poor roads. Conversely, a land power could be freed from its vulnerability to the Royal Navy in certain circumstances – the most notable example of this being the advantages which Russia accrued to itself by the construction of the trans-Siberian railway. The latter, so argued the Russian Finance Minister, Witte, in 1892, 'would not only bring about the opening of Siberia, but would revolutionize world trade, supersede the Suez Canal as the leading route to China, enable Russia to flood the Chinese market with textiles and metal goods, and secure political control of northern China.'[11]

These hopes were soon to be blunted by the war with Japan, the results of which reassured navalists everywhere; but in retrospect it is possible to see the Russian defeat being due more to unreadiness and inefficiency than to the workings of sea power. Even as it was, the Russian expansion by land was quite impressive, Mackinder later noting in one of his perceptive comparisons:

> It was an unprecedented thing in the year 1900 that Britain should maintain a quarter of a million men in her war with the Boers at a distance of six thousand miles over the ocean; but it was as remarkable a feat for Russia to place an army of more than a quarter of a million men against the Japanese in Manchuria in 1904 at a distance of four thousand miles by rail.[12]

More worrying still to the British was the threat which Russian railway-building offered to their control of India. For centuries this important possession had been only accessible by sea, but by 1900 the approaching Orenburg–Tashkent railway created a danger to which the British simply had no answer: the Royal Navy could not defend the North-West Frontier. Truly, the defence of an empire susceptible in so many places to attack from land was a desperate problem for a country that was basically a sea power, as the *Naval and Military Record* pointed out in 1901 in a leader which is worth quoting at some length:

> There has never been room for doubt that certain limitations must hamper the expansion of a naval Power. The familiar truth has been somewhat obscured by the writings of Captain Mahan, which may easily be misread by Englishmen who are naturally proud of their Navy and of their expanding Empire. It may be doubted, however, if Captain Mahan ever intended to suggest that an extensive Empire, scattered over all parts of the globe, can be held for centuries by sea power alone. The defence of India, as we recently pointed out, is based upon sea power, but it also involves the maintenance of 300,000 troops, and makes a considerable drain upon the limited supply of military recruits under our voluntary system of service. The Canadian frontier, again, could hardly be held with security in the event of war

against the United States. Our conquests in South Africa may oblige us to maintain a permanent garrison of 50,000 troops, and at present it is not very clear how that army is to be raised under the voluntary system. . . . Singapore, for example, is a valuable naval base, but it cannot be held by the Navy alone. The port requires a large garrison. Thus, the limitations of sea power begin to be felt when territorial expansion can no longer be safeguarded exclusively by the guns of the fleet, backed by minor garrisons.[13]

There were other changes, too, which had taken place or were still in progress in the nineteenth century, which might cause one to wonder if Mahan's strategical analysis of Britain's previous naval wars would be of much relevance in the future. Particularly significant here was the alteration in the effectiveness of the blockade, previously a slow but terrible weapon. The newer world powers, the United States and Germany, and the old enemy of Russia, having less of their national wealth bound up in overseas trade, were far less susceptible to defeat by naval pressure alone than ever Spain, Holland or even France had been. To seize the Spanish bullion convoy or to interrupt the Dutch trade with the Indies had been to deal the enemy's economy a very severe blow indeed; but now it was different, as was emphasized in an interesting lecture given at the United Services Institute by one Douglas Owen in 1905. As he explained, the trade which British privateers of the seventeenth and eighteenth centuries had harassed was that between ports which then belonged to her rivals – Ceylon, Mauritius, Cape Town, Guinea, Dominica, Trinidad, St Vincent, St Lucia, Demerara, Grenada, French Canada: since those times they had all become British. In the second place, colonial trade as a whole had declined in importance: the gold and silver from Latin America, the spices from the East Indies, the rum and tobacco and sugar from the West Indies had no modern equivalents – except perhaps the carriage of raw materials and foodstuffs to the British Isles itself. The best targets, in other words, were now nearly all British. Thirdly, the coming of the railway had reduced the effectiveness of the blockade and the possibility of paralysing the enemy's trade:

Since those times, railways have been introduced and so developed as to link together city, town, and port, whilst inland water-ways have on the Continent been created and developed to an extent of which most Englishmen have no conception. Even if it were possible for us to close absolutely our adversary's ports, his trade would go on with little interruption. . . . Today France can supply herself through Belgium; Germany, through Holland and Belgium; Holland, through Belgium and Germany; Russia, through Germany and the Low Countries. . . . The days of coastal blockade, in the case of European States, with any thought of starving out the enemy, or with any idea of making prizes of his coastal traffic, have gone for ever.[14]

This latter section was of course written under the belief that the clauses of the Declaration of Paris of 1856 concerning the 'freedom of the seas' would be observed in future wars; and that the enemy would simply proceed to lay up all his ships and to rely upon neutral carriers. But even if this was not to be the case, Owen's analysis still possessed a certain validity: continental states could obtain supplies much more easily from neutral neighbours under modern conditions of transport than they ever could have in the past. And it was laughable to think of trying to starve out Russia or the United States.

What was more, the new inventions of the mine, the torpedo, the submarine and the long-range coastal ordnance were making the operational application of the blockade very difficult – so much so that the Royal Navy gradually abandoned the idea of a close blockade of the German coast in the years before 1914.[15] Furthermore, although at first the new weapons seemed only to restrict the freedom of action of battleships operating off the enemy's ports, it was later recognized that there was no inherent reason why the mine and the torpedo could not be employed on the high seas also. Some far-sighted strategists quickly drew their own conclusions: Admiral Sir Percy Scott caused a minor furore by a letter to *The Times* of June 1914, in which he prophesied that submarines and aircraft would make the battleship worthless and pleaded instead for a strategy based upon a large air force, a fleet of submarines and many cruisers (for trade protection).[16] His critics protested that his case was not proven and that Mahan's principles would continue to be valid. To see the victory of the *guerre de course* theories at this time of the great power of the British battlefleet would have been too bitter a pill to swallow; but behind their protests one can also detect the deeper fear that the supremacy of the submarine, torpedo-boat and aeroplane on the naval battlefield would presage the fall of Britain's maritime supremacy. A battlefleet, after all, could only be built by a limited number of powers and took many years to create, giving the British time to take countermeasures; any reasonably ambitious country could afford aircraft and submarines, however, thus assuring to itself at least local naval dominance.

Industrialization had two further consequences which affected Britain's strategic capabilities. In the first place, the developments in shipping, taken together with her industrial growth and increased population and prosperity, led to an enormous increase in her dependence upon the import of foodstuffs and raw materials – and this meant that she was much more vulnerable to hostile naval pressures upon her own lines of communication with the outside world. The Royal Navy would now have thousands of merchant ships to protect in wartime, and the consequences of any interruption would be far more serious. In the second place, the Industrial Revolution, with its accompanying rise in population and mobility, not only permitted still larger armies to be recruited and transported than was hitherto the case, but it also provided the financial and material strength for them to be clothed, armed and fed for a very long time. In other words, as Ivan S. Bloch intuitively suggested in his book *Modern Weapons and Modern War*, future conflicts between Great Powers were going to be endurance tests, where the defensive would have the upper hand:

> instead of a war fought out to the bitter end in a series of decisive battles, we shall have as a substitute a long period of continually increasing strain upon the resources of the combatants. The war, instead of being a hand-to-hand contest in which the combatants measure their physical and moral superiority, will become a kind of stalemate in which, neither army being able to get at the other, both armies will be maintained in opposition to each other,

threatening each other, but never able to deliver a final and decisive attack.[17]

All this turned the small professional army which Britain possessed into a nonentity and reduced even further its ability to influence continental events through military pressure. If the British were to land their army on the German coast, Bismarck is reported to have quipped, he would call out the local police force and have it arrested.

From about 1900 onwards, the British government began to respond to certain of these challenges and to reduce some of its worldwide defence commitments: the Western Hemisphere was left to the United States; Japan assumed the task of protecting British interests in the Far East; even the Mediterranean, the 'windpipe' of the Empire, became a French naval responsibility after 1912; and Fisher's drastic reorganization of the Royal Navy saw the scattered gunboat fleets withdrawn and scrapped, and overseas stations amalgamated. The end of the age of *Pax Britannica* had arrived, hastened – and in some way concealed – by the parallel need to concentrate more and more of the fleet in the North Sea to meet the growing German challenge.

Yet this reduction in Britain's world role, serious though it was, did not compare with a far greater revolution in her defence policy after 1905 – the virtual abandonment of 'the British way of warfare'. Reversing previous strategy, the British government made the Royal Navy 'a subsidiary weapon, and grasped the glittering sword of Continental manufacture' by assuming an ever-greater commitment to engage in a full-scale military campaign in Europe.[18]

It was not the case, of course, that Whitehall deliberately planned such an astonishing change in its traditional policy – in fact, most statesmen and their advisers loathed the prospect of being embroiled in a continental conflict – but the circumstances gradually whittled down Britain's freedom of action until it appeared almost inevitable that an expeditionary force should be despatched across the Channel. The root of the problem, which the British had not needed to face for over a century, was that they could not make their homeland secure by naval measures alone: the

56

balance of power in Europe was also important. Yet that balance, in equilibrium since the fall of Napoleon, was collapsing again as a united and powerful Germany assumed the preponderance to which her enormous industrial base and population entitled her;[19] and this was accentuated by the sudden collapse of Russian military might in 1905. What would happen if Germany overran the whole of western Europe or (a likely possibility if Britain ignored the European situation) turned France and the Low Countries into political appendages? The answers were chilling to any Briton who pondered upon them: first, such an agglomeration of industrial strength would probably enable Germany to outbuild the British, whatever the efforts of the latter; and secondly, instead of being restricted to the North Sea, the High Seas Fleet could be based upon the harbours of Brest and Cherbourg while German torpedo-boats closed the Channel. Slowly, reluctantly, people began to realize that Britain's naval position and the balance of power in Europe were inextricably linked, though Radicals and extreme Imperialists continued to deny this. Grey made the connection clear in his important statement of 1912 to the Committee of Imperial Defence:

> if a European conflict, not of our making, arose, in which it was quite clear that the struggle was one for supremacy in Europe, in fact, that you got back to a situation something like that in the Napoleonic days, then . . . our concern is seeing that there did not arise a supremacy in Europe which entailed a combination that would deprive us of the command of the sea would be such that we might have to take part in that European war. That is why the naval position underlines our European policy. . . .[20]

But how was Britain to 'take part in that European war' unless she reorganized her army, which had been regarded hitherto as an imperial police force? The logic of the situation pointed to a total reorientation of British defence policy, from one based chiefly upon naval and imperial considerations to one which reflected the dominance of military and European factors. The change was of course fiercely resisted by the Admiralty; but it could not prevent the growing intimacy between British and French General Staffs, nor its own loss of influence. Indeed, at the famous meeting of the Committee of Imperial Defence on 23 August 1911, the army convincingly won this interservice dispute. As Hankey, the secretary to that body, noted afterwards,

> From that time onwards there was never any doubt what would be the Grand Strategy in the event of our being drawn into a continental war in support of France. Unquestionably the Expeditionary Force, or the greater part of it, would have been sent to France as it actually was in 1914.[21]

It may well be that the main consequence of the Anglo-French military conversations lay not so much in the *political* arena, where the British government still retained its freedom of action in 1914 even though the minds of the Cabinet had been conditioned by their concern for the independence of western Europe in the preceding decade; but in the *strategic* field, where the 'contours' of its intervention had already been decided. As Professor Williamson notes, 'In August 1914 the British government, no less than its French and German counterparts, was committed to a "plan".'[22] Once this step had been taken, of course, it was almost impossible to reverse it. As the critics had always warned, a continental commitment was quick to take roots and even quicker to escalate: the recruitment and despatch of twenty-five or more divisions made more sense, in terms of strict military logic, than that of only five or six divisions, if the Low Countries were to be held and the German army defeated. But this, naturally enough, also implied national conscription.

It is hardly surprising to learn that the naval lobby tried throughout the war to regain its primacy in defence strategy and to steer the nation back to 'the British way of warfare'. This time, however, the politics which had been implemented in the wars of the eighteenth and nineteenth centuries proved to be less successful and effective against Germany. There is little doubt that the traditional methods would have been enthusiastically supported by the vast majority of the public and politicians in Britain, had they offered any prospect of success and a viable alternative to the slaughter on the Western Front; but, one by one, the cheap, maritime-based, peripheral ways of defeating an enemy were discovered to be inadequate when dealing with a continental bloc as strong and as self-sufficient as the Central Powers.

The greatest disappointment came in the sphere of fleet operations itself, where the Admiralty had expected to meet and overwhelm the High Seas Fleet in a second and even greater Trafalgar, that Armageddon in the North Sea for which Fisher and his successors had been training the service for a whole decade. Yet this hope never came to anything – for quite understandable reasons. The first of these was Britain's favourable geographical position *vis-à-vis* Germany, which enabled her to close the enemy's lines of communication to the outside world by a distant blockade alone, instead of having to incur the risks from mines, submarines and torpedo-boats which a close blockade entailed. The second was the decisive British superiority in battleship numbers, which made a full toe-to-toe battle between the two fleets an extremely hazardous action for the Germans, who wisely sought to avoid such an event. The obvious conclusion to be drawn from this stalemate, as Professor Marder has put it, was 'that Britain's principal strategical aims at sea, offensive and defensive, could be met by keeping the two holes to the north and south blockaded'.[23] An avoidance of battle in the North Sea meant that Britain could not lose the surface naval war, whereas Germany could not win it. This underlying strategical reason, together with the fact that each side grew increasingly nervous of attack from enemy submarines, goes a long way to explaining why there was no decisive fleet encounter in the First World War; chance clashes, such as those at the Dogger Bank and Jutland, simply confirmed the basic pattern. Hence the 'feeling of incompleteness' confessed to by Admiral Weymss in 1918 when the High Seas Fleet surrendered: the opportunity to fight a great sea battle, like that at the Nile or Trafalgar, had not appeared. Compared with the burdens borne by the army, the navy had appeared in the public eye to have done little to win the war against Germany, and, by its poor performance in defending Allied merchant shipping, had almost lost the war.

The failure to stage a fleet confrontation was only the first of the unpleasant surprises to British navalists in this war. More were to come in those fields of colonial campaigns, commerce warfare, and peripheral operations which had also formed part of Mahan's historical panoply. Germany's overseas colonies were – with the exception of East Africa – quickly overrun by the Allies, but this hardly compared in importance with the Anglo-French struggles in earlier wars for India, the West Indies and Canada. The German colonial empire, although one million square miles in extent by 1914, housed only 21,000 Germans, took only 3·8 per cent of Germany's foreign investment and contributed to only 0·5 per cent of Germany's foreign trade. Losing such possessions was hardly a mortal blow to Berlin, therefore, especially when it is recalled that they provided few raw materials for German industry and that they had had to be heavily subsidized by the Reich, possibly to the tune of £100 million by 1914.[24] In strategic terms, they were considered irrelevant by the German government: Tirpitz had always argued that the challenge to Britain's world position had to be mounted in the North Sea and that, if they were successful there, they would be able to recoup all the territorial losses he anticipated in the extra-European fields. Samoa, South-West Africa and the rest were simply the first few unimportant pawns in a great and complex world struggle.

Equally insignificant, in terms of the total war effort, was the effect of the British destruction of the few German surface commerce-raiders. Here, too, geography had compelled Tirpitz deliberately to eschew any large-scale naval commitment overseas, and the vessels which were on foreign stations were to 'show the flag' – and were openly regarded in Berlin as hostages to fortune in the event of war. Of the ten German surface commerce-raiders operating in the early months of the war, only a few, notably the *Emden* and the *Karlsruhe*, achieved worthwhile successes; but even they were silenced, and the total of British vessels sunk by such raiders throughout the war (442,000 tons) was not a significant blow. The only tangible threat emerged in the form of Spee's East Asian Squadron; but after its victory at Coronel it was quickly wiped out by Sturdee's battlecruisers at the Falklands. These battles, it has been pointed out, were the last ones of the war between surface ships by gunfire alone: 'Thereafter, torpedoes, mines, submarines, and, to some extent, aircraft introduced complications unknown to Sturdee and Spee.'[25] The greatest change, of course, was the development of the U-boat as the commerce-raider *par excellence* – which was a predictable step once the German navy found it had no other obvious means of hitting its enemy, once the political opposition inside Germany had been overcome, and the necessary numbers of U-boats had been made ready. As soon as this campaign began in earnest, however, the British Admiralty's prewar preparations for the defence of sea-borne trade were shown to be quite out of date.

The other great weapon in the Royal Navy's armoury was the blockade. This, too, was now encrusted with tradition. While Napoleon's armies had ranged all over Europe, so Mahan had taught, 'there went on unceasingly that noiseless pressure upon the vitals of France, that compulsion whose silence, when once noted, becomes to the observer the most striking and awful mark of Sea Power'. Before the war the Admiralty firmly believed that this strategy would be deadly in its effects: did they not control the enemy's sea routes to the outside world, and did not Germany, like all modern industrialized nations, depend so heavily upon this traffic that its interruption would have the most disastrous consequences for its entire war industry? All this was true, but it was offset by many other factors and it was a mistake to equate her position with that of an island state such as Britain or Japan. Approximately 19 per cent of her national income derived from exports, but of these only 20 per cent were extra-European; and only 10 per cent of Germany's national wealth was in overseas investment (cf. 27 per cent of Britain's), the returns from which contributed to only 2 per cent of her national income.[26] Theoretically, then, the loss of about 6 per cent, or perhaps 8 per cent, of her national income was not a disaster. This would be swiftly altered if certain essential raw materials could not be obtained, but the Central Powers already possessed or soon took over vast resources (e.g. Romanian wheat and oil), and could also secure supplies via neutral neighbours. They had the technology, in addition, to create many *ersatz* goods. In the long term, naturally enough, the consequences of the Allied blockade were very serious but it was not until late in the war that German soldiers were affected by it. And it is worth suggesting that the civilian sufferings from the blockade would have been far fewer had not the great military campaigns swallowed up such astronomical amounts of foodstuffs, industrial products and especially the men who were needed to farm the land. Moreover, as Sir Herbert Richmond has wisely observed, the nineteenth-century improvements in land communications had greatly assisted the Central Powers and limited the implementation of an effective blockade *by Britain alone*; as a result,

> It was only owing to the fact that the land frontiers of the enemies were sealed by the armies, and that every nation of importance was either actively assisting with her navies at sea, or passively by withholding trade, that the eventual degree of isolation was procured which contributed to the victory.[27]

Richmond's statement, in fact, leads straight to the weak point of the navalists' arguments – that this weapon, unless it be used against an island state heavily dependent upon overseas trade, is bound to be only a subsidiary one. Only when used in conjunction with a land blockade, and as an additional means of pressure to the constant assaults of armies, was its long-term and formidable influence upon an enemy such as Germany to be felt. For not only did the bloody wars of attrition of the Western and Eastern Fronts sap the manpower, economy and morale of the Central Powers at a far higher rate than the maritime blockade ever did, but the latter could easily be neutralized by a German military victory in either theatre:

> The collapse of Russia, which burst the barriers in the East, broke this blockade, and then the supplies drawn from the Ukraine preserved Austria and relieved Germany. If the Western barrier could also have been broken, whatever might have happened to the armies, a vast territory would have fallen into German hands on which they could have lived and continued to hold out and defy the oceanic blockade. But it would have done still more; it would have aided to a high degree the German offensive at sea.[28]

It was a similar fear, this time of a successful enemy push into the

Balkans and Middle East, making Germany 'practically independent of maritime blockade and . . . able completely to outstrip the rest of Europe in the reconstruction of their economic and military resources', which caused the despatch of British troops into the Caucasus and towards the Caspian Sea in 1918.[29] Berlin, Britain's strategists could see, was in danger of dominating the 'Heartland'. The truth of the matter, as Richmond further observed,[30] was that sea power and land power were interdependent, that both were necessary to check the enemy challenge, and that the isolationists' hope of avoiding a continental commitment and relying upon maritime pressure alone would have led to the German domination of the European land-mass and beyond. Furthermore, while nothing was 'more misleading or objectionable than the attribution of success to one or the other separately' (Richmond), it was also true that in the First World War Britain was obliged *nolens volens* to commit an ever-increasing share of her resources to the land struggle, thereby giving that theatre an unprecedented military and political predominance.

The only solution remaining was for the navalists to argue for joint operations, to use the army, in Grey's phrase, as 'a projectile to be fired by the navy'. In the prewar years Admirals Fisher and Wilson had pressed for a large variety of amphibious schemes, all of which had foundered upon the opposition of the General Staff and the scepticism of the Cabinet. As General Nicholson had put it in 1914, 'The truth was that this class of operation possibly had some value a century ago, when land communications were indifferent, but now, when they were excellent, they were doomed to failure. Wherever we threatened to land, the Germans could concentrate superior force.'[31]

Yet if the army had gained the decisive first victory in this interservice dispute, the continental strategy was not to go unchallenged during the war itself. Indeed, the more the casualty figures on the Western Front rose, the more longingly the Cabinet looked towards the alternative, sea-based strategy: once again, political factors became enmeshed in the military considerations, as traditionalists like Esher appealed for a return to the policy of Pitt:

When the army of Sir John French was committed to war on the Continent there was no irrevocable breach of this great principle, but, as time went on, and reinforcement after reinforcement was sent to France, absorbing all the available military reserves of the country, its amphibious power was gradually sapped, and has, at the present time, practically been destroyed. . . . It is as true today as it was then (the Seven Years' War), that our military power, used amphibiously in combination with the Fleet, can produce results all out of proportion to the numerical strength of our Army. . . . The moment has come.[32]

The Allied strike against the Dardenelles in 1915 seemed to provide that 'moment' to emulate Pitt and 'to produce results all out of proportion' to the forces used – which is no doubt why it attracted a Cabinet looking for a cheaper way to win the war. Unfortunately for this scheme, the forceful Churchill managed to persuade and convince the Cabinet that it could be done even more cheaply than that – by the navy alone. The result, almost inevitably, was disaster, a confirmation of all that the experts had predicted would happen when warships attempted to force their way past strongly held land defences and floating mines. By the time a hastily improvised amphibious force arrived, the Turks had immeasurably strengthened their defences and the Allied troops which landed were virtually confined to the beaches until their evacuation at the end of 1915. The disaster at Gallipoli simply reinforced the views of those who insisted that any diversion of troops from the Western Front weakened the Allied war effort.

This did not fully stop the efforts to find a 'back-door' route to Berlin, however. In fact, part of Fisher's own hesitating attitude towards the Dardanelles operation was due to his wish to deploy the ships and the men elsewhere – on the Pomeranian coast! Admiral Wilson, for his part, preferred an assault upon Heligoland while their political chief, Churchill, predictably enough, was in favour of virtually any daring stroke. Later in the war there were again to be proposals for a large-scale intervention in the Baltic to keep Russia in the war or at least to forestall a German seizure of its fleet. All such ideas fell down in the face of the enormous practical disadvantages, even on the naval side alone. As the Deputy Chief of Naval Staff reported:

> Any attempt to enter the Baltic in force was ruled out by the undoubted presence of minefields whose positions were unknown, by the distance which disabled ships would find themselves from our bases, and by the strategical advantages possessed by the enemy in the existence of the Kiel Canal, which enabled him to move his Battle Fleet at will in a comparatively short time, through the canal, to the North Sea or the Baltic. A project for attacking one or other of the German naval bases was considered impracticable for similar reasons and on account of their heavy coast defences.[33]

In addition, there still remained that even greater obstacle, which the navy had never been able to overcome: the army positively refused to have anything to do with amphibious operations which not only would weaken the major land onslaught upon Germany but which also threatened to throw away many fine units. And while British generals regarded the schemes as a nonsense, the French political and military leaders saw such diversions as a virtual betrayal.

Gallipoli had ended in failure; the Salonika expedition was an inglorious waste of troops; and Baltic operations were deemed impracticable. Only in one region, in fact, were the 'Easterners' able to come into their own – the Middle East. Mesopotamia and Palestine were in their way the modern equivalents of Canada and Louisiana, of Bengal and the Cape. In terms of naval strategy, such gains could only be applauded: they strengthened the British hold upon Egypt and the Suez Canal, they sheltered the Indian Ocean from any northern challenger, and they made safe the oilfields. But the 'sideshows' of which Lloyd George was so proud were, as the 'Westerners' duly pointed out, an expensive business: by early 1918, just before Ludendorff's final great offensive, there were over 750,000 Empire troops (including twelve British divisions) serving in the Middle East and Salonika. Moreover, in no way could the campaigns of Maude, Allenby and Lawrence be described as combined or amphibious: they were essentially land affairs, with the navy's role a very minor one indeed. Once again, it found little opportunity to increase its stature, and was to remain in the army's shadow.

The world conflict of 1914–18 proved in the main to be no cheap and swift campaign, but a hard and bloody war of attrition by mass armies in which sea power appeared to be a subsidiary factor. It is perfectly true, of course, that had the U-boats won the Battle of the Atlantic, the war as a whole would have been lost by the Allies; and in both world wars the security of the sea routes to Britain was clearly London's first objective, without which little else could be done. Yet two points counted against the navy here. In the first place, this aim was essentially a negative one. The Senior Service could lose the war, but it could not win it: that had to be done by the army, which garnered all the credit thereby. In the second place, this war against the U-boats was a continuous series of small-scale actions which were hardly capable of exciting a public which had been brought up to expect glorious fleet battles and did not understand that these were not necessary to achieve that basic negative aim. In this respect, it would be no exaggeration to state that the course of the First World War substantially discredited that mighty host of great grey battleships, swinging on their anchors in the distant harbour of Scapa.

In addition to these fairly obvious aspects of the decline in the effectiveness of British sea power, there were two further, and equally serious developments: the financial and industrial losses Britain suffered during the war, and her increasing dependence upon the goodwill of other naval powers while she concentrated her fleets in European waters. The exact balance-sheet of Britain's losses during the war is still a matter for debate;[34] but what is clear is that instead of boosting the country to the front rank of the world's military/naval and commercial/industrial powers as the Napoleonic conflict had done, it caused grievous strain. About 745,000 Britons (9 per cent of the men under forty-five) were killed in the war, and a further 1,600,000 injured, many very seriously; merchant shipping of 7¾ million tons was sunk; British exports were also lost, in a direct sense, to central Europe, and in an indirect sense through the concentration of her industries upon war production; and, despite heavy tax increases, the National Debt rose alarmingly from £650 million to £7435 million. The United States replaced Britain in many world markets and took over as the greatest creditor nation, while the pound steadily weakened in value against the dollar.

A somewhat similar trend could be observed with regard to Britain's increasing dependence upon foreign navies on overseas stations. Here, too, was a continuation of that prewar development described earlier; but now that she was engaged in actual fighting, the dependence was much more real than when she was simply instituting a precautionary concentration of force against a rising German navy. In the Far East, for example, the Admiralty was forced after 1914 to rely more and more upon Japan, even though it reassured itself with the thought that this was only a temporary eclipse of its influence which would have to be restored after the war. But for the Cabinet and the Committee of Imperial Defence, at least, as one scholar has recently shown, the real problem was to evolve 'a diplomacy and strategy to underpin the permanent decline of British power in this region'.[35] In this sense, the war had only acted as an accelerator rather than as a catalyst; and the more Britain poured her resources into the European struggle, the relatively weaker her Far Eastern position became.

More alarming still by the closing stages of the war was the attitude of the United States, where the 'big navy' circles had persuaded Congress and the President to accept the idea of 'a navy second to none' – an aim which even Tirpitz, though he privately hoped for it, had never publicly outlined. Given the vast industrial resources of the United States, this ambition was clearly realizable: already by the end of the war the US Navy had a fleet equal in size to the combined navies of France, Italy and Japan, and the Navy Department was asking Congress for an eventual force of thirty-nine Dreadnoughts and twelve battlecruisers. Such a fleet 'dwarfed even the Grand Fleet in its prime', notes Professor Marder, particularly since all these vessels were modern whereas the majority of the British capital ships had been built before the war. And while Professor Schilling has argued that the real objective of this enormous progamme was 'to force Great Britain to support the League of Nations project and then to collaborate in a general reduction of armaments on the basis of naval equality with the United States', it is clear that Anglophobes like Admiral Benson were out to get the decisive *superiority* that this total implied.[36]

Here was the greatest naval challenge to the Royal Navy's mastery yet seen – and launched at the worst possible time, when Britain was heavily in debt to the United States, physically and psychologically exhausted by the war, and desperate to reduce her enormous defence expenditure. To emerge from the most destructive war in history with the prospect looming ahead of a ruinous naval race, with all its financial and domestic consequences, simply appalled British politicians and admirals, yet this seemed very probable unless an agreement could be reached with the touchy and suspicious Americans. The scuttling of the High Seas Fleet at Scapa eased the problem, but even before then Lloyd George had declared that he was satisfied with American promises to abandon or substantially to modify the 1918 additional programme instead of the basic 1916 fleet plan. The 'freedom of the seas' difference was simply shelved. Although the Cabinet as a whole professed its satisfaction with this compromise, it was apparent to all involved that only a truce rather than a lasting settlement had been reached, and that it was impossible to persuade the United States to acknowledge British maritime supremacy. Equally obvious was the underlying reason for Lloyd George's conciliation:

> What Britain needed to compete successfully with the United States Navy was a throbbing economy capable of undertaking new ships comparable to the Dreadnoughts and battlecruisers already authorized by Congress and far more. This Lloyd George did not have. . . . In 1919 British statesmen and naval men fought to retain acknowledged first place for the Royal Navy, but they failed because the exhausted island kingdom was unable to match the great resources of the continental United States. By 1919, in short, the trident was passing peacefully from Britain to the United States.[37]

In the interwar years those two long-term trends pinpointed earlier by Mackinder – the decline in Britain's relative position in world politics, and the challenge to the traditional navalist doctrines –

continued unabated. On the one hand, the Depression not only seemed to have more deleterious effects upon industry in Britain than elsewhere, but the collapse of international trade severely reduced the earning power of its financial and shipping services. On the other hand, despite the worldwide slump, those countries which were rich in land, population and technology – the United States and, to a lesser extent, Russia and Nazi Germany – had increased their relative economic strength by 1939 compared with such declining powers as Britain and France. Moreover, the introduction of the aeroplane as a military weapon was throwing into question the whole future of the surface fleets so praised by Mahan, although the admirals in all countries fought a strenuous rearguard action to preserve their capital ships. Add to this the failure to ban the submarine as a weapon of war, and the widespread public demand in Britain for drastic cuts in defence expenditures, and it is plain to see why the 1920s and 1930s are regarded as a 'black spot' in British military and naval history.

But the most unfortunate aspect of British defence policy in the interwar years was the failure to learn certain basic lessons from the 1914–18 conflict. The greatest of these was the impracticality of 'the British way of warfare' in a struggle involving continental powers with great industries and large armies which posed a threat to Britain's interests. As John Terraine has put it,

> the historical truth is there *was* no shorter way, until the possession and use of the atomic bomb by one side created it. . . . What the past has shown is that armies of millions, equipped by modern technology, cannot be defeated quickly, and that war economies show almost incredible capacity for survival even under the most intense duress, as Germany proved in 1944 and 1945. It requires the fullest, sustained pressure on both the military and economic fronts to achieve 'victory'.[38]

Instead, the British nation and its leaders, recoiling from the slaughter of the trenches, strove to recreate the golden days of splendid isolation. The army was reduced once again to being an imperial police force; the navy returned to the Mediterranean and to 'showing the flag'; and the Royal Air Force, although only effective in its forays against Arab tribes in the Middle East, was supposed to be a deterrent against any aggressor in Europe itself – a cheap and controllable substitute for a well-equipped expeditionary force. What they failed to see was that the Versailles settlement had not fundamentally altered the power balance in Europe. To those imbued in the traditions of Palmerston and Disraeli, perhaps this did not matter so much: they had gained German colonies, bases and coaling stations; and they had expanded into the Middle East. Under such circumstances, imperialists such as Curzon, Smuts, Milner and, by extension, Lloyd George, were willing to tolerate the continued existence of Bismarck's empire in Europe with only a few transfers of disaffected border regions. Yet this was the country which, as Professor Northedge points out,

> for the four and a half years of the First World War, with no considerable assistance from her allies, had held the rest of the world at bay, had beaten Russia, had driven France, the military colossus of Europe for more than two centuries, to the end of her tether, and in 1917, had come within an ace of starving Britain into surrender. It would have required a coalition of all these states, together with the United States, to contain Germany after 1918, even had the Nazis never come to power.[39]

Ironically enough, one of Mackinder's final books was to pinpoint again the nub of this problem. In 1919 he returned to his main theme with a plea for the Allied victors to create and actively to support East European 'buffer' states in order to prevent Germany from again seeking to dominate the continent: 'The test of the League', he warned, 'will be in the Heartland of the Continent.'[40] While Hitler and Nazi geopoliticians such as Haushofer accepted Mackinder's ideas with enthusiasm, the British disregarded them and remained cool to the notion of a continental commitment despite the fact that Germany's central position, large population and immense industrial potential would, if ever utilized by expansionist politicians, once again tend towards the domination of Europe. Against such a development, an isolationist, Empire-centred, pacifistic foreign policy by London would be a simple recipe for disaster, particularly when the new advances in tank strategy were to make land forces more mobile and hard-hitting than ever before.

There was no sudden change of attitude in London when Hitler's expansion commenced and the German threat to France became more marked as the balance of power tilted further towards Berlin through the reoccupation or conquest of the Saarland, the Rhineland, Austria and the Sudetenland. Even when the British began to respond, attitudes were confused and contradictory. On the one hand there was a growing awareness of how far she had fallen behind Germany in armaments production, and of the need to buy time until her weaknesses in this field were made good. On the other hand there lingered that dislike of a continental commitment and a distinct preference for a mainly maritime-based form of warfare – a tendency which the simultaneous threats from Italy and Japan only strengthened. It was as late as the spring of 1939, in fact, before the British Cabinet reconciled itself to the notion of sending an expeditionary force to France and instituting a limited form of military conscription, in a belated recognition of the need to preserve the balance of power in western Europe.[41] Nevertheless, the small size of this force suggested that its main purpose was political – to give 'moral' support to wavering and nervous allies.

The only comfort, so far as the Chiefs of Staff were concerned, was to be found in the fact that a war with Germany would be a lengthy conflict, in which the Allies would reveal the superior staying power. By using the traditional economic weapon of the naval blockade, by steadily augmenting the worldwide resources of the British and French empires, and by dealing with Italy first if that power dared to engage in war, the strategic experts hoped to find the best method of achieving eventual victory without too excessive a cost.[42]

For this reason alone, as for many others, the Second World War was very much a repeat of the first. It might seem that, in terms of actions fought and battles won, the performance of the Royal Navy in this conflict was incomparably better than in the first. So it was; but this was mainly due to the fact that that overwhelming superiority in ships and men, which had permitted the Admiralty to adopt a predominantly passive strategy between 1914 and 1918 and to reap the benefits therefrom, no longer existed. Now that they were stretched and strained throughout the globe, the British displayed an ingenuity and a ruthlessness which more comfortable situations rarely bring forth. Yet as soon as we take our eyes from the battles and the ships and the men, and turn to scrutinize those factors which form the basis for naval mastery, it becomes clear that, far from emerging in an enhanced position in 1945, British sea power had been grievously stricken by the war. Those trends which Mackinder had detected at the turn of the century had just received their greatest confirmation.

Essentially, all that the navy had done – and could do – in strategical terms was to keep open the sea routes to Britain from the outside world, just as it had done in the First World War. This was a quite vital function – in Churchill's words it was the 'foundation' upon which victory was based – yet it remained a negative, defensive contribution basically. Even here, however, the struggle was much more in the balance than it had been during the earlier conflict: the Mediterranean and Far Eastern routes were interrupted, the Arctic route had to be suspended occasionally, and the Atlantic losses were far heavier than in 1914–18 despite the swift adoption of the convoy system. What is also clear is that Britain only survived the U-boat onslaughts because of weapons and countermeasures which had little to do with the traditional ways with which she had maintained command of the sea: the introduction of American-built very long range Liberators to close the Atlantic 'gap'; escort carriers, again American-built in most cases; the strategic bombing campaign, which caused delays to the German submarine construction programme; and the launching of sufficient merchant vessels to keep pace with the sinkings, an activity where the United States equalled and then surpassed its staggering First World War production performance. The development of new methods of detecting submarines, the exhausting labours of convoy duty and the grim fights with the enemy were overwhelmingly an affair of the Royal Navy; but it is doubtful whether they would have sufficed without the assistance of these non-British, non-naval factors.

The most important of these new elements, predictably enough, was air power, indicated perhaps by the fact that whereas 246 U-boats were sunk by Allied surface craft, 288 were sunk by Allied aircraft (excluding bombing raids).[43] The Second World War saw the full arrival and exploitation of this revolutionary weapon and the fulfilment of the prophecies of Douhet, Mitchell, Trenchard and others that aircraft were vital to achieve dominance over land and sea theatres. As such, this did not invalidate Mahan's doctrine that command of the sea meant control of those 'broad highways', the lines of communication between homeland and overseas ports; but it did spell the end of the navy's claim to a monopoly role in preserving such sea mastery. And the Admiralty's established belief that a fleet of battleships provided the ultimate force to control the ocean seaways was made to look more old-fashioned than ever – and very erroneous and dangerous. Time and time again, off Norway, Dunkirk and Crete, during the Arctic and Mediterranean convoys, in the early stages of the war against Japan, the threat from the air was made plain. In the Pacific war the Americans demonstrated the supremacy of the aircraft-carrier while demoting their battleships to the role of preinvasion bombardment vessels. Yet when the British Admiralty belatedly sought to enhance its own fleet carrier numbers, it discovered that its shipyards were too cramped to do more than complete existing orders by the end of the war.[44]

If the Second World War demonstrated that command of the sea was dependent upon a prior command of the air, it also failed to confirm the superiority and effectiveness of maritime power in its more ancient relationship – with continental land power. In the American campaign against the widely dispersed Japanese Empire, of course, the outcome was different; but the British seemed never to have understood the basic geographical contrast between their two main enemies. Thus it was that the strategical role played by the Royal Navy against Germany was a mere repetition of that in the years 1914–18: holding the line. The fact that it was much more difficult and called for more frequent displays of heroism to accomplish this task – because the odds were greater, the convoy routes more dangerous and attacks from the air more common – should not obscure this basic point. In all other respects, too, the navy's tasks – and accomplishments – were to be repeated. There was no need to overrun enemy-held colonies (except those of Italy), but even if Germany had possessed overseas territories it is doubtful whether their capture by the British would have had any profound effect upon the war. Nevertheless, there remained the more important naval weapons of the blockade and the landing of troops, either for peripheral raids or for larger-scale strategical purposes. Yet in neither case was the part played by the navy as decisive as one might have imagined.

In view of the experiences of the First World War, of Germany's dominant military and economic position in Europe by 1939 and of the fact that she was bordered by neutrals, it is difficult to understand how British leaders could have been so confident of the effects of a naval blockade, even in the long term. Yet before the outbreak of war, as we have seen, the Chiefs of Staff had declared their faith in this weapon; and the swift overrunning of Poland did nothing to check their opinion that it was economic pressure 'upon which we mainly rely for the ultimate defeat of Germany'.[45] The American Neutrality Acts, which had the political effect of making the 'freedom of the seas' dispute an irrelevancy, were adjudged to be an additional advantage. As a consequence, Whitehall possessed a quite unjustified optimism about the struggle with Germany, the sole result of which was to make it disinclined to end the period of the Phoney War. 'What we ought to do is just to throw back the peace offers and continue the blockade,' noted Chamberlain. 'I do not believe that holocausts are required.' 'The Allies are bound to win in the end. . . .'[46] Despite the commitment of the expeditionary force to France, there lingered that traditional fear of trench warfare on a massive scale; which, together with the exaggerated notion of the effects of the 'Hunger Blockade' upon Germany in 1918–19, combined to persuade the British that it would not be necessary to oppose the enemy's vast armies until his resources and morale were crumbling.

The flaw in this calculation was a massive one and became even more apparent after the fall of France in 1940: London's estimate of the enemy's military strength contrasted sharply with its estimate of his economic power, even though those two elements had been so closely fused together that they were virtually indistinguishable. The well-known Russian and American charges of British tergiversation and reluctance to open a Second Front, although undeniably true, were easy to understand. To oppose a much enlarged *Wehrmacht* in complete control of the continent with a far smaller British Empire force was, even apart from the problems of air command and logistical support, a suicidal gesture, and Churchill was correct in resisting the pressure from his allies for a premature invasion. But it was precisely because Germany was in such a dominant position and controlled the destinies and economies of the greater part of Europe that the British should have been wary of any hopes of Nazi rule collapsing due to maritime pressure alone. Mahanite methods were ineffectual against a power which had adopted a Mackinderite programme.

On the face of it, the British experts reckoned, Germany was very susceptible to blockading pressure: like any modern industrialized state, she traded extensively with the outside world, and her war economy was dependent upon some absolutely vital raw materials.[47] Over 66 per cent of her ores for steel production came from abroad, as did 25 per cent of her zinc, 50 per cent of her lead, 70 per cent of her copper, 90 per cent of her tin, 95 per cent of her nickel, 99 per cent of her bauxite, 66 per cent of her oil, 80 per cent of her rubber and even 10–20 per cent of her foodstuffs. She was also heavily dependent upon imports of cotton, wool, mercury, mica, sulphur and manganese. Presented with these facts, it may not be surprising to learn that 'both government and country regarded the blockade as Britain's chief offensive weapon, and looked to it for decisive, or at any rate dramatic results.'[48] Yet this presumption could only be justified if Germany was an island; if the German leaders had been unable to take precautionary measures; if they could not secure supplies, either from friendly neutrals or conquered territories; and if her armed forces were so heavily engaged in battle that her stocks were being run down and her productivity insufficient. However, none of these provisos was to be true until the later stages of the war, when reliance upon the blockade had been abandoned for more direct measures in any case.

From the outset of his policy of aggression, Hitler had realized the dangers that might come about from the cutting off of overseas supplies and he strove, through the Four Year Plan and other measures, to combat the effects of a possible blockade. His aim, widely proclaimed, was economic autarky – an absolute freedom from dependence upon other states – and as such a direct contrast to the liberal concepts of international economic interdependence which influenced British attitudes. Such a target was to be achieved in part by the creation of substitutes, despite the higher costs involved: synthetic wool (from a wood base), rubber (from buna) and fuel (through hydrogenation) were the main products here. On similar grounds, low-grade iron ores which hitherto had been considered unusable were now exploited, and domestic foodstuffs production was intensified. Secondly, there was a ready flow of materials from pro-Axis and neutral states: ores from Sweden; oil, foodstuffs and copper from Romania, Russia and Yugoslavia; molybdenum from Norway; nickel and chrome from the Balkans; wolfram from Spain and Portugal: bauxite from Italy and Hungary. Only by a decisive blow in Scandinavia to cut the flow of Swedish iron ore to Germany could great damage be done to the Nazi economy by the Royal Navy – which goes far to justifying the Allies' Norwegian policy and at least part of the way to explaining Churchill's reckless scheme for operations in the Baltic.[49] The threat from German air power quashed this latter project, however, as it did the whole Norwegian venture.

Finally, there was conquest: the looting of Europe to enrich the 'Thousand Year' Reich and to create a completely autarkic economy. Once again, Hitler was quite clear about his plans. Russia, the Heartland, he enthused, would be the key: 'We shall be the most self-supporting state, in every respect, including cotton, in the world. . . .'[50] But on the way to this great aim many other countries could be pillaged. The victories in the west in 1940, for example, were not simply the military ones of defeating enemy armies or the strategical one of gaining access to the Atlantic; there was also the acquisition of the Lorraine-Luxembourg-Minette iron ore deposits; the stockpiles of various important metals in Belgium; more oil reserves in France than the *Wehrmacht* had used in the Polish, Norwegian and French campaigns together; and the opening of a land route to the tungsten and ores and wolfram of Spain and Portugal and the bauxite of North Africa. Similarly, the seizure of Norway secured the supply of molybdenum and nickel, the overrunning of Yugoslavia and Greece provided bauxite and other metals, and the virtual takeover of Romania greatly eased the

76

oil situation. As agents of this new *Herrenvolk*, the occupation forces and offices had no scruples about intensive exploitation of captured resources; the 'contributions' from these territories to Germany's national income rose from 8 per cent in the early years of the war to 20 per cent by 1942.

Nor was it true, until after 1942 at least, that the actual operations of war were draining the Nazi economy: until the battles of Moscow and Stalingrad the Germans were leisurely waging war, enjoying both the guns *and* butter that a *Blitzkrieg* strategy allowed. As a result British war production, far behind in the prewar years, caught Germany up and by 1942 Britain was actually spending half as much again on munitions, giving her a 60 per cent superiority in aircraft and small arms production and a 33 per cent superiority in tank output. In that year, however, with the defeats on the Eastern Front and the entry of the United States combining to convince the Nazi leadership of the need to organize for a long struggle, German production shot ahead again. Under Speer's leadership, the vast German labour force of 41·2 million (cf. Britain's 22·6 million; both 1943) and enormous industrial potential of half a continent was made much more efficient. On the eve of the Normandy invasion, ironically enough, Germany was better stocked in most types of military equipment than ever before – making the strategy of wearing down her resistance by blockade appear quite absurd.

Yet if British war production was being outpaced by a reorganized German industry, this provided little consolation in Berlin when Russian and American output was growing even faster. In the years 1942–4, Germany's annual production averages of 26,000 aircraft and 12,000 tanks and self-propelled guns were far behind the Russian averages of 40,000 and 30,000 respectively.[51] American war production was simply phenomenal: in 1941 it was only 75 per cent of Germany's, but by the following year it was already two and a half times as great and still in its early stages. Whereas the Americans had built only 2100 aircraft in 1939, this had risen to 48,000 in 1942, 86,000 in 1943 and to a staggering 96,300 in 1944. In fact, in the five years from 1940 to 1945 the United States produced 297,000 aircraft, 86,000 tanks, 17,400,000 small arms, 64,500 landing vessels and 5200 larger ships (of nearly

53 million tons).[52] In terms of military potential, therefore, the Americans were in a virtually unchallengeable position, with Russia second, Germany third and Britain only a modest fourth.

Nevertheless, if the 1939 beliefs in the effectiveness of a blockade and in the long-term British economic superiority over Germany were illusions, it remains true that the Nazi industrial machine collapsed into ruins between 1944 and 1945. The first cause of this was obvious: the losses in men and materials in the prolonged fighting against the Allies, particularly on the Eastern Front, were by then far in excess of Germany's resources. Furthermore, as the *Wehrmacht* was forced to surrender territory, so correspondingly did Speer lose supplies of raw materials – a trend which was aggravated by the increasing unwillingness of neutrals to provide help to a failing empire. Rivalries within the Nazi hierarchy, and the diversion of workers from production into fighting in October 1944, were equally deleterious in their effects. Most important of all, however, was the strategic bombing campaign, which after a disappointing first few years had by 1944 achieved the strength and the accuracy which its prophets had forecast for it two decades earlier. In February of that year the assaults upon the German aircraft industry caused structural damage in 75 per cent of all airframe component and assembly plants. Later in the year the bombers switched to oil production, causing such a crisis that German tanks, aircraft and warships were frequently unable to operate in crucial campaigns due to the lack of this commodity; and in early 1945 they struck at the German transport system with devastating effect, isolating the coalfields from industry. 'The development of the long-range bomber', Milward writes, 'provided a means of economic warfare infinitely more effective than the traditional blockade.' It was far more positive and specific, and the fact that 'many of the calculations on which the naval blockade had been based had been nullified by Germany's extension of her territorial area of control' made no difference to it. 'It effected a virtual revolution in economic warfare.'[53] Yet if Allied statesmen could rejoice at the achievements of this new weapon and encourage its use – and Britain is estimated to have devoted 50–60 per cent of its entire war production to the RAF – this simply served to illustrate the decline in the importance of the naval blockade and of sea power itself. The best that could be said about the traditional policy was that to abandon it might have eased the economic pressure upon the enemy. Nevertheless, the system of contraband control and pre-emptive buying at source was more effective than naval measures, and the official British historian of this topic has concluded that 'At no stage of the war was Germany decisively weakened by shortages due to the blockade alone.' Her Achilles heel was struck 'by the bomber and not by the blockade'.[54] Only Japan and Britain herself, being island states heavily dependent upon seaborne trade, proved economically susceptible to enemy naval pressure in the Second World War, although in both cases it was the submarine and not surface warships which provided the danger.

In almost the same way, the navy's inportance in amphibious operations was also overtaken by air and land power. Crete and Norway showed that such steps could only be taken when command of the air had been secured; Dieppe and Greece showed that small-scale interventions would always be punished by superior enemy forces able to rush swiftly to the point of attack. All signified, as the British Chiefs of Staff could see, that an invasion of western Europe would have to be a massive one and that they would have to wait upon the Americans. Yet the success of Overlord, when it came, was heavily dependent upon Allied air superiority, which had been steadily won in the preceding two years. British and American bombers devastated the enemy's communications system before the invasion started; their fighters protected the massive convoys and the bridgehead from aerial interference; and their bombers were again at work in the period after D-Day, checking the enemy's counterattack and forcing him to travel at night. By comparison, the navy's role was far less significant; its supporting gunfire was certainly of use to the invading troops, 'but the decisive factor was the paralysing effect of the Allied air forces . . .'[55] In any case, despite the undeniable success of the Overlord operation, the real stuffing was knocked out of the German army on its Eastern Front, where it suffered over four-fifths of its casualties and where Soviet military casualties were greater than those of *all* combatants in the First World War. Compared with this struggle for Mackinder's Heartland, the

British-led campaigns in North Africa and Italy were mere side-shows in the Churchill–Lloyd George tradition of avoiding the slaughter of frontal confrontations. Yet if the Second World War did anything – apart from illustrating the overall decline in the effectiveness of warships alone – it was to break the myth of the efficacy of the 'British way of warfare' against a power which straddled half a continent.

The greatest flaw in the British overestimation of the effects of their sea power lay in the associated calculation that, while the blockade was steadily sapping the enemy's strength, the superior economic resources of the Empire would be assembled to provide the eventual retribution; that, just as Britain's combined maritime and financial pressures had caused the collapse of the Dutch and French challenges in the seventeenth and eighteenth centuries, so too it would undermine the German threat in the twentieth. Yet this assumption, accepted by almost everyone from armchair strategists to the Chiefs of Staff, was based upon the fallacy that Britain's productive strength, her control of raw materials and especially her financial resources, were as well equipped to withstand war now as they had been in the era of her rise to economic supremacy in the Western world – which clearly was no longer the case. Contrary to expectations, it was she who experienced shortages of raw materials, caused partly by the Japanese conquest of Far Eastern sources of rubber, tin, sisal, hemp, tungsten and hardwood; and partly by the successful German 'counterblockade' of the U-boats. Moreover, as we have seen above, Britain could not match the munitions production of her enemy once Speer had reorganized the German armaments industry; nor could she, even with substantial Commonwealth reinforcements, hope to field an army strong enough to challenge the *Wehrmacht* on the continent. In May 1942, as the rapid rise in munitions output was beginning to reach that plateau dictated by the size of Britain's population, the Minister of Labour warned Churchill that further demands for manpower for the armed forces must be met mainly by diverting workers from industry, and thereby reducing production.[56] To keep up the war effort, to achieve the proclaimed aim of 'victory at all costs', they were forced more and more to rely upon the United States: she alone had the industrial capacity and the manpower to ensure the defeat of Germany in the west. In the second quarter of 1942 American military output caught up with the British; by the end of 1943, her production of aircraft was double, her launchings of merchant vessels six times, that of Britain; and by 1944 her overall armaments production was six times as large.[57] The full potential of her continent-wide resources, her great population, her more modern industry, was at last being realized – to produce a superpower which was as far ahead of Britain as the latter had been of the declining and smaller states of Spain, Portugal and the Netherlands centuries earlier.

The chief consequence of this disparity in strength was that Britain became dependent upon American aid to an ever-increasing degree: in 1941 10 per cent of the Empire's munitions came from that source, but it had risen to 27 per cent in 1943 and to 28·7 per cent in 1944. More specifically, the United States supplied – without any apparent strain to its own forces – 47 per cent of the Empire's total consumption of tanks, 21 per cent of small arms, 38 per cent of landing craft and ships, 18 per cent of combat and 60 per cent of transport aircraft. But the financial results of the 'victory at all costs' programme and the increasing dependence upon American production were disastrous for Britain: her position as an independent Great Power was shattered. Only emergency shipments of gold, and borrowing from Canada and the Belgian government, helped to keep her solvent by 1941, when her gold and dollar reserves dipped to a mere $12 million. In March of that year, however, Roosevelt had succumbed to Churchill's pleadings and to his own fears of a Nazi victory, and he persuaded Congress to pass the famous Lend-Lease Act. Yet the conditions of this aid, and in particular the restrictions upon Britain's exports, crippled the country still further in the long run and increased the extent of her dependence. The decline in exports, Correlli Barnett has noted, 'testified . . . to the degree to which, like a patient on a heart-lung machine, she was now dependent for life itself upon the United States'.[58]

Even the briefest survey of Britain's economic position in 1945 would indicate just how deleterious the conflict had been for her. Only in the number of human casualties could it be said to have been an improvement upon the First World War[59] – and that because of the determination to avoid mass assaults until the enemy's resistance had been sapped by the Russian army and the bombing campaign. Her losses in merchant ships totalled 11,455,906 tons, bringing the size of the fleet down to 70 per cent of its 1939 figure despite frantic rebuilding. Bombing had caused extensive damage to housing and industrial property, and the strain of six years of war had worn out much of Britain's plant and led to a heavy depreciation of capital equipment – which together destroyed some 10 per cent of her prewar national wealth at home and left her in a poor position to recapture her world markets. Lend-lease conditions and the single-minded determination to prosecute the war regardless of the financial consequences had led to the collapse of her export trade, which declined in value from £471 million in 1938 to £258 million in 1945. During the same period, imports rose from £858 million to £1299 million, overseas debt increased nearly fivefold, to £3355 million, and capital assets to the tune of £1299 million were liquidated, thereby halving the net overseas income from this source and making it even more difficult to achieve a balance of payments. She had probably lost about one-quarter (£7300 million) of her prewar wealth and was now in the unenviable position of being the world's largest debtor nation. And all hopes of a gradual transition to a peacetime economy were shattered by the unexpectedly swift defeat of Japan only three months after the German collapse, at which Truman cut off all lend-lease.

The writing was on the wall in other respects, too. The production of the atomic bomb – which appeared to render both sea power and land power irrelevant in a Great Power struggle – illustrated another arena where the British were being gradually left behind.[60] The Second World War also dealt the final blow to the notion of imperial unity: while nationalist unrest was provoked in Egypt, India and Burma, the self-governing Dominions found it prudent to reinsure with the rising star of the United States when it was apparent that Britain no longer possessed the strength to protect them.[61] Nor was the political picture more promising nearer home. By 1944 it seemed clear that the enormous superiority in men and materials of the Americans would soon bring them victory over a rapidly weakening Germany; but the steady rise in suspicion between Russia and the West led Churchill and others to the conclusion that the tyranny of the Nazi *Gauleiter* over central and eastern Europe was about to be replaced by that of the Soviet Commissar. The 'big battalions', to use Stalin's phrase, had decided who would control the Heartland and the Red Army was now advancing into Poland, Hungary and the Balkans – a development which the British had as little power to prevent as they had had in defending the Polish Corridor in 1939. Until the United States could be persuaded to recognize the possible danger and to support the liberties of Europe in both economic and military terms, there was little that Churchill could do except to try to arrange a 'deal' with Stalin in the hope of defining the limits of Russian expansion.[62] As the most exhausting war in her history was drawing to its close, therefore, Britain was as far away as ever from preserving that continental balance of power which was so congenial to her world interests and for which she had entered the struggle against Germany in the first place.

With the United States dominating the overseas world and Soviet Russia likely to dominate Europe, the age of the super-powers, predicted many decades earlier by de Tocqueville, Seeley and others, had at last arrived – and the British Empire was not among their number. Instead she was swiftly declining to the ranks of the second-class powers. The contrasts with the United States – and with Britain's own growth in an earlier age through the catalyst of war – were glaring enough to provoke the official historians to point them out at the end of their study of the British war economy:

> Despite all the contrasts of technology and of economic magnitude between the wars of the Napoleonic Age and those of the twentieth century there are some striking parallels between the situation of the United Kingdom in the earlier age and the situation of the United States in the later one. Each of these two countries, in its own fortunate time, was able to use the expansion of its exports as an instrument of war; each found itself, at the conclusion of the war, in some degree compensated for its efforts and sacrifices by an immense enhancement of its comparative economic strength among the nations. But the United Kingdom in the twentieth century found itself in quite the

opposite situation. The nation's struggle after the Second World War to overcome the consequences of an effort which had so heavily overtaxed its economic strength was bound to be a long one.[63]

Even at the height of the war, the US Military Staff could confidently predict that the profoundly changing world would soon see America and Russia as 'the only military powers of the first magnitude', a fact they attributed in each case to a Mackinder-like 'combination of geographical position and extent, and vast munitioning potential'. At the same time, there was little likelihood that either could emerge supreme since 'the relative strength and geographical position of these two powers precluded the military defeat of one . . . by the other.' To which prediction they offered the further statement that 'Both in an absolute sense and relative to the United States and Russia, the British Empire will emerge from the war having lost ground both economically and militarily.'[64] All great conflicts in the past had witnessed the rise and fall of empires: now it was the turn of two new states to achieve prominence, and of a third to withdraw from the centre of the international stage which she had dominated for so long.

The above essay, like all historical accounts not written at the time of an event, has enjoyed the immense benefit of hindsight. From our present-day vantage point, no one would dispute that Britain and her Empire collapsed more swiftly than the political prophets writing around 1900 could have imagined; or that the influence of sea power upon world affairs was also to be steadily curtailed over a similar period. Yet it would be churlish to upbraid Mahan for not having been able to forecast the future more accurately: economic and political events have been so varied and frequent since his time that a man loses little credit for being wrong about the direction in which the world is to move next. Mahan will always remain respected as the most important historian of British sea power, and as one who exerted a profound influence upon contemporary strategic thought, even though he was far less successful as a political and strategical pundit than as an analyst of the past.

In this latter respect, it appears that Mackinder, observing with fascination the way in which industrialization was steadily exploiting the potential of continental land-masses, was the better prophet. As such, he deserves a certain rehabilitation among military and naval thinkers, and a more widespread acknowledgement of the percipience of his writings. Although our complex world is changing very rapidly, we may still have a lot to learn from him – which is another way of saying that it is not infrequently the case that the accepted orthodoxy of the time is often less relevant and acclaimed in retrospect than a doctrine which was then obscure or unpopular. If there is one thing that historians should learn from their subject, it is an awareness of the constant modification of the course of events by new elements, and of the fact that the past is unlikely to repeat itself to any great degree in the future.

3

Far too often, the study of military history and the study of economic history are allowed to go their separate ways, with little effort being made to understand the connections between the two. This is, admittedly, much less true of the early modern period, where impressive work has been done on such topics as the financing of Philip II's military campaigns, and 'war and the English economy' in the eighteenth century. But perhaps it is one intellectual consequence of the study of the post-mercantilist age that financial and business matters have generally been kept apart from the world of strategy and diplomacy, just as the *laissez-faire* 'Manchester men' and the Whitehall mandarins preferred.

To students of Britain's Great Power decline in the twentieth century, however, economic issues can no longer be ignored: for the latter overshadowed, at first incipiently and then more persistently, almost every major decision in British grand strategy and diplomacy. If this has become very clear from the records of British 'appeasement' policy in the 1930s, where the role of the Treasury was vital (see essay 1), it was also true, implicitly, in the years before 1914; and, as the documents reveal, the Committee of Imperial Defence even in Asquith's time could not reconcile Britain's strategical interests with its financial requirements. To a large extent, as this article argues, the two were *irreconcilable*.

Although at first in some danger of falling into the 'gap' which looms between military history journals and economic history journals, the article was rescued by Professor Edward Ingram for the *International History Review*, where it appeared in 1981.

Strategy *versus* Finance
in Twentieth-century Britain

This article tries to trace some of the processes in the decline of a great world power.[1] Although the most obvious manifestations of Britain's demise occur *after* 1945, the object here has been to analyse certain long-term, structural weaknesses which go back beyond even the interwar years to the late-Victorian period. Being a general interpretation, the present essay has benefited from the flood of publications upon British external policy in the twentieth century which has appeared since the release of public records under the 'thirty-year rule'; but it has, of necessity, supplemented the findings of those books by further documentary evidence on specific points. In addition, since the natural tendency of military historians is to write military history, and of economic historians to write economic history, the thrust of this article is to demonstrate the interrelationship between the two subjects. For it is in the vicious circle of the repeated contradictions between British strategic planning and the nation's economic requirements in the era of the two world wars that one most clearly sees the inexorable process of decline from its earlier world primacy.

Before discussing the decline, however, it would be proper to recall the background of that British pre-eminence. Many reasons have been given for the country's rise, but it is worth emphasizing in particular that in the period between Elizabeth I's reign and the coming of free trade, British financial and strategic policies complemented each other more than in the years examined here. Both in the theory and in the practice of the mercantilist state in wartime, there was no inherent contradiction between the aims of the financial arm and of the fighting arm of the country: they were mutually supporting organs of the British grand strategy.[2] This presumed, of course, victory in the actual battles, especially those at sea; but, happily for the British, this *was* usually what happened. During the eighteenth-century wars, while its European rivals saw their economies weakened, their overseas trade and colonial empires reduced, and their naval power eradicated, Britain went – except in the War of American Independence – from strength to strength. The whole development provided a beautiful example of alternating cause and effect. The navy's decisive victories in these wars had given its merchants the lion's share in the booming overseas trade, which itself had stimulated the Industrial Revolution; yet this in turn was to provide the foundations for the country's continuing and increasing economic growth. Industrialization not only furthered the British ascendancy in commerce and finance and shipping, but it also underpinned its own naval supremacy with a previously unheard-of economic potential.[3]

Furthermore, this indigenous strength of the British economy, its usually successful wartime record, the fact that its overseas trade at the end of most of these wars was actually higher than at the beginning, all meant that the government's credit in the financial world remained high even in wartime, when it needed to raise loans in a hurry. Recent research shows how crucial was the government's reliance upon the money market to cover the gap between its wartime revenue and its expenditure.[4] In the short term, war was an expensive business; in the long term, because a mercantilist victory enhanced British overseas possessions and trade, and because the rise in customs and excise receipts could be added to the other available forms of taxation, war seemed to pay for itself. At any rate, it did not scare away the financiers, who readily subscribed to British government loans when other governments found it impossible to raise the cash. The Amsterdam money-lenders, for example, preferred to subscribe to British government loans even when their two countries were at war in the late eighteenth century, and even the suspension of cash payments by the Bank of England in the crisis year of 1797 did not undermine public confidence. On its credit and its navy, Lord Selborne later reflected,[5] the country rested; and each was dependent upon the other. Finally, one should note that, once the struggles with France came to a close after 1815, this position of pre-eminence could be held incredibly cheaply: the naval budget during the years of the so-called *Pax Britannica* averaged around £8 million per annum, a reasonable insurance policy indeed for a position of unmatched global pre-eminence.

This retrospective view of Britain's triumphal progress from the time of Elizabeth to that of Palmerston will doubtless appear too rosy to scholars of the period, who can point to certain less impressive factors: the wars with France (especially the Napoleonic War) produced domestic fissures and instability; the nation's wealth and strength would most probably have been even greater had peace prevailed; and the growing richness of Britain was not necessarily evidence of its *power*, which was still limited on the sea and even more limited on land (in India, for example). Yet despite such valid points, the overriding fact was that the country was growing *relative to its rivals*, whose own progress was distinctly retarded in consequence of the wars with Britain.[6] Furthermore, and of equal importance to the main theme of this essay, most of them failed to achieve victories – or gained at best a Carthaginian victory – primarily because they did not have the financial and productive resources to sustain such drawn-out conflicts. Thus, even if by 'Britain's rise' we really mean its increasing relative advantages over less favoured rivals rather than some preordained and trouble-free assumption of the Number One position in world affairs, it is this change in relative strength which is the most important factor. Similarly, in the twentieth century, it was the corresponding British decline compared with other nations which was more significant than changes in wealth, fire power or other indices of greatness.

It was from around the 1860s onwards that Great Britain's extremely favourable status began to alter, slowly but ineluctably, and the basic reason for this new development again lay in the economic sphere: in the final three or four decades of the nineteenth century its position as an *industrial* power of the first order – indeed in a class of its own – shrank rapidly as other nations overtook it in various fields of industry and technology, which are, after all, the foundations of modern military strength. British exports were forced, first of all, out of their favourable position in European and American markets while those countries themselves industrialized, often behind high tariff barriers; then out of certain overseas markets, where its rivals competed both commercially and, in further imitation of British habits, by establishing their own colonies and placing tariffs around them; and, finally, British industry found itself weakened by an ever-rising flood of imported foreign manufactures. This latter fact – the inability of the British to retain their domestic market in certain spheres – was the clearest sign of all that their industry was becoming inefficient and uncompetitive. It is not intended, however, to venture here into that much-debated question of the reasons for the slowing-down of British productivity in the later nineteenth century, which involves such complex matters as national character, generation differences, the social ethos and the educational structure as well as more specific failures of low investment, out-of-date plant, bad labour relations, poor salesmanship and the rest: a sorry tale which has a familiar echo about it today. Instead, one may simply note that whereas in 1870 the UK contained 32 per cent of the world's manufacturing capacity, this share was down to 15 per cent by 1910, when the USA had 35 per cent of the world's manufacturing capacity; and whereas Britain's share of world trade in 1870 was 25 per cent, by 1913 this had shrunk to 14 per cent.[7] These figures, once again, indicate relative decline, not an absolute fall-off in productivity and wealth; but in so many significant ways industrial capacity and strength, and the national power that attaches to it, is a relative thing. Britain is far richer, produces many more goods, and has more powerful defence forces today, for example, than in 1815 or 1860; but no sensible British government would conclude from such absolute increases that it could still act like Canning and Palmerston when its relative position is now so much less.

It is, indeed, this relative factor which renders unnecessary a detailed investigation of the internal reasons for Britain's economic decline in the later nineteenth century. In a certain sense this had always been quite probable, for its economic domination of the world after 1815 had rested upon a unique concatenation of circumstances very favourable to itself. It was not to be expected that Britain would remain eternally either the only or even the greatest industrialized nation; when others with larger populations and more resources took the same path, a relative decline was inevitable. As Professor Mathias has put it, 'When half a continent starts to develop, then it can produce more than a small island.'[8] In some ways Britain itself made decisive contributions to this process, both by building railways in foreign countries which were to enable their industries and agriculture to rival its own, and by establishing and developing those foreign industries with repeated financial injections. One might go further and argue that, hypothetically, it might have been better for Britain's world position in the long term had the Industrial Revolution not taken place at all; it was, after all, at or near the top of the tree in 1760, when industrial 'take-off' was beginning. And while the coming of steam power, the factory system, railways, later electricity, enabled the British to overcome natural, physical obstacles to higher productivity, and therefore increased its wealth and strength, such inventions helped the United States, Russia and central Europe even more, because the natural, physical obstacles to the development of their landlocked potential were much greater. What industrialization did was to equalize the chances to exploit one's indigenous resources and, as argued elsewhere,[9] to take away some of the advantages hitherto enjoyed by those small, peripheral, naval-cum-commercial states such as Britain and the Netherlands and to give them to the great land-based states.

What is perhaps more pertinent for the purposes of this paper was the second economic development, the growth of London in the nineteenth century to be the centre of the world's financial and commercial system. This had been helped already by Britain's early economic lead, by the ready availability of capital, and by the development of a sophisticated market for foreign loan issues and for international commercial transactions. It was boosted by two further factors: the wholehearted acceptance by the British establishment of *laissez-faire* commercial doctrines, which meant that London suffered from little or no governmental restrictions in becoming the centre of world finance; and, secondly, the growth in the economies and the trade of other countries, which then sought the services which the City of London could so easily provide. The economic benefits to Britain from this latter development were, naturally, very considerable. The massive rise in earnings from such 'invisible' services as shipping, insurance, commodity-dealing, banking and especially overseas investments more than compensated for the otherwise alarming increase in the balance-of-payments deficit on 'visible' trade.[10] To put it crudely, while many British industries were suffering from foreign competition, the City of London before 1914 was in its heyday, funding and arranging and insuring and shipping – and thus profiting from the growth in – the trade of foreign countries. Yet if the overall trade surplus of Britain prior to 1914 was actually rising because of the City's earnings, this was not in itself a guarantee of Britain's status as a Great Power, capable if necessary of taking on another Great Power. As one commentator has put it,

> For good or ill the root of success for the new industrial state was in the efficiency of its productive machine. . . . The point was, that the springs of wealth from financial income were less secure, less resilient, more subject to disturbance under the stress of political insecurity abroad or the shock of war than the solid indigenous strength of an efficient system of production and trade.[11]

After all, ploughshares can be turned into swords, car factories into tank factories, chemical plants into explosives works, if industry existed to be transformed from a peacetime to a wartime basis; but the centre of an international credit system, which is what Britain was, depends for its functioning upon there being not even a threat of war, for that upsets the markets and hurts credit. Here, hidden under the rising receipts of the City, was a fundamental contradiction between Britain's peculiar economic structure and its power-political status.

One can illustrate this point by reference to a series of investigations conducted by the Committee of Imperial Defence (CID) after 1911, when the second Moroccan crisis had suggested the necessity of taking account of the financial consequences of an Anglo-German war.[12] The strategic planners then discovered three alarming facts.

First, that whereas the gold stocks held by such state banks as the Bank of France and the *Reichsbank* in Berlin were very considerable, were considered as part of a national reserve, and were supervised to ensure that they would not be run down, the

gold reserves held by the Bank of England were minimal in relation
to the size of Britain's GNP and foreign trade; and further, that
there was no control to prevent such stocks being shipped out of
the country within a couple of days of a foreign bank's order for
gold. Yet all the efforts of the strategists to increase the centrally
held gold stock, or to control a sudden run upon it, were resisted by
a Treasury brought up in the *laissez-faire* assumption that gold
lying in a bank was a useless commodity compared with that in free
circulation, generating trade; and that any hint of controls would
ruin London's place as the central, and only really free, market for
gold.[13]

Second, the CID discovered that a large part of that booming
German foreign trade which was pressing certain British industries
so heavily was financed by London banks, in that German orders
for Australian wool, Peruvian silver and many other raw materials
were paid for by bills drawn on account in London, partly because
of the City's worldwide connections, and partly because farmers
and traders overseas wished to be paid only in sterling. Such
funding was naturally favoured by the City, for the banks' interest
charges on these transactions were bringing profits to themselves
and 'invisible' earnings to the country. But this meant, of course,
that at the outset of an Anglo-German war British banks would be
owed millions of pounds by German industry, which would not or
could not settle its debts because of Berlin's moratorium on foreign
payments; it meant, in other words, that the first stage of an
Anglo-German war might be the collapse of several important
London banks.

Third, the CID discovered that Lloyds of London not only
insured the British merchant marine but also much of the German;
and that its underwriters had declared themselves willing to pay
out for losses incurred in wartime by the action of *any* hostile power
(including the Royal Navy), whereas the Admiralty's strategy was
precisely to capture as many German merchantmen as possible at
the outbreak of war. Here was another glaring example of the
dichotomy between Britain's strategic needs and economic needs;
and throughout the CID investigations it is difficult to say who
were the more aghast, the strategists or the financiers, at the
assumptions of the other! It is, perhaps, worth recording the

delicious interchange which took place between Viscount Desart, the Chairman of this sub-committee, and Mr Ogilvie, a leading Lloyds underwriter:

CHAIRMAN: I want to put to you the particular case of a German ship which has been insured in England, captured by a British cruiser and either destroyed or condemned: do you consider your honourable obligation extends as far as paying in that case?
MR OGILVIE: If we had insured her before the war, I think so, certainly.
CHAIRMAN: Just consider the meaning of that. . . . We are at war with Germany; the navy of your country is endeavouring to put pressure on the Germans by destroying their trade, and in pursuance of that has captured a ship and destroyed it or condemned it, whichever it may be: do you not see that you destroy the whole effect of that act of war by compensating the German owner for the loss he has experienced?
MR OGILVIE: I quite see that point, and I saw it all through; but that is rather governed, from our point of view, by the honourable carrying out of our bargain.[14]

What this suggests is that the late-nineteenth-century transformation of Britain's economy from being the industrial centre of the world to being its financial centre – a transformation which, as mentioned before, handsomely covered its massive trade gap in 'visible' goods – meant that it was much more dependent upon international prosperity, much more a hostage to a continuing boom in global trade, and therefore much more vulnerable economically to the shock of war and the collapse of international credit, than those more tightly controlled, protectionist – one might say, mercantilist – economies of Germany, Russia, the United States and the other Great Powers (which is not to say that they would not have their own economic problems in wartime). Since the 1840s Great Britain had pinned its flag to the mast of international free trade, which was why, of course, even when its economy was suffering from foreign tariffs, 'dumped' manufactures and cheap agricultural imports in the later nineteenth century, it had felt unable to go protectionist itself. The implication of this free-trade policy, as Cobden had forecast, was that war would now be much more daunting to undertake than in the age of mercantilism, because the British economy was becoming ever more predicated upon eternal peace between the Great Powers. Just as, in territorial and strategic terms, the British Empire was sensitive as no other power to challenges in every part of the globe, so, too, was it financially unique and extraordinarily vulnerable to the collapse of the global trading system in the event of war. Yet, as the Assistant Under-Secretary of the Foreign Office, Sir Eyre Crowe, pointed out in 1914, a country which feels it cannot go to war under any circumstances has abdicated as a Great Power.[15] It was perhaps all right to be the centre of the world's credit system if one was scrupulously neutral, like Switzerland; but if one had an empire to protect, alliance and *entente* obligations to fulfil, and, more serious still, a traditional interest in preserving the European balance even in the era of mass armies and vast expenditure of resources in battle, how could one retain one's unique financial position?

The First World War gave the answer to that question: one could not. The economic consequences of the war, which is all that can be mentioned here, were extremely deleterious for Great Britain's world power status. It was true that many of the industrial deficiencies of the country were overcome, such as that embarrassing reliance upon neutral and even German production of vital items like ball-bearings, magnetos, aircraft engines, optical equipment, drugs and dyestuffs during the first part of the war; it was true, also, that rationalization of old, and creation of new industries under government direction led to some remarkable advances; and it was true, finally, that the country's accumulated wealth was by then so enormous that it weathered the economic storm without financial collapse. On the other hand, despite the vast rise in all forms of taxation, only 36 per cent of the costs of the war could be met from revenue, and the National Debt rose alarmingly from £650 million to over £7400 million, on which the annual interest payments alone were to consume 40 per cent of the central government budget in the 1920s. Secondly, its pre-eminence in merchant shipping and shipbuilding – both traditional sources of foreign currency – was badly hit, by the losses to U-boats and by the fact that British yards had to give priority to warship construction, leaving the Americans, Japanese and Scandinavians to fill the gap in merchant vessels. Similarly, the export of British manufactures declined, not merely to the markets of central Europe, but also to the rest of the world, for its own industry was forced to concentrate upon war production, thus enabling the Americans to dominate the Latin American markets and the Japanese and Indians to undermine Lancashire's supremacy in textiles in the Asian market. Finally, Britain's financial position was greatly weakened in relation to the United States, from whom it had been obliged to purchase a large variety of vital products, in part through the sale of dollar securities. Therefore, as the United States replaced Britain in many world markets and took over as the greatest creditor nation, the pound steadily weakened against the dollar and Britain's trade balance with dollar countries worsened. Its industrial predominance had long since gone, but it was hard to admit that its financial supremacy was also slipping away. And all this had occurred at a time when, if anything, its global obligations – in the Middle East, India, Ireland, the Far East – had increased. At the end of the First World War the British Empire stood at its territorial zenith; but that also meant that the gap between its commitments and its capacities was wider than ever. Fortunately for it, there arose no crisis large enough to expose that gap, in the decade following at least.[16]

What was worse, the interwar years were characterized, not by a revival of prosperity which, by creating wealth, might close that gap, but by a worldwide economic crisis of unprecedented severity from 1929 onwards. The traditional Victorian economy, as Hobsbawm puts it, 'crashed into ruins between the two world wars'.[17] It not only ceased to grow, it actually contracted for a while. The stable industries – textiles, shipbuilding, coal, iron and steel, still the mainstay of the British economy – found their export trade disappear due to foreign competition, tariffs and international financial uncertainties. Moreover, the world crisis, which saw trade in manufactures fall by one-third and in primary products by over a half, ravaged the service industries of the City, since they relied almost totally upon a high level of international trade and prosperity: annual earnings from shipping, commissions, insurance and overseas investments fell by some £250 million after 1929, and in 1931 Britain actually had a deficit of £103 million on 'visible' and 'invisible' trade combined. Restoring this alarming trend as soon as possible became the Number One priority of the British government.

Most histories of interwar Britain adequately cover the consequences of this economic crisis upon the country's foreign and defence policies. It obviously made the settlement of international disputes by conciliation ever more urgent. It reinforced the demand, by Treasury and public alike, for the further reduction in defence expenditures in order to secure a balanced budget; a demand which can also be connected with the widespread revulsion against war which the experiences of 1914–18 had produced, and with the rising demands of a fully blown democracy for social and economic reforms in preference to military expenditures. This alteration may be best expressed statistically, by comparing the breakdown of British public expenditure before the First World War with that of the interwar period:[18]

Public Expenditure (£ million)

	1913	1933
Defence	91·3 (29·9%)	112·4 (10·5%)
Social services	100·8 (33%)	497·2 (46·6%)
Economic services	39·9 (12·9%)	111·8 (10·5%)
National Debt	18·7 (6·1%)	228·4 (21·4%)
TOTAL	305·4 (100%)	1066 (100%)

Despite the toll taken by price inflation,* British defence expenditure had really only increased between 1913 and 1933 insofar as a third service (the Royal Air Force) existed, consuming £17·1 million by the latter date.

The consequence of this relative neglect of the armed services was that when there arose, only slightly later and almost simultaneously, threats to world peace in the Far East, the Mediterra-

*Index of current prices [1900=100]: 1913=109; 1933=174.

nean and central Europe, the fighting strength of the British Empire was weaker in relation to its potential enemies than at any time since 1779. A whole series of investigations by the Chiefs of Staff in the early 1930s catalogued a multitude of deficiencies in defence; but a fear of upsetting public opinion, and the obstinate resistance of the Treasury, together with the inefficiency of the British industrial machine by this time, meant that it was to take years before even the most glaring of those deficiencies was made good. In that intervening period, the British government was forced to temporize, to concede, to 'appease' the demands of the dictators.[19]

That military weaknesses decisively influenced British foreign policy in the 1930s cannot be doubted; but there is a danger, particularly in the 'guilty men' historiography of appeasement, of ignoring the awful fact that in the long run the Treasury was absolutely right in its Cassandra-like forebodings of the consequences of large-scale defence spending by an economically weak state such as Britain. When it conceded in 1932 that the Ten Year Rule should be abandoned, it was not exaggerating in simultaneously warning that 'today's financial and economic risks are the most serious and urgent that the country has to face'.[20] It is true that in the early 1930s some extra expenditure on the forces would have had beneficial effects in strategic and industrial and employment terms; but the amount of cash that was needed to rebuild a two-ocean navy, to provide the RAF with both its fighter defences and its long-range bombers, and to equip the army for a European field role – all of which was demanded by the Chiefs of Staff in the months after Munich – was well beyond the industrial and financial capacity of the country. The great increases in government expenditure in the late 1930s, the enormous defence loans, did cause inflation; the many orders abroad for machine tools, steel, aircraft, instruments, which a weakened British industry could not produce itself, drastically raised the amount of imports; yet the transition of the economy from a peacetime to a wartime basis meant that the proportion of manufactures devoted to exports was falling rapidly; and the general level of international trade and finance at the time gave no hope that Britain's earnings from 'invisibles' would cover the yawning trade gap. The economy, Sir

Thomas Inskip remarked in 1937, was 'the fourth arm of defence'[21] because its strength was needed to underpin the other three arms, particularly in a long war; and the Chiefs of Staff, aware of their military inferiority against the German army, could only envisage victory if the war was to be a long one, in which the blockade would sap the enemy's strength while the worldwide resources of the Empire would be steadily assembled in order to deal the final blow.[22] But by the late 1930s it could hardly be said that the economy was underpinning Britain's military effort – far from it.

Leaving aside the not inconsiderable fact that a naval blockade was to be quite useless against the autarkic economic policy of Nazi Germany, we can now see from the recently released official documents that the most glaring dichotomy of all between Britain's economic and strategic aims actually emerged in the period when the government was abandoning appeasement, after Munich and Prague. The Treasury's resistance to massive defence spending had by then been overcome; but it still had an opinion, and it still continued to advise its political masters about the state of the economy. The financial trends were, from its viewpoint, horrifying: the balance of payments was worsening rapidly, the standard rate of income tax was higher than at any time since 1919, and there was no way in which the swelling defence expenditures could be paid for except by going to the money markets. Yet borrowing itself placed a further question-mark over the government's commitment to economic stability and, thus, over its long-term credit, which was no longer as highly esteemed as in the eighteenth century. The Czech crisis of 1938 led to the withdrawal of £150 million to 'safer' places of deposit, and by 1939 a further £150 million had left the country. 'Everyone knew', the Treasury pointed out, 'how shaky our position was and world opinion was so susceptible that no one could tell when the slide might not begin.'[23] A sterling crisis, draconian fiscal controls, high interest rates, all loomed before the Treasury's eyes; and this in turn would have a reciprocal effect upon the nation's long-term military strength. As one alarmed Under-Secretary at the Treasury noted, in March 1939,

Defence expenditure is now at a level which must seriously call into question the country's ability to meet it, and a continuance at this level may well result in a situation in which the completion of our material preparations against attack is frustrated by a weakening of our economic stability, which renders us incapable of standing the strain of war or even of maintaining those material defences in peace.[24]

In view of such messages, which were bound in any case to echo Neville Chamberlain's longstanding apprehensions, it is scarcely surprising to observe how the Prime Minister sought throughout the first eight months of 1939 to improve the atmosphere between Britain and Germany; and it is even less surprising that the British pursuit of appeasement by economic means was secretly accelerated.[25]

Although Hitler's further aggressions and the angry reaction to them of the British public dashed Chamberlain's hopes of preserving peace, the entry into war in no way eased the basic dilemma which has been mentioned above. A long war, the only one the Chiefs of Staff thought they might have a chance of winning, would lead in all probability to economic collapse: as the Treasury coldly pointed out in April 1939, 'If we were under the impression that we were as well able as in 1914 to conduct a long war, we were burying our heads in the sand.'[26] Yet a short war, the only one the British economy perhaps could afford, was not one which the country would be able, in the opinion of the Chiefs of Staff, to win. This was a grim prospect for a nation which once had been called 'the workshop of the world'.

A similar sort of dilemma to the budgetary one also existed in regard to commercial policy in the 1930s. It was true that in many respects the structure of British foreign trade had altered since the pre-1914 period. Protection had returned, at least to a limited extent, after the Ottawa Conference of 1932; trade with the Empire was more valuable than that with Europe; and foreign trade as a whole formed a much smaller part of the country's wealth than a quarter-century earlier. Yet the weakened nature of the British economy, its vulnerability to foreign competition on the one hand and to the loss of international confidence in sterling on the other, and especially its need to pay for imports by increasing exports, meant that the government favoured any policy which would lead to further foreign trade. In addition, there was that political and moral calculation behind 'economic appeasement' which derived from the teachings of Adam Smith, Cobden and Woodrow Wilson: increasing international commerce would, it was argued, improve the economies and standards of living of all the peoples concerned, thus drawing the sting out of the resentments of the dissatisfied nations of the world and creating a better climate for the settlement of international differences. In the mid to late 1930s, it was hoped that the development of Anglo-German trade, and possible loans to assist the recovery of the German economy, would not only establish friendly relations and a sense of interdependence, but it might also aid the so-called 'moderates' (Schacht, Goering, *et. al.*) within the Nazi hierarchy in their supposed argument that it was more profitable to cooperate with the Western democracies than to fight them.[27] Yet this hope, understandable no doubt from the viewpoint of a British economy predicated upon international trade and cooperation, ignored – as Cobden himself had ignored – the awful possibility that other political cultures might not adhere to such enlightened principles.

One example may be sufficient to illustrate this dilemma. At the end of 1938 and beginning of 1939, Magowan, the commercial counsellor at the British embassy in Berlin, strongly questioned the continuance of the 1934 Anglo-German payments agreement, which had been made to keep trade between the two countries at a high and mutually satisfactory level. What had actually happened was that the Germans had used their access to sterling, which the payments agreement gave them, to maintain their own mercantilist economic policy, to purchase raw materials and strategic goods for stockpiling, and to maximize their armed strength. A future war, not eternal peace, was apparently uppermost in the German mind; yet when Magowan argued for an embargo on raw materials exports to Germany, this was resisted by the Treasury and the Board of Trade and he was, in fact, reprimanded.[28] A small affair in itself, it reveals once again the twin horns of the dilemma upon which the British were impaled. The country's economic needs required peace, stability, and flourishing international trade with all, including (more than ever perhaps) potential enemies, so as to ameliorate tensions; but its strategical requirements necessitated planning and in some cases preparations for a conflict with those states, preparations which were economic as well as military and which could well be at a cost to one's own trading interests. Yet the dilemma did not end there: if it is assumed that war is inevitable and preparations are made, then (as the Treasury warned) with a weak economy such as Great Britain's, certain measures could actually be further undermining national prosperity and the prospects of enduring a lengthy conflict; if, however, it is assumed that peace is not only desirable but also still feasible, then there is no desire to break trade links or hasten the pace of rearmament, but that runs the risk of aiding the potential foe's economy and leaving one's own country with weaker armaments should this assumption about continued peace prove wrong.

To this catalogue of problems about reconciling Britain's economic and strategical needs, one further point of difficulty should be added. Appeasement, as is well known, involved concessions, readjustments within the international system, attempts by the 'satisfied' powers to meet the demands of the 'dissatisfied' ones in various parts of the globe. Yet this did not mean concession and retreat at all levels. Recent studies of appeasement have shown that, even if London was prepared to concede predominant political influence, in the Far East to Japan,[29] in eastern Europe to Germany,[30] it was desperately keen to preserve Britain's economic position in those areas. Whether naive or not, this hope was based upon an acute recognition of the unique importance to the British economy of trade and investment in the non-industrialized world outside Europe and, slightly less so, in the quasi-independent economies of eastern Europe. The contradiction here is obvious. Militarily, the British admitted that they could not influence the course of events in eastern Europe and the Balkans. This was probably also true in regard to Japanese expansionism in the Orient and tacitly admitted since the Manchurian crisis or perhaps since the Russo-Japanese War. Yet, paradoxically, in the interwar years the British needed to retain their commercial and financial interests in those regions more than ever before. After showing how much British statesmen in the late 1930s sought to cling on economically to what they could not preserve militarily, it is not surprising that certain of these newer studies disagree with the older picture of appeasement as being one of surrender.[31] On the other hand, this resolve to preserve British trade and investments could not be taken to the brink of war, for that would be even more disastrous economically: hence the financial pull-out from Czechoslovakia after Munich; hence the retreat in the Tientsin crisis of 1939, when the Admiralty warned the Foreign Office and Cabinet that it was impossible to wage war in the Far East. Again and again, Whitehall had to measure the costs of retreat against the (incalculable but no doubt enormous) costs of standing firm to the point of going to war. In each case, the British would lose something.

This, indeed, is the general conclusion which emerges from all of these examples of the contradictions between Britain's economic needs and strategical requirements by the late 1930s. The blunt fact of the matter is that the Treasury was perfectly right in its appeal to preserve financial stability, and the Chiefs of Staff also were perfectly right to urge the need for further armaments. Each course brought its share of disadvantages: there was only a choice of evils. The crisis in the British global position by this time was such that it was, in the last resort, insoluble, in the sense that there was no good or 'proper' solution. Naturally, the British were intent upon preserving the *status quo*, but the point was that they lacked the power to do so. By 1939 it is doubtful, to say the least, whether they could have won a war against Germany alone. They would even have found it difficult to take on Japan alone. The prospect, therefore, of a conflict with Germany, Japan and Italy combined was horrifying. France could not swing the balance, Russia was unpredictable, the USA was still wreathed in isolation, and the Empire was more of a liability than an asset in military terms. Is it all that surprising that the defence chiefs pressed for armaments spending, which the Treasury could see was beyond the country's resources to produce; or that the Treasury, in striving to preserve financial stability, was criticized by the strategists for obstructing vital defence measures? Each side had its case. Whatever course the government took, it was liable to criticism; and, in the pressing circumstances of 1939, it not surprisingly elected to achieve military security even if that prejudiced its economic security.

The solution, such as it was, could not be found in the country itself but came in March 1941 when the Lend-Lease Act was passed by Congress – by which time, it may be noted, Britain's gold and dollar reserves totalled a mere $12 million, and it was only that high because of borrowing and gifts from Canada and from the Belgian government-in-exile (which had prudently brought its gold stocks with it when abandoning Brussels in 1940).

By 1945, it was clear that Churchill's decision to keep on fighting after the disastrous summer of 1940 had been vindicated, and Britain had played a major role in holding the dictator-states in check. It had, indeed, made economic sacrifices to that end which few of the other combatants matched; but it had only been able to keep up that struggle with repeated injections of American financial aid and an increasing reliance upon American armaments, rather like its own German or Dutch allies in the eighteenth-century wars whom it had so easily subsidized. The harder the British fought, the more they had bankrupted themselves.

During the Second World War, indeed, only the United States – like Britain 150 years earlier – had really been powerful enough to be able to keep economic and strategical requirements in harmony, due to industrial productivity, military successes and a clever quasi-mercantilistic commercial policy. For Britain, the results were different, in part because of its overall decline relatively as an industrial and power-political unit, and in part because of its peculiarly cosmopolitan and vulnerable economic system which had evolved since the middle of the nineteenth century. In an ironic way, it may be said that Cobden had been quite correct in his belief that Britain's abandonment of mercantilism would increase the incentives for not going to war: where he and many others had been too optimistic was in the assumption that everyone else would feel the same way about it. In the years immediately preceding the two world wars, the documents suggest, British statesmen and their officials became aware of the awful dilemma which arose when an economy predicated upon eternal peace coexisted in an international situation where major war was a real possibility. Since they could neither amend this basic economic structure, nor successfully ease the international tensions, it was clear that they were in for a rough time – as is the fate of most declining empires. But one doubts if even the planners knew how rough it was going to be.

II

Germany and England: the Naval Aspects

4

The essay which follows is a small-scale experiment in two types of history: the biographical, which is so popular in the Anglo-Saxon tradition; and the comparative, which (while often advocated) is far less widely practised, chiefly because of the difficulties involved. The main purpose of this exercise was not so much to analyse the characters of the two admirals in question as to show how they both reflected the prominence given to technical and *matériel* development in the naval thought and practices of the time. Although much comparative history is concerned with institutions and social groups, there is no inherent reason why the methodology cannot be applied to particular individuals in history.

This article was originally written at the invitation of Professor Gerald Jordan, for inclusion in *Naval Warfare in the Twentieth Century 1900–1945. Essays in Honour of Arthur Marder* (London and New York, 1977).

Fisher and Tirpitz Compared

On 29 March 1916 that restless and controversial character, Admiral 'Jacky' Fisher, penned the following letter to his old rival, Admiral Alfred von Tirpitz:[1]

Dear Old Tirps,
   We are both in the same boat! What a time we've been colleagues, old boy! However, we did you in the eye over the battle cruisers and I know you've said you'll never forgive me for it when bang went the *Blücher* and Von Spee and all his host!
   Cheer up, old chap! Say '*Resurgam*'! You're the one German sailor who understands war! Kill your enemy without being killed yourself. *I don't blame you for the submarine business*. I'd have done the same myself, only our idiots in England wouldn't believe it when I told 'em!
   Well! So long!
   Yours till hell freezes,
                                        Fisher

It was not a particularly profound or percipient message in itself, yet nonetheless it gives us a clue to some of the remarkable similarities in the careers of the two most famous admirals of the early twentieth century – similarities which at first sight appear the more marked because the men concerned were on opposing sides and represented countries so different in their historical, strategical and political traditions. Even a reader ignorant of the detailed past of these two personalities could appreciate how ironic it was that, while the great Anglo-German maritime conflict for which Fisher and Tirpitz had been preparing their respective navies for so long was now raging, both men were 'on the sidelines' and no longer in a position to influence the direction of the war.

Yet the similarities do, in fact, run through the entire careers of the two men, so much so that it appears to be unlikely that they can be satisfactorily explained solely on the grounds of an amazing personal coincidence. Indeed, it is equally probable that Fisher and Tirpitz both rose to power because of the particular historical conditions in which they lived – conditions of which they took full advantage and which were available neither to the preceding nor to the succeeding generations of admirals in the British and German navies. If the title of this contribution seems strongly biographical, therefore, it is not its main purpose to present character sketches pure and simple but rather to examine the circumstances in which Fisher and Tirpitz flourished for so long. Despite the personal characteristics peculiar to each of them, they were very much 'men of their time'.

The similarities between Fisher and Tirpitz may be said to have originated in their family backgrounds.[2] Both came, not from the traditional decision-making élite, the aristocracy, but from those middle-class professional and service families which provided so much of the character and energies of nineteenth-century European society. Fisher's mother was the daughter of a London wine-merchant; his father, although descended from the Warwickshire gentry, an army officer turned coffee planter in Ceylon. Tirpitz's mother was the daughter of a physician; his father a judge. The traditions of this class in both countries emphasized individual initiative and self-help, service and duty to society, and a general 'liberal' outlook upon politics, at least if understood in the context of the time. Success in their chosen profession would mean a rise through the ranks of the middle class, recognition and honour from the state, possibly even ennoblement: Fisher, for example, received his knighthood in 1894 and was raised to the peerage in 1909; Tirpitz was ennobled in 1900. As a consequence of their distinction, both men came to mix freely with their respective monarchs, cabinet ministers and other people of influence. Nevertheless, neither was fully 'integrated' into the establishment but remained to a certain extent an outsider, critical of what Fisher termed 'the old gang' which rested upon its laurels and possessed neither the will, nor the imagination, nor the expertise to carry out great national tasks. For both admirals, being kept out of power by the middle years of the war simply confirmed this impression in their minds.

To a very large extent, this sense of expertise and the professional pride felt by Fisher and Tirpitz was justified by their rigorous training, wide experience and successful careers. From an early stage, they had both been recognized as exceptionally gifted officers within their respective navies and 'tipped' for high positions. Fisher's career was the more varied. After his early years as a midshipman, lieutenant and commander on board a variety of vessels, he became Captain of the Royal Navy's gunnery school HMS *Excellent* (1883), Director of Naval Ordnance (1886), Admiral Superintendent of Portsmouth Dockyard (1891), Controller and Third Sea Lord (1892), Commander-in-Chief, North America and West Indies (1897), Commander-in-Chief, Mediterranean (1899), Second Sea Lord (1902), Commander-in-Chief, Portsmouth (1903), and finally, First Sea Lord (1904). Tirpitz similarly followed his early career at sea with predominantly shore-based positions; in 1878, as officer in charge of the German navy's embryonic torpedo section; in 1890, after a year at sea in the Mediterranean, as Director of Dockyards and, only a few months later, as Chief of Staff of the Baltic Station; in 1892, as Chief of Staff of the High Command, where he was responsible for developing the tactics of the battlefleet; in 1896, as Commander-in-Chief of the East Asian Squadron; and finally, in 1897, as Secretary of State at the Reich Navy Office. In each post which the two men occupied, they produced a virtual explosion of activity, innovation and radical improvements. As organizers, they were clearly superb. In each case, too, despite assuming the most prestigious overseas command of both navies (the Mediterranean Fleet and the East Asian Squadron respectively), they spent most of their time on shore, which was no doubt inevitable as they climbed up the higher rungs of their naval hierarchies.

More important still, their early careers shaped and confirmed both Fisher and Tirpitz as leading advocates of the *matériel* school. In an age of rapid technological change, when improved gunnery, torpedoes, electricity, turbines, mines, submarines and radio were to have an enormous impact upon naval warfare,[3] this was no doubt unavoidable – indeed, one of the reasons for their own rise was precisely this ability to see the importance of utilizing such new inventions. Yet it is worth suggesting that both men were so busy encouraging and adapting to the technological innovations, organizing their battlefleets, perfecting tactical manoeuvres, improving the gunnery, torpedo, signalling, supply and engineering sections, ensuring adequate logistical and dockyard support for the warships, and striving to retain the sympathy of politicians and the public, that they had little or no time – or inclination – to consider the fundamentals of naval strategy and the extent to which the new technology was revolutionizing the conduct of naval warfare.

The strategical conceptions of Fisher and Tirpitz will be examined later. In the years before the outbreak of war, the importance of this aspect was somewhat overshadowed by the impression of sheer productivity, efficiency and innovation which both men exuded. What struck most observers was the way in which they were getting down to their respective tasks: Fisher to bring the prestigious but dilapidated Royal Navy, kicking and screaming, into the twentieth century; Tirpitz to fashion what was virtually a new service. Both men, too, seemed to know where they were going, to have a 'blueprint' or a 'plan'. Fisher's shoals of memoranda, all stamped with his colourful personality, bowled over his contemporaries and still make delightful reading today.[4] Yet Tirpitz also, if less flamboyant about it, demonstrated from the beginning of his long years as Secretary of State that he had a well thought out system; indeed, as V. R. Berghahn and J. Steinberg have shown, even in 1897 he was planning towards the giant German battlefleet which would exist in two or three decades' time.[5] Little wonder, then, that the Kaiser, bitterly angry over the Reich Navy Office's previous lack of imagination and inability to obtain Reichstag assent to a large fleet in the early and mid-1890s, was delighted when Tirpitz could produce a coherent naval development programme and then secure parliamentary approval, not only for the First Navy Law, but also for all subsequent extensions to it.

If Fisher and Tirpitz were recognized as men who 'got things done', it would be a mistake to explain this solely in terms of their professional skills as naval administrators. The sheer force of their personalities was also a vital ingredient in their success, although 'force' may be an ill-chosen word in respect of Tirpitz, who was cautious, steady and liked to ponder for a long time before making a decision. Nevertheless, each was determined to carry out his chosen task regardless of the opposition. Neither tolerated fools easily; nor, unfortunately, did they take kindly to criticism which had more reason behind it. Both were hypersensitive to real or imagined threats to their personal position, and took ruthless action – ranging from direct opposition to secret discrediting of their foes – to counter such challenges. Few men came away from talking with Fisher without feeling impressed, and sometimes overwhelmed, by his articulate and spicy language, wild imagination, engaging frankness and boundless energy in conversation ('Will you kindly leave off shaking your fist in my face?' Edward VII once protested); yet observers were also impressed by Tirpitz's quieter presence, his command of a subject, and his self-evident determination to get his way which was in no degree contradicted by his diplomatic handling of those whom he thought he could win over to his point of view. If he did not terrify in personal conversation, as Fisher often did, he was formidable on paper. Both admirals clearly had a sense of mission, a feeling that they alone could carry out their great task although the obstacles were great and time was closing in. Fisher, certainly, gave the impression of an old man in a hurry and, after all, by the occasion of the great Anglo-German naval 'scare' of 1909, he was already sixty-nine years old; yet Tirpitz was sixty-one by then and all too aware of the internal and external threats to his own plans, especially since he had no 'safe' successor to continue his work in the way that Fisher counted upon Admiral Wilson.

Few people had neutral feelings about Fisher or Tirpitz; they either attracted or repelled. Both left a trail of crushed opponents in their wake: those naval officers who were not in the 'Fishpond', or others, outside the service, who stood in Fisher's way; and Tirpitz's own long list of rivals, professional and political. Fisher's ruthless treatment of opponents is well known to British readers:

'If you oppose my education scheme I will crush you,' he spat at one unfortunate, Captain Egerton, in 1903.[6] The great controversy with Beresford, that equally colourful and forthright admiral, is the most notorious of the many storms which surrounded Fisher, but he made many other enemies and rarely forgave them. Custance, Lambton, Sturdee, Berkeley Milne, he persecuted relentlessly; Sir George Clarke he broke with when that official criticized the Admiralty's lack of strategic planning; the army he held in contempt, to which he added a deep animosity when it began to work out a 'continental' strategy with the French after 1905; when the Committee of Imperial Defence appeared to support the army, he cold-shouldered that institution as well; and during the bitter controversies of the war itself, he broke with such old friends as Balfour and Jellicoe.

For Tirpitz the challenges from rivals which had to be beaten off were, if anything, the greater, since he was not (like Fisher, as First Sea Lord) the professional head of the service but simply the chief of *one* of the numerous naval departments which stood immediately below the Kaiser in the latter's capacity as Commander-in-Chief. Admittedly, this Byzantine system of divided authority, which Wilhelm refused to alter lest it detract from his personal control, was likely in any case to lead to clashes between, say, the strategical and the financial branches of the navy; what Tirpitz added to this was a determination not to be thwarted in any of his aims. While still a captain, he showed himself to be a clever political tactician and a resolute defender, and enhancer, of his own power-base. As Chief of Staff of the High Command he strongly maintained that institution's claims but, as soon as he became Secretary of State of the Reich Navy Office, he began to whittle away at the powers of the High Command, which as a result was re-formed in 1899. This, however, was only the beginning of a constant struggle against rival departments, particularly the Admiralty Staff (which took over strategic planning from the High Command in 1899) and the Marine Cabinet (which was responsible for personnel matters), for there were of course many points at which their respective areas of competence overlapped in practice. Tirpitz also dealt vigorously with such naval officers as Valois and Maltzahn, who wrote against his battlefleet strategy and in favour of their own *guerre de course* ideas; indeed, the Kaiser was persuaded by Tirpitz to promulgate an order forbidding naval officers to have their opinions published without obtaining prior permission. Like Fisher, too, Tirpitz struggled against the rival claims of the army, seeking at the Rominten audience with Wilhelm of September 1899 to divert a larger porportion of the defence budget to the navy, opposing after 1911 the General Staff's demand for priority to be given again to continental rather than 'world' policy, criticizing the decision to go to war in 1914 and deploring the inferior role which the navy had to play in it. But perhaps his greatest fight was with those civilians who attempted to frustrate his construction schedules in order to improve relations with Britain: that is, with the Foreign Ministry and its ambassador in London, Count Metternich, and especially with the Chancellor, Bethmann Hollweg, for whom Tirpitz conceived an unrelenting hostility. What preserved the admiral for so long was the fact that he alone appeared capable of creating the powerful, homogeneous battlefleet which the Kaiser desired. When, after 1911 or so, that aim became less important, Tirpitz's position began to crumble; but it received an even heavier blow at the outbreak of war itself, both because of the emphasis given to the land campaigns and also because ship construction seemed less crucial than operations and strategy, which were in the hands of the Admiralty Staff and the Commander-in-Chief, High Seas Fleet.[7]

Nevertheless, although Fisher once described himself as 'Athanasius contra mundum', neither he nor Tirpitz were ever in the weak, isolated and defenceless position they occasionally liked to portray. Both enjoyed substantial support from crucial sections of the body politic, with which they in turn took great care to cultivate close ties.

The first of these was their respective monarchs. This support, as mentioned above, was vital for Tirpitz, for the Emperor was the mainspring of the post-1871 German constitution and enjoyed almost untrammelled powers in respect of the armed services – powers which the ambitious and impulsive Wilhelm II was determined to exert. From 1897 onwards, perhaps earlier, Wilhelm had recognized Tirpitz as being the only naval officer who could obtain for him a large navy and, while this was being built, the admiral's position was secure. Maintaining the confidence of such an erratic monarch was not an easy task for any of the imperial ministers and advisers, some of whom were literally shattered by Wilhelm's lifestyle and mannerisms, and Tirpitz was careful to keep his relationship with the Kaiser in good repair. Sometimes it was disturbed by strictly naval questions – such as Wilhelm's temporary enthusiasm for fast armoured cruisers in 1903; sometimes by the influence of rivals – so that Tirpitz once told the British naval attaché that he did not dare leave Kiel regatta early lest some other naval officer pour the wrong ideas into his imperial master's impressionable mind;[8] but, compared with so many other ministers, Tirpitz was astonishingly success-ful in his tactics until 1913 or so. Fisher's relationship with King Edward VII, by contrast, was less subject to such problems and had less significance in strictly constitutional terms; but the infor-mal influence of the monarch, prodding his ministers in this or that direction by means of letters and conversations, was still enormous and Fisher always valued this source of support. From 1903, when the King summoned Fisher to Balmoral and encour-aged him to write out his ideas as private memoranda, until 1910, when Edward died and the admiral mourned his loss for months thereafter, the friendship was unshakeable; he was 'my best friend', Fisher claimed.[9] This fact alone kept many of his foes in society and politics from pressing their criticisms to the limit.

Second, Fisher and Tirpitz nourished good relations with the political 'powers that be'. For Fisher, as the chief official of a great department of state, this meant, first and foremost, his political head, the First Lord; and by extension, the Prime Minis-ter and other members of the Cabinet. Luckily, none of the First Lords during Fisher's time at the Admiralty fell out with him, and even Selborne, although in no way overwhelmed by Fisher's enthusiasms and exaggerations, was wise enough to give the admiral his head. Balfour, driven on by the need to make the armed services more efficient after the Boer War, was most impressed by Fisher and gained a great deal from their frequent interchanges, although the education was by no means a one-way process. The relationship with Asquith, whose mind was not drawn to strategic matters, was less close, and there were other ministers – Haldane, for instance – whom Fisher disliked intensely.

For Tirpitz, who was an actual Secretary of State, friendship with fellow ministers was less important than support from the main parties in the Reichstag. Since there existed no Cabinet system of government and since Tirpitz enjoyed the support of the Kaiser and had the right of direct audience with him, the admiral's chief political function was not to agree with the other ministers so much as to get his fleet bills and naval budgets passed by the legislative assembly. Even the friendship of the Chancellor was less vital, although this is not to say that Bülow's assistance, especially around the turn of the century, was not useful; yet even when Tirpitz was involved in a fierce political struggle with Bethmann Hollweg, his position remained unshaken. Had the Reichstag thrown out or substantially modified his fleet bills, as had happened to the unfortunate Hollmann, then matters would have been very different. Thus, from the beginning of his time at the Reich Navy Office, Tirpitz took care to impress the party leaders in the Reichstag: reasoned memoranda were sent for their perusal; private conversations encouraged; all queries answered; visits to imperial shipyards were laid on for Reichstag deputies; and his speeches to the assembly were always clear and competent. Moreover, in manoeuvring for support for the crucial first two navy laws, Tirpitz was brilliantly successful in persuading the greater part of the hitherto hostile Centre Party into voting for a large fleet, which, taken together with the votes of the traditionally patriotic Conservatives and National Liberals, ensured safe majorities.

In an age of mass primary education, near-universal male suffrage and regular general elections, however, the parties were bound to reflect the sentiments and aspirations of that wider 'public opinion' to which all politicians now paid tribute; and this, to a very large extent, meant cultivating the pressure-groups and the press. Both Fisher and Tirpitz were very 'modern' in this regard, having none of the scruples or reservations of their predecessors about the correct relationship between state officials and newspaper editors. Fisher, of course, had played a part in W. T. Stead's 'The Truth about the Navy' agitation in the *Pall Mall*

Gazette in 1884 and from that time onwards took great pains to maintain contact with the press. While Commander-in-Chief, Mediterranean, he bombarded journalists such as Arnold White and J. R. Thursfield (*The Times* correspondent) with advice upon the line they ought to take over Britain's naval weaknesses – a tactic which occasionally backfired upon the admiral, such as the occasion when his recent political chief, Goschen, observed that White's articles bore 'a strong Mediterranean flavour' and that the journalist 'might even be supposed to have read all the public and private letters' which Fisher had been despatching to the Admiralty![10] And, as the criticisms about Fisher's policies as First Sea Lord mounted after 1906 or so, he used these journalists to hit back repeatedly at his foes who were, ironically enough, making the same sort of alarmist noises about the state of the navy as he himself had made twenty years before.

Tirpitz's method of cultivating public opinion was less direct, although he certainly had personal contacts with Graf Reventlow and many other imperialist and navalist writers. Instead, he established within the Reich Navy Office the euphemistically entitled *Nachrichtenbureau* (News Bureau), whose task it was to convert the German public to the idea of a large fleet and to answer all the attacks made upon it by the hostile Social Democrats and Radical Liberals. Reporters were encouraged to call upon the News Bureau, and hints were given there as to how naval matters should be treated; lectures were arranged all over the country; and contacts were established with the German Colonial Society, the Pan-German League and (after its founding in 1898) especially the Navy League, all of which willingly supported the cause and procured information from Tirpitz's subordinates, even if their campaigns at times became so virulent that the government was forced to disavow them. There is little doubt, in other words, that a considerable amount of the apparently spontaneous enthusiasm for the Kaiser's *Flottenpolitik* was the result of a carefully organized propaganda policy from above.[11]

If these were the strengths of the two admirals, what were their weaknesses? Once again, curiously enough, they were very similar. Both men, because of their determination to have their own way, had been chiefly responsible for the frequent quarrels which occurred within their navies at this time. Nelson's 'Happy Band of Brothers' found no real equivalent in the navies which Fisher and Tirpitz were creating and the consequences for the morale and organizational coherence of the two services can only have been deleterious. The Fisher–Beresford 'row', for example,. caused many politicians in Britain to fear that the navy would be less effective than hoped for in time of war. Yet Tirpitz, although never engaged in so public a controversy, probably did even more damage to his own service by his constant emphasis to the Kaiser of the necessity of maintaining and even increasing the division of responsibilities between its chief administrative and operational branches. While the admiral's crude argument of *divide et impera* was bound to find favour with Wilhelm, Tirpitz obviously hoped that in the event of war he would be given supreme direction of the navy. The failure of this hope was not only a personal blow to him but it also left the service with a confused command structure. In 1917, while ruminating during his retirement, Tirpitz confessed to Trotha that the old *Admiralität* (i.e. the unified, pre-1889 structure) had really been the best of all;[12] but it was not until after the war – and after a complete failure of the 'Tirpitz Plan' – that the German navy received a centralized administrative and command system.

The other major weakness of both men lay in their lack of strategical insight – the reverse side, so to speak, of their great knowledge and distinction in matters material, technical, organizational and political. This was not an uncommon failing in an era of rapid technological change, for few naval officers appeared to have appreciated how the new weapons of the submarine, torpedo, mine and aeroplane might affect the operations of battlefleets; let alone the ironic fact that, as Professor Graham has pointed out, Mahan's classic writings upon sea power appeared 'at the very time when new instruments of the Industrial Revolution were beginning to erode principles and theories upon which his doctrines were based'.[13] Furthermore, the creation of a sensible naval strategy was affected by the determination of Fisher and Tirpitz to brook no rivals within the naval establishment: the former constantly refusing to establish a War Staff and resenting any intrusion into matters of maritime strategy by the Committee of Imperial

Defence even after the interservice clash of August 1911;[14] and the latter constantly weakening the position of the Admiralty Staff and even permitting the Reich Navy Office, which legally had no competence in strategical affairs, to draft its own war plans on one occasion.[15]

Tirpitz's strategy, in fact, was based upon a series of miscalculations: that the massive German shipbuilding programme would somehow be unnoticed by the British until he had brought it through the 'danger zone'; that the Admiralty in London would be unable to concentrate the greater part of the Royal Navy in home waters to meet the German challenge; and that the British would always take the offensive in wartime, steaming recklessly into the dangerous waters of the Heligoland Bight to seek out their foe.[16] When all three of these assumptions proved erroneous, the value of his entire battlefleet-centred policy became worthless. Only the U-boats, ignored by Tirpitz for so long, saved the German navy from total strategical impotence during the First World War. Fisher's case is more complex. He, too, concentrated enthusiastically upon the construction of the biggest battleships possible, effecting a virtual revolution in naval architecture with his Dreadnought conception; yet it is also true that he forecast, well before most of his peers, that the embryonic submarine and aeroplane would be immensely important in the future. Nevertheless, he appears to have had little *consistent* appreciation of the many practical ways in which this newer weaponry would undermine the effectiveness of his beloved Royal Navy: for example, that neither the German *nor* the British fleets dare cruise in the North Sea when those waters were infested by submarines; that a close blockade was a thing of the past; that amphibious landings – Fisher's favourite alternative to the army's plan for a continental commitment – would be immensely difficult, if not impossible to carry out in the face of the enemy; and that in the U-boat lay a far more dangerous instrument of the *guerre de course* than anything hitherto. It was, rather, a layman such as Balfour who pushed things to their logical conclusion when he informed Fisher in 1913, 'The question that really troubles me is not whether *our* submarines could render the enemy's position intolerable, but whether *their* submarines could not render *our* position untenable.'[17] Occasionally the admiral admitted, and sometimes appeared warmly to welcome, the fact that the whole nature of maritime warfare might be changing; yet – perhaps because of his fear that only the army would benefit from this strategical uncertainty? – he never pushed things to their logical conclusion and worked out what the fleet might do under the altered circumstances. Certainly, his bold assertions about the future potential of submarines and aircraft sit uneasily alongside his fantastic plans to push a fleet into the Baltic and to land troops on the Pomeranian coast – a scheme which he was still talking about as late as 1916!

The only marked differences between Fisher and Tirpitz emerge when their attitudes to domestic politics and ideology are examined. In certain obvious questions, such as the annual debate over the navy budget, their views were bound to be similar; neither admiral, although keen to economize where possible, could agree with the radicals and pacifists that naval expenditure was excessively high in the turbulent years before 1914. They were both too attached, by tradition and upbringing, to the service in which they had spent all their lives, and they genuinely held that the expenses incurred by a large navy were akin to those of an insurance policy. Yet in respect of political matters not directly related to the navy, there was no longer this similarity between the two men. Fisher, for all his royal contacts, dancing with duchesses, and professed contempt for politicians, remained something of a radical until his death. He detested the 'mandarins' and 'fuddy-duddies' who occupied important positions because of their birth rather than their intelligence and ability. He seems to have preferred the company of Liberal politicians such as McKenna and Grey, and later Churchill and Lloyd George, to that of many Tories, which earned him sharp criticism from the reactionaries within the fold of the Imperial Maritime League. His closest journalist friends were either pronounced radicals such as Stead or unorthodox right-wingers such as Arnold White. He genuinely wished to introduce democracy into officer recruitment and raged at all those traditionalists who obstructed his enlightened reforms.[18] In the same way, the substantial improvements he made in lower-deck conditions were humane and, to the extent that they helped to avoid the unrest which broke out in the German navy during the war, inherently sensible. Even during the last few months of his life, he was bombarding *The Times* with letters like the following:[19]

> Sir,
> Quite nice people are quite shocked that the common herd (the unvoiced ones), who invariably control every General Election, have thrown in their lot with the Labour Party. . . .
> Ireland in rebellion. . . . We alienate America and all our sister nations in not allowing Ireland to be as free as they are. The simple and so obvious plan of getting rid of industrial unrest by the working man sharing in the profits is carped at and denied. . . . Are you surprised at the universal determination to sack the lot?

Tirpitz, on the other hand, was not only monarchical in a personal sense but also sought to uphold the conservative Prusso-German constitution and was alarmed at domestic trends which threatened to undermine it. Indeed, with his argument that the sentimental and economic benefits accruing from his fleet policy would 'offer a strong palliative against educated and uneducated Social Democrats', Tirpitz has been regarded by some scholars as a person actuated primarily by a desire to forestall radical social and political changes within the German system.[20] This did not mean that he identified wholeheartedly with the reactionary East-Elbian Junkers (who were closely linked with agriculture and the army, rather than trade and the navy), but it did mean that he can be placed alongside other 'social-imperialists' of this age, who sought to solve domestic problems by success in external policies.

More important still, as his published writings and still more his private correspondence reveals, Tirpitz was a fundamental Social-Darwinist, convinced of the superiority of German *Kultur*, imbued with the notion of the 'struggle for survival' in the twentieth-century world of the superpowers, and bitterly opposed to the liberal, cosmopolitan doctrines of the Manchester School with its advocacy of materialistic individualism, denial of state power and lack of fervent patriotism. For this reason he was anti-English in a way that Fisher was never anti-German, for Tirpitz came to regard Britain not only as being a real power-political and commercial threat to Germany but also as representing in the most extreme degree an ideological, almost a spiritual, foe. As he became older, the admiral's right-wing convictions hardened: he was a leading member of the ultra-patriotic *Vaterlandspartei* during the war; he became a Reichstag deputy for the *Deutschnationale Volks-Partei* in 1924; he corresponded with such luminaries of 'radical Right' politics as Ludendorff, Housten Stewart Chamberlain, Oswald Spengler, Graf Reventlow and Dietrich Schäfer; and he railed against the internal foes and the 'unsoundness' which had caused the collapse of 1918. In short, he was a fully fledged exponent of the 'politics of cultural despair', that ideological movement which in its German context drove frustrated monarchists towards the Nazis in the years following Versailles.[21] It was not because of the National Socialists' aims but because of their crude methods of street-brawling, he informed Hitler's assistant Hess in 1922, that he did not support their organization,[22] but he increasingly did wonder whether the hoped-for 'regeneration' of the German people would come in the future from Bavaria instead of Prussia. No study of Tirpitz is complete without an appreciation of his ideology, which stands in marked contrast with that of Fisher.

With this exception admitted, however, the comparisons which can be made between the two men are striking. Yet, as was suggested above, this is scarcely surprising in view of the age in which they lived. In the period of the 'new navalism' before 1914 maritime power was widely regarded as being of particular importance to national strength and well-being, and leading officers were subjected to a blaze of publicity from which their equivalents in the 1870s and the 1950s were spared. Decisive and colourful personalities were therefore being played up by, and were themselves utilizing, the fast growing 'Yellow Press' and the mushrooming patriotic pressure-groups. Moreover, because the technical and *matériel* school was then so dominant in all navies, officers such as Fisher and Tirpitz were bound to be brought forward on account of their expertise; while the great emphasis laid upon efficiency and organization in this heady age of competitive imperialism and spiralling arms-races naturally enhanced their particular claims to influence and power within their respective navies. Even where –

as in domestic politics – Fisher and Tirpitz differed in their attitudes, they each reflected significant currents of contemporary thought. To sum up: no two individuals are alike, still less such giants as these. Yet however unusual and individualistic in personality these two admirals were, a comparative study of their careers and achievements can usefully contribute towards a better understanding of the *general* naval and political history of those momentous years from 1890 to 1918.[23]

5

For many years after the Second World War, research upon the Imperial German Navy had suffered from the fact that its records were in the hands of the Allied authorities. By the 1960s, however, most of the files had been returned to the archives in Freiburg and interest in German policy before 1914 had been greatly stimulated by the controversy over Fritz Fischer's work *Germany's Aims in the First World War* (German edition, 1961; English edition, London and New York, 1967). Around the early 1970s, therefore, there was a veritable explosion of published works and unpublished dissertations upon many aspects of German naval policy – the technical, financial and domestic-political factors, the role of navalist propaganda and pressure-groups, the relationship between maritime strategy and the Reich's foreign and colonial policies, and so on. Responding to this groundswell, and in particular to the arguments put forward in Volker Berghahn's impressive book *Der Tirpitz-Plan* (1971), the Military History Research Office in Freiburg arranged a conference during which these various researches and viewpoints were brought together. The papers were then assembled and edited by H. Schottelius and W. Deist, and published as *Marine und Marinepolitik im kaiserlichen Deutschland 1871–1914* (Düsseldorf, 1972; paperback edition, 1981).

This particular contribution to the symposium was intended as a sustained critique of Tirpitz's strategic assumptions, using both newly opened German and British records to buttress the argument. Previously, the Grand Admiral's apologists had maintained that his strategy was perfectly logical, but that it had been undermined by later events (the coming of the *ententes*, the British abandonment of a close blockade, etc.) which could not have been foreseen at the turn of the century. As the record shows, Tirpitz's assumptions were riddled with contradictions from the beginning, and many of them were pointed out by the Admiralty Staff planners. Only if we accept that Tirpitz's secret, real aim was one day to have a fleet as big as the British navy are these contradictions resolved. But if that was his long-term goal, then older views of the extent of his ambitions for Germany need to be revised.

Strategic Aspects of the Anglo-German Naval Race

On 26 June 1897, the greatest naval force the world had ever seen was assembled off Spithead to celebrate the Diamond Jubilee of Queen Victoria. Over 165 British warships, including 21 first-class battleships and 54 cruisers, demonstrated the immense size and fighting power of the Royal Navy; thirty miles of ships were stretched out in six great lines, each over five miles in length. Foreign observers were very impressed by it all, and few were inclined to deny the proud boast of *The Times* that

> The Fleet . . . is certainly the most formidable force in all its elements and qualities that has ever been brought together, and such as no combination of other powers can rival. It is at once the most powerful and far-reaching weapon which the world has ever seen.[1]

This vast naval force was complemented by, and in turn offered protection to, the world's greatest merchant marine, for Britain was also the leading trading nation and derived most of its national wealth necessary to finance the Royal Navy's building programmes from overseas commerce and investment. In addition, Britain also possessed incomparably the largest colonial empire, providing among other benefits the most important collection of naval bases on the globe: 'Five strategic keys lock up the globe!' gloated Admiral Fisher, and they (Dover, Gibraltar, the Cape, Alexandria, Singapore) were all in British hands.[2] Moreover, that empire and those bases were being rapidly linked together by an intricate imperial cable communications network, which even further enhanced British strategic domination of the world's oceans.[3]

Even its geographical position offered the island nation immense advantages. Separated from the continent of Europe, Britain could

129

safely avoid the maintenance of a large and expensive standing army which burdened the budgets of other powers, nor need she enter into entangling military commitments except in the rare event of the European balance being disturbed.[4] Conversely, her geographical situation, and her very necessary possession of a great fleet to protect herself, inevitably meant that most European nations were to a greater or lesser extent dependent upon her goodwill with regard to their maritime communications with the outside world. Mahan's acute observation in 1902 about Germany's unfavourable position was true of other continental powers: 'The dilemma of Great Britain is that she cannot help commanding the approaches to Germany by the mere possession of the very means essential to her own existence as a state of the first order.'[5] Yet, frustrating though all these facts were to many Europeans, there appeared to be little that could be done about it: Britain seemed to hold so many trumps, and the eclipse of Spanish, Dutch and French sea power in earlier centuries pointed to the futility of attempting to challenge Britain's maritime supremacy.

On the other side of the North Sea, however, a new opponent was preparing to enter the lists, deterred neither by geographical disadvantages nor by historical precedents. In the same month as the Spithead review, the newly appointed State Secretary of the *Reichsmarineamt*, Rear-Admiral Tirpitz, had submitted to Wilhelm II a crucial memorandum in which he argued that 'For Germany the most dangerous naval enemy at the present time is England.' He also proposed to develop his challenge to the Royal Navy's supremacy in home waters – 'between Heligoland and the Thames' – and to concentrate upon the creation of a homogeneous fleet of battleships, condemning as 'hopeless' the rival strategy of commerce raiding.[6] From that time onwards, the German navy was to assume an ever-increasing anti-British orientation.

The motives and driving forces behind German naval policy after 1897 have been the subject of much historical debate. Some writers have seen the growth of the Kaiser's battlefleet as a natural and inevitable event, a consequence of the widespread acceptance of Mahan's doctrines in this age of the 'new imperialism' and the 'new navalism' and of the massive industrial and commercial expansion of the Second Reich; that England occupied the centre of Berlin's calculations was due either to the need to prepare for the most difficult situation in war or to a healthy defensive reaction to the apparently aggressive British policy around the turn of the century.[7] In contrast, a growing number of scholars feel that the motives behind German naval policy were much more positive and aggressive.[8] However, neither Tirpitz's *Ressortseifer*,[9] nor his internal political plans,[10] nor his Social-Darwinistic leanings,[11] concern us at this stage. What is remarkable is his decision to alter drastically Germany's sea-power relationship to Great Britain at all, and particularly in such a direct and deliberate way, in view of the size of the respective fleets of the two powers. In 1898, as Tirpitz was supervising the passage of the First Navy Law, Britain had thirty-eight first-class battleships, Germany seven; Britain had thirty-four first-class cruisers, Germany two.[12] Even after that law had been passed, the future German fleet would consist of nineteen battleships, hardly enough to seize the trident from Britannia. How could Tirpitz's anti-English policy work then? How did it have a chance?

The first thing to stress in Tirpitz's defence is that his policy was a long-term one; he did not expect to change the international power balance overnight, or even within a few years. 'The construction of a fleet is in general the work of a generation,' he insisted.[13] For him, therefore, the First Navy Law was more important in giving the service a single, clear, strategic aim and in removing the future shipbuilding programme from Reichstag control than in establishing a battlefleet of sufficient size to realize Germany's needs. As he admitted later, 'It was always clear to me . . . that the First Navy Law did not create the final, full fleet.'[14] Shortly after that measure had been passed by the Reichstag, he began preparations for the next stage and, exploiting the international situation and domestic anglophobia at the turn of the century, succeeded in obtaining legislative sanction for a battlefleet twice its size, thirty-eight battleships strong, by the Second Navy Law of 1900.[15] Yet even this was nowhere near Tirpitz's final target. In his important *Immediatvortrag* with the Kaiser in September 1899 he had talked of a fleet of forty-five battleships with accompanying heavy cruisers;[16] and a few years later he and his staff were coolly discussing the possibility of obtaining a third double-squadron. This was postponed by Tirpitz in view of the serious state of Anglo-German relations; but by 1907 he himself was recommending a fixed three-battleships-a-year programme, with a ship's life reduced to twenty years – in effect a fleet of sixty capital ships.[17] The 1908 and 1912 fleet measures, with their appeals to the dual needs to prevent redundancies in the shipyards and to build more quickly than planned against the English 'menace', were further steps in this direction and further examples of his habit of accelerating the momentum for the battlefleet.[18] Naturally, the timing and size of the later increases were greatly influenced by subsequent internal and external factors, yet it seems clear that even in 1898 Tirpitz had plans to make the German navy far larger than that contemplated by the First Navy Law.

Moreover, the admiral hoped to enlarge the battlefleet as quietly and undramatically as possible, thereby avoiding diplomatic crises and naval scares which would lead to a vigorous British response. A clash with that power at present, the Reichstag's Budget Commission was confidentially told in March 1900, 'would be more disadvantageous and dangerous for us than any other possible eventuality, since in view of our present maritime inferiority England could do more damage to us than any other power. . . .'[19] Although the need to exploit the anglophobia in Germany occasionally, to obtain public support for the fleet measures, made this policy of avoiding provocations to the British a difficult one to carry out, it was expected that Bülow would manage to keep relations between Berlin and London upon reasonably good terms during the expected 'danger zone'; the Chancellor was certainly aware that 'in view of our naval inferiority, we must operate so carefully, like the caterpillar before it has grown into the butterfly'.[20] In this connection, it is not surprising to learn that Tirpitz opposed overseas adventures such as the Boxer and Venezuela expeditions and drastic changes of policy such as the proposed alliance with Russia in 1904.[21]

What was more, provided that Bülow kept on friendly terms with Britain on the one hand and the German battlefleet was steadily augmented on the other, the time would come when Germany was clear of this danger zone and her fleet would be so large that Tirpitz's famous 'risk theory' would have come into play.

According to this theory, Germany must equip herself with a fleet at least strong enough not only to defend her coasts but also able to threaten the *overall* maritime superiority of the most powerful navy existing. In other words, Britain, in attacking such a fleet, might lose so many warships that the Royal Navy would be inferior to its other rivals, particularly the Franco-Russian naval forces.[22] The mere existence of a considerable battlefleet based at Wilhelmshaven and Kiel would be enough, Tirpitz calculated, to ensure the first, essentially negative stage in Germany's development as a sea power – security from a British attack.

Another important aspect of the admiral's calculations was the decision, as mentioned above, to concentrate Germany's naval force in the North Sea. In considering a conflict against Britain, this seemed the natural thing to do; as he put it in 1897, 'Commerce raiding and transatlantic war against England is so hopeless, because of the shortage of bases on our side and the superfluity on England's side. . . .'[23] Assaults upon the peripheries of the British Empire, pinprick attacks upon that power's vast floating commerce, offered little chance of success: a direct threat to Britain's coastal waters did, for it would not only deter a British attack but it would also make London conciliatory and amenable in world affairs. This is what he meant when he wrote: 'The lever of our *Weltpolitik* was the North Sea; it influenced the entire globe without us needing to be directly engaged in any other place.'[24]

The corollary of this belief that Germany's naval effort would best be seen to effect in the North Sea was the assumption that Britain, in contrast, would be unable to concentrate her enormous battlefleets in those waters. If by chance she did, then the German navy would be so heavily outnumbered in the foreseeable future that it would be virtually forced to stay in harbour, thus forfeiting the military-political benefits anticipated in the 'risk theory'; but Tirpitz seems to have been confident that this situation would never occur. By the turn of the century, Britain appeared to have too many pressing overseas commitments to allow her to bring back her forces into the North Sea: the Boer War, the Mediterranean naval balance, the situation in the Far East, were all fraught with danger for the British Empire. In particular, she was threatened by the combined naval forces of France and Russia, only slightly inferior in size to her own. It seemed plain to Tirpitz that 'on account of her foreign policy commitments [England] can only utilize a very small part of these ships in the North Sea. England's weak point is therefore the North Sea, for here we can concentrate our entire force.'[25]

Also vital for Tirpitz's entire strategy was the belief that, immediately upon the outbreak of hostilities, the Royal Navy would institute a close blockade of Germany's harbours. This seemed to be in line with the traditions of Drake and Nelson, with the probable strategy of the stronger naval force, and with the (supposed) aggressive spirit of the English nation. It also made political sense:

> England can . . . only compel us to sue for peace if it pursues war in Europe as energetically as possible. The more forcefully this takes place along our own coasts, the quicker will peace probably be brought about and thus the less likely is it that Germany might bring together alliances which could be dangerous for England.[26]

Consequently, the early operations plans of the *Oberkommando*, which involved a virtually suicidal offensive against the Thames estuary at the outset of war, were altered in late 1899 to take account of Tirpitz's long-term programme and his strategic concepts.[27] In the admiral's official calculations around the turn of the century, at least, there is no sign that he ever thought the British might *not* attack immediately. There did, however, exist the belief that the attacking force far from base required a 3:2 numerical superiority to gain a decisive victory over the defensive force operating in or near its own coastal waters; and Tirpitz was reasonably certain, given the above-mentioned considerations, that the German navy would have enough battleships to meet the expected British strength.[28] Moreover, he also believed that it would be possible to reduce the numbers of enemy battleships in these waters before the large-scale battle commenced. As Professor Marder notes, a close blockade by the Royal Navy

> would give [the High Seas Fleet] opportunities for continuous guerrilla attacks on the British fleet in the vicinity of the Bight.

When the 'brutal superiority' of the Grand Fleet had been whittled down to a *Kräfteausgleich*, an approximate equalization of forces, as well as through such tactics as the use of minefields, massed flotilla attacks, and other devices, the High Seas Fleet could risk a major battle in open waters.[29]

Even so, Tirpitz wished to take no chances in any decisive engagement with the British in the North Sea, and he was determined to achieve as great a technical and tactical superiority over the Royal Navy's battle squadrons as he possibly could. Even in 1899, he felt that in a future struggle they would have a good chance even against England 'through geographical position, military structure, mobilization, torpedo-boats, tactical training, systematically organized improvement, and unified leadership through the monarch'.[30] By 1914, the results could be seen: all German capital ships had been constructed and armoured to be as 'sink-proof' as possible, with a better system of watertight subdivisions than their British counterparts; their gunnery was first class, due to constant training and an efficient rangefinder; German shells, torpedoes and mines were superior to British ones; training for night engagements was encouraged, as was the employment of massed torpedo attacks by the destroyer flotillas; and the German North Sea bases and repair yards were modern and efficient.[31]

It was in view of all these factors that Tirpitz looked forward with a reasonable degree of confidence to Germany's future ability to challenge the Royal Navy and to avoid further dependence upon Britain's political goodwill in world affairs. Compelled by the very consideration of these same factors to accord Germany a far greater respect and civility than hitherto, the British would be less arrogant and would cease to be such a threat to Germany's overseas trade, colonies and merchant marine. There would be no further blows to national pride, such as occurred in the Samoan crisis of 1899 or in the seizure of the German steamers off Delagoa Bay in early 1900. Freed from the almost suffocating domination of the Royal Navy, the German government would be able to extend its overseas interests and to carry out a genuine *Weltpolitik*. She would at last have her rightful place in the sun, secured and maintained by Tirpitz's brilliant naval policy.

If, on the other hand, a war with Britain did occur in the future, the prospects would no longer be so fearsome as those portrayed by Bülow in 1900, who had felt that

> A calamitous war with England would, through the elimination of our large and ever-growing overseas interests, through the destruction of our trade, the damage to our export industries, throw us back generations in our economic and political development, and have similar effects as the Thirty Years War had in its time.[32]

Presuming that Tirpitz's calculations were correct, the Royal Navy would receive a decisive defeat shortly after it had instituted a close blockade in the Heligoland Bight region; a defeat which the hasty recall of squadrons from the Far East and Mediterranean would probably not recoup; a defeat which could possibly lead to peace talks and which would certainly compensate for the temporary loss of any German colonies; a defeat which, if swiftly followed up, might lead to more daring operations and further successes, perhaps even the invasion of England itself.[33] All this, it seems fair to conclude from the knowledge we possess of German naval planning around the turn of the century, was what Tirpitz and his colleagues generally hoped for: recognition and respect in peacetime, and a good chance of victory in wartime. These were not unusual aims, although their proponents did seem to have anticipated achieving them in a relatively short time.

In fact, as is well known, things worked out quite differently from the way Tirpitz had hoped. Despite Bülow's cautious foreign policy and the efforts of the press bureaus, it proved impossible to avoid raising English suspicions and by 1902 the Admiralty had come to the conclusion that the German fleet was being built against them and began to consider countermeasures.[34] The danger zone had commenced but without any foreseeable end; for the larger the German battlefleet grew, the more the British reacted; and the more ships the British constructed as an answer, the harder it was for Germany to come clear of the danger zone. An enormously expensive naval race began which strained Tirpitz's delicate financial calculations, and also prejudiced his internal policy; while the 'Dreadnought Spring' threw doubt upon his hopes of achieving technical superiority over the Royal Navy. On the diplomatic front, Germany lost her place as *tertius gaudens*, while Britain steadily improved relations with America, Japan, France and even Russia; by 1907, Germany seemed encircled. The British brought home more and more battleships and Tirpitz could no longer cling to the hope that only part of the Royal Navy would be available in the North Sea. Finally, the developments in mines, torpedoes and submarines increased the dangers to surface warships and caused the British to abandon any ideas of a close blockade. Instead, they would seal off the entrances to the North Sea and wait for the High Seas Fleet to emerge to fight. If it did, it would be on very unfavourable terms indeed; if it did not, then Tirpitz's entire naval policy would have been in vain. The course of the surface war in the North Sea in the years 1914–18 merely confirmed the disastrous position in which the High Seas Fleet had been placed due to Tirpitz's earlier miscalculations.[35]

It is easy, we all know, to show where the admiral made mistakes. It is also quite easy, however, to absolve him from much of the blame for the catastrophic alterations in Germany's position; after all, how could he have foreseen in 1897 the future Anglo-French *entente*, Fisher's reforms in the Royal Navy or the abandonment of the strategy of the close blockade? Was he not right in suggesting that it was the flamboyant foreign policy and failure of the *Auswärtiges Amt* to keep on good relations with other powers that was the real cause of Germany's downfall?[36] This line of argument is plausible enough at first sight but it must be denied; for a study of the German and British naval documents in the period when Tirpitz's scheme was first put into practice – between 1897 and 1904 – suggests a different interpretation: *that his strategic and political ideas were riddled with weak points, false assumptions and glaring contradictions from the very start, which the normal passage of time would expose*. In any case, to say that he could not have foreseen future changes is to ignore the point that it was precisely his ambitious fleet plans which caused or accelerated many of them. The final irony is that so many of Tirpitz's ideas seem to be a *mis*interpretation of the writings of Mahan, whose follower he claimed to be.

In the first place, serious doubts arise about the validity of the idea of a 'danger zone' through which Germany would eventually pass. As described by Tirpitz, this policy seemed an easy one to carry out, provided that a cautious overseas policy was adopted in its early years:

> In introducing the Navy Law of 1900 it was quite clear to us that political tensions would at first be increased by it. . . . It was also clear that technically the fleet-construction had to be done as swiftly as possible, in order to shorten the danger zone. . . .
>
> It was important to avoid [confrontations], and indeed to accept possible restrictions upon our actions, so long as the foundations of our power were inadequate. Only when that was established through our fleet and political leanings could we move more freely on the oceans and demand equality of rights.[37]

Yet the premises upon which this theory was based were extremely dubious. The German government was already finding it impossible to control and suppress the rabid anglophobia in Germany during the years of the Boer War and, in fact, had exploited this very feeling to secure fresh support for the fleet increases. It was therefore most unwise to assume that this would not be noticed by the English press and public, as indeed it was; even in 1899–1900 there was a growing number of journalists in Britain who were warning their readers of Germany's plans. The retort of *The Times* to Bülow's 'hammer and anvil' speech in support of the Second Navy Law gave an indication *then* that the danger zone might be indefinitely prolonged: 'Whatever our position may be at a given moment, we must be ready to make it still stronger, if other sea powers build more ships.' This was the Admiralty's view also.[38]

Secondly, as Tirpitz well knew, Germany had begun with its fleet programme a gradual and lengthy policy whose target would only be reached after many years. This was another reason to doubt that this increasing challenge to British naval superiority could be kept secret. The annual statistical tables laid before parliament, or in *Brassey's Naval Annual*, would expose the great growth of the German fleet long before that time, never precisely defined by Tirpitz, when Germany would be out of the danger zone and free to demand 'equality of rights'.

This is reinforced by a third consideration: that, irrespective of public suspicion and dislike of Germany, Britain would have to take that nation into account as soon as her fleet affected the Two Power Standard. As the First Lord, Selborne, reminded the Cabinet in 1902, 'It is an error to suppose that the Two Power Standard . . . has ever had reference only to France and Russia. It has always referred to the two strongest naval powers at any given moment.'[39] In other words, Admiralty policy would *automatically* operate against Germany as soon as she developed the third largest navy in the world, that is, long before the building programme of the Second Navy Law was completed. Moreover, British navalists often insisted upon a 10 per cent superiority over the next two powers, to prevent a fourth navy from holding the balance – precisely one of Tirpitz's calculations. Thus, as early as March 1897, there was disquiet in the British press and Admiralty when Hollmann's estimates were announced.[40]

Fourthly, it was surely a great error to assume that the British would be forced into concessions by the creation of the 'lever' of a battlefleet, as Tirpitz blandly did when he wrote:

> Apart from the battle circumstances, which would by no means be hopeless for us, England would (for general political reasons and from the purely practical standpoint of the businessman) have lost any inclination to attack us; and would in consequence accord to Your Majesty such a measure of sea power and thus enable Your Majesty to carry out a great overseas policy. . . .[41]

Tirpitz had regarded it as perfectly natural, in fact as his duty, to neutralize what he saw to be the British threat to Germany's expanding world interests.[42] But why did he assume that the British, so touchy about their naval supremacy, so full of nationalistic pride at the turn of the century, would behave any differently? The far more dangerous Franco-Russian naval threat had not made them amenable to the wishes of Paris and St

Petersburg; and the public outcry and the creation of a 'flying squadron' after the Kruger Telegram were far better indications of how they would react when challenged by Germany.

Also doubtful *at the time* was Tirpitz's second major strategic calculation, that the British would never be able to assemble the greater part of the Royal Navy in the North Sea; most of its seven overseas squadrons, so he told Büchsel in 1899, would remain on foreign stations even in wartime.[43] Of course, in the closing years of the nineteenth century, it was normal for the British to station ten first-class battleships at Malta, to be reinforced if necessary by the eight first-class battleships of the Channel Fleet, while the number in the Far East had risen to four. In contrast, it was considered that a Home Reserve Squadron of eleven second-class battleships was strong enough to protect British interests in the North Sea.[44] In such a situation, Germany's battlefleet would find it easy to gain a decisive victory. However, all this presupposes that the British could not or would not recall their overseas squadrons if a grave threat arose nearer home – an assumption that was strategically and politically so wide of the mark that it seems incredible that Tirpitz should have based all his hopes upon it.

The very existence of those overseas squadrons was due, not to the bizarre whims of the Admiralty, but to the need to protect British interests, especially the important trade routes; but had not Mahan declared that 'The vital centre of English commerce is in the waters surrounding the British islands'?[45] Threats in the Far East were of no comparison; Selborne, in admitting to the Cabinet the need to maintain an adequate force in that region, felt bound to declare:

If the British Navy were defeated in the Mediterranean and Channel the stress of our position would not be alleviated by any amount of superiority in the Chinese seas. If, on the other hand, it were to prove supreme in the Mediterranean and Channel, even serious disasters in Chinese seas would matter little.[46]

Even withdrawal from the Mediterranean was regarded as a possibility during the 1890s, as the German navy was well aware.[47] In contrast, an Admiralty memorandum of March 1902, that is, *before* the German navy was regarded by the naval chiefs in London as a threat aimed specifically at Britain, insisted that

> It is a fundamental principle of Admiralty policy that sufficient force shall at all times be maintained in home waters to ensure the command of those seas. And in no other way than by defeat can our naval force be rendered unable to meet the enemy at sea.[48]

What was more, the whole reasoning behind Tirpitz's *Risikoflotte*, that the only really effective threat to Britain's naval superiority could be posed in the North Sea and English Channel, was in a negative way a recognition of where the strategic centre of British sea power lay. As Levetzow put it, if England lost a battle in the South Seas, it would not be fatal; if she lost in the Channel, she would be forced to sue for peace.[49] Yet if the Germans perceived that this was the crucial area, how did they ever believe that the Royal Navy would attach more importance to the Far East or Mediterranean? The choice lay between regions where *potential* threats to British interests existed, and a region (the North Sea) where British *national security* was involved, and there could be no doubt to the Admiralty that the latter was the most important. The more effective the risk, the more the British would react; for example, Arnold-Forster's first action after his visit to Germany in 1902 was to advocate the creation of 'a modern and powerful fleet in home waters' to counter any possible challenge from the Kaiser's navy.[50]

This strategy of flexible response was so obvious that the Admiralty could not resist publicly lecturing the world about it in the Cawdor Memorandum:

> The periods of European rest as well as the stable grouping of international interests during the latter part of the last century, had assigned certain degrees of relative importance to our various squadrons and the scale of their strength has been reflected in the rank and capabilities of the Admirals selected to command them. So much has this been the case that today people are apt to look on a definite number of ships on any

141

given station as a fixed quantity rather than a strategic exigency.

This idea must be entirely dispelled. Squadrons of varying strength are strategically required in certain waters; but the kaleidoscopic nature of international relations, as well as variations or new developments in Seapower, not only forbids any permanent allocation of numbers, but in fact points the necessity for periodic redistribution of ships between our Fleets to meet the political requirements of the moment.[51]

In the following year, the Admiralty said the same thing: they could not base their plans 'upon the shifting sands of any temporary and unofficial international relations'; they 'cannot build for the moment'.[52] Flexibility was essential for a world power with so many commitments. This being the case, however, the mere development of the German navy as a result of Tirpitz's policy alone would have been bound to lead to a 'periodic redistribution'; when it was combined with the unmistakable anglophobia in Germany and the Kaiser's alarming foreign policy, a reaction such as Fisher's was inevitable:

Our only probable enemy is Germany. Germany keeps her whole fleet always concentrated within a few hours of England. We must therefore keep a fleet twice as powerful as that of Germany always concentrated within a few hours of Germany.[53]

The result, of course, had a catastrophic effect upon German naval strategy, destroying Tirpitz's hope of being able to engage only a part of the Royal Navy in the North Sea. Instead, public attention was focused upon that region, the British concentrated more and more warships there, and a feverish naval race developed which steadily worsened relations between the two peoples and governments. Little wonder that the Kaiser tried, with characteristic clumsiness and unconscious irony, to persuade the British naval attaché in Berlin to advise his government to disperse its squadrons again:

Your great mistake [Wilhelm said] was when you withdrew your ships from foreign stations and brought them into the North

Sea, because then Germany realized it was a threat to her. But it is also a mistake strategically, because it was an upsetting of carefully balanced strategical calculations.[54]

When one looks at the German records around the turn of the century, too, it is interesting to see that a number of experienced staff officers were not so convinced that Britain would be able to deploy only part of the Royal Navy in the North Sea. Their viewpoints were often disputed by other officers and made no impression upon the established strategy in these years; but it does suggest once again that Tirpitz's calculations were not as obvious and 'natural' as his defenders have claimed. As early as March 1896, one *Oberkommando* expert criticized the idea of a swift offensive against the Thames with a reason that equally applied when Germany assumed a defensive strategy:

It must also be borne in mind that England will never declare war before it has assembled a fleet of overwhelming superiority in the Channel and Thames estuary.[55]

German officers also pointed out that during the Transvaal crisis the Channel Fleet did not leave Portland between November 1895 and June 1896, an ominous precedent for any future confrontation; and also that, according to existing fleet dispositions, a bare English superiority of two battleships on the fifth day of a war with Germany alone would change to an overwhelming twenty-four-battleship superiority by the fifteenth day, something of which the British must also have been aware. Both were considerations which cast doubt upon the belief that the Royal Navy could be destroyed piecemeal, and in 1898 Scheder asserted that it would be foolish to hold that Britain would not be fully prepared if war came.[56]

Moreover, in 1902 Souchon solemnly warned that they could not exclude the possibility that the British might bring home the Mediterranean Fleet, too:

In my view, concentration of forces is no less correct for England than for Germany. England often concentrates its European fleets in peacetime for manoeuvres, and it will certainly concentrate its forces first in wartime, be it war conducted against the Dual Alliance, the Triple Alliance, against France or Germany alone. It will only decline to concentrate its forces if it is a war against a very weak foe, and I do not believe that England regards us as a weak opponent.

England is in the position to deploy more than three times as many vessels against us in our waters, and still have enough forces to protect its own coast and trade-routes. If the above is accepted, then we ought not to reckon on the favourable chance of encountering a weaker part of the English fleet with our entire forces.[57]

Nor did Souchon believe that it was imperative for the British to finish off the war quickly with its Home Fleet, pointing out: 'The longer the war lasts, the more thoroughly German trade will be ruined. England has plenty time to crush us slowly.'[58] Because of Germany's poor alliance prospects, Abeken too came to a similar conclusion:

This exercise must in principle be made with the most unfavourable assumption for us, that the war will be fought with the complete neutrality of the other Great Powers, so that England could also deploy against us, fully or in part, more than its Home Fleet (for example, its Mediterranean Fleet also).[59]

By 1905, therefore, when many of Tirpitz's calculations were already shown to be false, the Chief of the *Admiralstab* could only console himself that the enforced British naval concentration in home waters was weakening that power's influence in the rest of the world – which was no help strategically to the German navy and quite the reverse of the former argument that such overseas interests would keep the Royal Navy weak in the North Sea![60] The only possible alternative, in purely military terms, might have been a surprise attack upon the British Home Fleet before declaring war; but, although both sides occasionally feared that the other might attempt such a *coup de main*, they never adopted such a strategy themselves.

Tirpitz's third major miscalculation was that the Royal Navy would always act offensively, establishing a close blockade and taking the fight into German coastal waters where it would face unfavourable circumstances. On the face of it, this is the most feasible of all his assumptions and seems borne out by a number of contemporary pronouncements on the British side. Had not the delegates to the 1902 Colonial Conference been publicly told that

> the primary object of the British Navy is not to defend anything, but to attack the fleets of the enemy, and, by defeating them, to afford protection to British Dominions, supplies and commerce. This is the ultimate aim. . . . The traditional role of the Royal Navy is not to act on the defensive, but to prepare to attack the force which threatens – in other words, to assume the offensive.[61]

And did not all naval officers, British as well as German, hold that the defeat of the enemy's battlefleet was the primary task in war, with the Admiralty's War Orders stressing that 'all other operations are subsidiary to this end'?[62] Judging from the articles written by naval 'experts' in the British press at the time, one might be forgiven for believing that the Royal Navy would implement nothing less than an immediate and vigorous blockade of the enemy's coasts in war.

Against this, however, must be made a number of important points. In the first place, public discussion or even published official statements by the Admiralty did not always represent the true strategy, or only represented it in a very one-sided way; the pronouncements at the 1902 Colonial Conference, for example, had been aimed at dissuading the Dominions from creating their own local and piecemeal naval defence forces by arguing that only a worldwide policy based upon centrally directed battle squadrons would offer full security to the British Empire.[63] In the second place, much of the contemporary discussion about the necessity of hunting down and bringing to battle the enemy's warships had in mind a *guerre de course* situation, one which the feverish construction of fast armoured cruisers by the French and Russians at the turn of the century suggested as being quite possible; in such a case, the Royal Navy's squadrons would certainly need to go on to the offensive immediately to keep intact their sea communications. But it would not be so necessary if the enemy scorned commerce raiding and kept his battlefleet in the waters around Heligoland.

This leads on to a third, and very major, point: Tirpitz's strategy failed to understand what 'command of the sea' really means: it is not *necessarily* the defeat of the enemy's squadrons, though this certainly helps to secure it; it is rather the control of trade routes and communications at sea, and the capacity to defend all threats to that control. As Mahan himself puts it,

> It is the possession of that overbearing power on the sea which drives the enemy's flag from it, or allows it only to appear as a fugitive; and which, by controlling the great common, closes the highways by which commerce moves to and from the enemy's shores.[64]

In other words, to quote Mahan again, one should distinguish between the basic *object* of a belligerent like Britain – in this case, retaining command of the sea – and the military *objectives* to be secured or *methods* to be used to achieve that overall aim.[65] The latter might mean a close blockade; it might however mean a distant one, depending upon the geographical situation and the balance of forces. It might mean a swift and reckless offensive; it might instead mean waiting for a more favourable moment for battle, if one was secure in the knowledge that, until the enemy emerged, command of the sea would be unchallenged. All depended upon the particular circumstances – especially the geography – of the combatants. In the wars against France and Spain, the Royal Navy had had to maintain a tight blockading policy, because it would otherwise have been unable to anticipate and frustrate assaults upon its sea routes; unless Britain had done this, her command of the sea would have been in danger. With Germany, though, it was quite different: both German overseas commerce, and the German naval threat, could be controlled simply by foreclosing the exits from the North Sea. The onus was therefore upon the High Seas Fleet to come out and fight the British; the latter did not need to secure their *object*, retaining command of the sea, by the *objective* of destroying the German fleet or the *method* of the close blockade, and might in fact prejudice their overall aim by a rash move into the Heligoland Bight. Like Tromp in the Anglo-Dutch wars, Germany had to give battle – or a strategic stalemate would ensue in the North Sea, which would in effect leave Britain's command of the sea unchallenged.[66]

Thus, even an Admiralty statement such as 'the first duty of British fleets and squadrons will be to seek out the corresponding fleets of the enemy with a view to bringing them to action and fighting for that which is the only really decisive factor – command of the sea'[67] has to be subjected to a wider scrutiny. In fact, the first real British naval operations plan against Germany (1906) indicates that an assault upon German bases was not favourably regarded, even if Admiral A. K. Wilson clung to this idea until he was replaced on account of his strategic incompetence in 1911:

They [the Germans] being the weaker Power at sea, will act strictly on the defensive, and our strategy must be directed to making them abandon this attitude and come out to attack us in a position of our choosing and under conditions agreeable to us.

If their fleet remains in harbour, then it can exercise no influence on the war and we must leave it there, where it is doing no harm. If we, on the other hand, attempt to attack it, then we shall run a very great risk of suffering severe loss in undertaking operations that do not directly affect the object at issue, and we may find our strength so much reduced that they might have a chance of meeting us on fairly equal terms at sea, and then the conditions would become changed very much to our disadvantage.[68]

It might conceivably be worthwhile for the British to seize an offshore island such as Bochum – there is considerable correspondence upon such schemes in the British records for the years 1905–7 – but this would not occur in a purely Anglo-German war and it was in any case only a move to tempt the High Seas Fleet out to give battle and not an end in itself.[69]

Nor was a close blockade outside the German ports ever a fixed policy in London, despite Tirpitz's hopes. A clear-cut and rigid war plan against Germany was never prepared and, although some officers such as Wilson clung to this old notion, an increasing number of people regarded it with suspicion. After all, as Mahan had pointed out in his most famous book, even 'The bulk of Nelson's fleet was fifty miles from Cadiz two days before Trafalgar', relying upon reports from frigates about the enemy's fleet; and improvements in communications and the speed of warships strengthened the tendency to blockade 'at much greater distances and with fewer ships than formerly'.[70] Moreover, recoaling difficulties for an entire battlefleet would be immense, and the development of mines, torpedoes and long-range coastal ordnance made a close blockade an even more dangerous policy. As early as 1893, the First Lord, Spencer, had thought 'an effective blockade with steam power will be extremely difficult, if not impossible', and *The Times* said the same publicly in 1896. Most interesting of all, Mahan had also voiced his doubts about it in a well-known article published in 1895. 'Blockade was pretty well *passé* by 1900,' Professor Marder informs us.[71] As the Royal Navy could see, it would itself be *on the defensive* as soon as it assumed a blockading position. Hence the interim decision to keep the Home Fleet not less than 170 miles away from the German coast, relying upon cruisers for reconnaissance; and the later, fairly inevitable acknowledgement that the distant blockade would be enough to retain command of the sea while a method was devised to tempt the High Seas Fleet into giving battle.[72]

Certain other factors, too, suggest that Tirpitz was too optimistic in holding that the British would institute a close blockade of the German coast. He himself in 1897 had sharply criticized the *Oberkommando*'s plans for a war against France with the following words:

The operations plan of the High Command bases itself upon the strategic defensive in the Baltic and North Sea. One is supposed to wait here for the foe, and then attack. The purpose is to keep open our import-trade. I strongly believe that this enemy will not at first come, and that we will then be waiting around with our large fleet while France blocks two-thirds to three-quarters of our imports in the Channel and to the north of England without great efforts.[73]

If the admiral believed that the French navy would prefer to wait, to pick off the German merchant marine and assemble their whole fleet in the meantime, why should this strategy not be adopted by the Royal Navy also?

The final and most damning objection to the viability of this German naval strategy lies, ironically enough, in the postulations of Tirpitz's risk theory. The German navy was to be so large and strong that even the greatest maritime power would have its control of the oceans endangered by attacking it. Why, then, was it believed that the enemy would adopt an aggressive war strategy at all? After all, Great Britain was supposed to make her calculations 'from the purely practical standpoint of the businessman'. Herein lies the basic paradox in Tirpitz's strategical views: *for the more he believed in the risk theory and the deterring of a British attack, the less convincing was his assumption that the Royal Navy would immediately rush into dangerous German waters*. Whether a state of war or peace existed, the two notions cannot be reconciled; if one idea worked, then the other could not. If a *Risikoflotte* really had existed, how likely was it that the Royal Navy under such cautious men as Goschen and Selborne would throw their warships into the German Bight when (in Tirpitz's calculation) a large part of their fleet would be away on other stations?

What was more, one finds that Tirpitz's conviction that the Royal Navy would institute a close blockade of the German coast was not shared by a number of *Admiralstab* officers. Büchsel himself minuted in 1901:

I am not sure if this is true. The cause of war is purely economic. If England comprehends it properly, it will only wage economic warfare, that is, a blockade – and from a central position in the North Sea. It will not divide its fleet. The battlefleet will be in the central position, and the cruisers will carry out a blockade.[74]

Boedecker, too, thought that the British would institute a distant blockade against German commerce and would last out the war better than Germany: 'England does not need to strive to arrange that the war against Germany would quickly be ended.' Despite this, he also believed that the Royal Navy's fleets would act aggressively, even forcing themselves into the Baltic.[75] Heeringen reached a similar, orthodox conclusion, although he also pointed out that 'England itself has no interest in a swift end to the war, since the longer it interrupts German trade, the more thoroughly the latter will be ruined; and England will then have more time to establish itself in German overseas markets.'[76] Why Britain should need to make an immediate sortie into German waters, an obvious question in the light of the above statement, he did not bother to consider. By early 1904, though, Büchsel was pressing for vigorous commerce raiding in time of war because 'through it one could force England to adopt a close blockade, which it might otherwise avoid.'[77] Thus, although the established German strategy was in no way changed in the 1906 plans, it was at least recognized that:

> Should England for any reason desire to achieve its aim without considerable fleet losses, then it will not employ a direct offensive regardless of the costs but instead its admirals will, despite numerical superiority, avoid engagements with coastal defences and under unfavourable circumstances, and will try to catch our fleet on the high seas and destroy it there.[78]

Nevertheless, for the next three years, the German operations plan against England was based on the belief that the Royal Navy would come over. Only in 1908–9 was the probability of a distant blockade accepted, and an offensive strategy evolved for the High Seas Fleet; but in 1912 this was again reversed. As late as August 1914, *Admiralstabschef* Pohl could agree that 'The English fleet's "Defensive" begins on the enemy's coast.' The alternative, felt another officer, Heeringen, hardly bore thinking about: 'If the English really devote themselves to a distant blockade, then the role of our dear High Seas Fleet could be a very unhappy one.'[79]

Many further criticisms have been made of Tirpitz's naval policy: that his financial calculations, particularly upon the relative capacity of Germany and Britain to withstand a protracted naval race, were unsound; that the fleet took away money from the army, thus weakening Germany's land defences, without ever being able to protect Germany's interests at sea and in the colonies; that, in an age of rapid technological change, it was unwise to assume that Germany would permanently possess technical superiority, as the 'Dreadnought Spring' was to show; that the internal political implications of this policy were also founded upon dubious calculations; that he cannot have been unaware that the leaders of Germany's foreign policy at the turn of the century opposed any alliance with France and Russia which would have provided a far better shield during the danger zone and the only real opportunity to challenge the Royal Navy's superiority; and that it caused the 'encirclement' of Germany, forfeiting that country's position as the *tertius gaudens* in European diplomacy and placing it in a far more hazardous situation than in 1897.[80] But they are not the main concern of this paper, which concentrates upon the strategic aspects of Tirpitz's policy.

In this regard, the basic error was the admiral's expectation that Britain would maintain the same naval dispositions, the same strategy, and the same foreign policy when Germany became a great and powerful threat to British maritime supremacy as when she had no navy worth speaking of at all. Yet the British were, in many ways, not so inflexible as Tirpitz; those dispositions, that strategy, that foreign policy were not fixed and unalterable rules to which Britain had always adhered but in fact necessary measures to meet the greatest threat at the time – the Franco-Russian alliance. If, however, an even greater threat arose, there was no absolute reason why the British would be unable to alter those measures accordingly. Tirpitz's calculations here were based upon premises which sheer commonsense, not to mention a considerable amount of contemporary British and German writings upon strategy, contradicted. In fact, it is not just a matter of how the admiral could have adopted such strategic views which requires investigation but also how his theories managed to prevail, almost unchallenged, inside Germany for so long – to which this writer can only suggest the following: the fragmented organization of the Imperial German Navy, which made much of the *Admiralstab*'s work mere theoretical musings; the lack of informed civilian probing into strategic matters, such as existed in the English press and parliament; the crushing of the early and somewhat fatuous strategical criticisms of people such as Valois and Maltzahn; and Tirpitz's great prestige and influence inside the navy, and with the Kaiser, because of his acknowledged abilities and achievements.

The latter point can hardly be denied: the admiral was an outstanding character. He had immensely winning ways, as his long period in the Kaiser's favour suggests; he was a superb planner and organizer, a clever tactician and propagandist, and possibly the most skilful politician of his time. To create the world's second largest navy in such a few years was little short of genius; and one might also claim that he did more than anyone else to bring the era of *Pax Britannica* to a close, forcing the British to scrap most of their gun-boats and to withdraw from the Western Hemisphere, the Far East, even the Mediterranean, to concentrate upon the North Sea.[81] But he was a poor strategist, unable to see the contradictions in his own scheme or to perceive how the British would react; he had imbibed only the superficial lessons of Mahan, and ignored the importance of geography; and he possessed an erroneous notion of what 'command of the sea' really meant, assuming that it was always identical with battleship strength.[82]

He was, moreover, unbelievably inflexible in his strategic tenets. The changing circumstances of history, 'the kaleidoscopic nature of international relations', could render any strategy out of date. It is one of the functions of operational planners to keep these circumstances and needs under review, and to adjust war strategy accordingly. This Tirpitz never did; he only had *one* strategy. The British swiftly altered their plans and dispositions, but he could not. His scheme for the political utilization of the German fleet was as fixed and inflexible as the Navy Laws themselves. The relatively quick British response to the German challenge, the redeployment of the Royal Navy in the North Sea and the reorganization of the entire British defence policy, the move by Britain closer to France and eventually to Russia, could not shake his determination to carry on according to his plan, however tighter this tugged the knot of encirclement around Germany.

Was there any way out of Tirpitz's dilemma, in strategical terms? The Achilles heel of *any* German naval strategy against Britain lay in the former's extremely disadvantageous geographical position. If this could not be improved, Germany would find it difficult to employ either her battlefleet or a policy of commerce raiding while she remained inferior in strength to the Royal Navy. But how could this basic geographical disadvantage be overcome? One way, suggested by Wolfgang Wegener, might have been the possession of bases in Norway, which would at one blow have allowed the German navy to be free of the suffocating confines of the North Sea and possibly have provoked the British into attacking under unfavourable conditions to forestall raids into the Atlantic.[83] However, the political objections to the seizure were enormous, and no one seems to have considered this alternative at the time. Only in the Second World War was this strategy carried out; but for coal-fired warships the logistical problems would have been large.

A second way out might have been the seizure of Belgium and the north-west coastline of France, breaking the British distant blockade and threatening the Channel sea-lanes. Here again, though, there is as yet no concrete evidence of planning or pressure by the German naval authorities before August 1914 to effect this alteration; in fact, the *Admiralstab* hoped in 1906 that the army would not occupy Belgium since the port of Antwerp would be a valuable entrepot for scarce raw materials in time of war with Britain.[84] However, as soon as the war did break out, the German navy pressed hard for the occupation of this region and the utilization of its ports. The *Admiralstab* pondered over the question and Tirpitz insisted upon 'the affiliation of Belgium in one form or other'.[85] By 1915 it had become an essential part of his aim to challenge the Anglo-Saxon powers and Russia for the control of the world's destinies and to create an even bigger 'risk' for Britain:

> Then Belgium can become the cornerstone on which our foes' schemes are ruined now and forever; and the foundation upon which a German world position is built, equal to that of the Anglo-Saxons and the Russians. The flank-position of the Belgian ports to the English east coast will always remain decisive,

as will the fact that the distance from them to the Thames estuary is only seventy miles, one-quarter of the stretch from Heligoland to the Thames.[86]

Only by this, he insisted, could Germany overcome 'the disadvantages of geography and of strategic positions', one of the rare occasions when he admitted that those actually existed.[87]

On the other hand, this strategy was not followed through; for to really break the British distant blockade, Germany would need to acquire bases even further to the west, such as Brest and Cherbourg, which the British would have to cover in some way. Tirpitz wondered if the Belgian ports might take battleships but the *Admiralstab* welcomed the possession of these bases for merely *Kleinkrieg* methods, using destroyers and submarines to attack English commerce. It seems fair to conclude, therefore, that little serious thought was given by the German navy to countering the wide blockade by the seizure of territory bordering one of the exits from the North Sea, certainly before 1914. What is less certain, in the light of the findings of Fritz Fischer and his school, is whether any conscious or half-conscious decision was made by Germany's leaders after 1911 or so to establish some form of continental hegemony first of all, before the navy's strategical dilemma could be finally solved.

One further alternative remained, the one solution which would remove the disadvantages of Germany's geographical position, would allow her to play the role of a world power unhindered by fears of the Royal Navy and would secure her that 'world-political freedom': namely, *a battlefleet at least as powerful as, and a great deal more efficient and better built than, the British fleet*. If one could credit Tirpitz with the long-term vision of creating the world's largest navy, then he cannot be faulted strategically – although the financial and political consequences would be immense. But if it is to be admitted that he merely sought for a fleet of thirty-eight battleships or so, then most of his strategical ideas and calculations must be labelled as unwise and short-sighted even at the time of their formulation. Only by outbuilding the British could Tirpitz provide the real answer.

Such an interpretation, voiced by excitable British newspapers in the pre-1914 period, has found little support in subsequent historical treatments of the problem, especially in Germany. The idea sounds too fantastic, too enormous; how could he have even thought of building a fleet the same size as or larger than the Royal Navy? Fantastic though it is, it seems to this writer that it should be given more serious consideration than hitherto, at least as a possibility. Despite the large amount of archival material available, it does not seem likely that there will ever be sufficient evidence to permit a conclusive judgement on this problem, particularly since what is under discussion is Tirpitz's *hoped-for final aim*; but the hints we possess are considerable.

In the first place, it would be utterly logical. The essence of the naval race, as Tirpitz must have known, was that the German and British aims were absolutely incompatible. For Germany to be safe from an English attack, and secure enough to carry out her *Weltpolitik* without hindrance, she had to create a real threat to the Royal Navy's supremacy and to the security of the British Isles. In the *Admiralstab*'s words,

> If it is possible for us to create a battlefleet which is in a position to oppose the British Home Fleet successfully, and which opens up for England the risk of losing its fleet and thus the country's shield, then we shall be secure against an English attack.[88]

However, it was and always had been a *conditio sine qua non* for the British that their naval supremacy should not be lost or put at risk. Had not Halifax said (1694): 'Look to your moat. The first article of an Englishman's political creed must be that he believeth in the sea.' The navalist press in the 1880s and 1890s had chanted: 'by the navy we stand or fall'; Grey restated the case in 1913: 'the Navy is our one and only means of defence and our life depends upon it and on it alone'; Fisher put it more bluntly: 'The Navy is the first, second, third, fourth, fifth . . . ad infinitum Line of Defence! . . . It's not invasion we have to fear if our Navy's beaten, IT'S STARVATION!'[89] The same point was reported frequently to Tirpitz; Coerper, for example, told him in 1907:

The steadily increasing sea-power of Germany constitutes the greatest hindrance to England's freedom of political action. That is the central point of the unsatisfactory relations of the two nations to one another.[90]

In other words, what it was vital for Tirpitz to achieve for Germany's sake, it was essential for the British Admiralty to deny for England's sake; what the German government wanted, the British government would never willingly surrender, and *vice-versa*; security for one meant danger to the other. Hence the grimly fought and costly naval race, which could only end in the defeat of one of them.

It was therefore a nonsense for Tirpitz and the Kaiser to insist that only by the construction of a great fleet could England be forced to be friendly. It is also a nonsense to suggest that they sought for a lasting understanding with the British; such would have been only a short-lived and one-sided affair, an uneasy truce. For Tirpitz, with his Darwinistic view of political developments, could not accept the idea that Britain and Germany could permanently cooperate. Their commercial rivalry, which he saw as the root of their antagonism, prevented an alliance from coming into being and would always exist. Without being as emotional and anglophobic about it as, say, Senden, he nevertheless recognized Britain from a very early stage in his career as the greatest obstacle to Germany's future. What mattered above all else was to create a state of security for German overseas interests, and to fulfil this condition the Royal Navy had to be overhauled and contained.

Secondly, it would also be logical in the strictly strategical sense; for the fleet provided in the Second Navy Law could not defeat the British provided the latter took the necessary precautions which an Anglo-German confrontation called for. The only methods by which Germany could bring Britain to her knees were either blockade or invasion. The former was logistically impossible, due to the geographical distances involved; the latter was operationally impossible, in the opinion of both Schlieffen and the *Admiralstab*, without a superior fleet, not just for the first few days but for a far longer time. Yet if Germany could carry out neither, she could not defeat Britain. The only safe way out was to have a more powerful fleet, and this Tirpitz and other strategists could not have failed to recognize. After all, Mahan had pointed this out in a famous article in 1902:

> Sea defence for Germany, in case of war with France or England, means established naval predominance at least in the North Sea; nor can it be considered complete unless extended through the Channel and as far as Great Britain will have to project hers into the Atlantic. This is Germany's initial disadvantage of position, to be overcome only by adequate superiority of numbers.[91]

In the third place, this interpretation fits in with the non-strategic aspects of the admiral's naval policy: with his Social-Darwinism and conviction that he had to provide Germany with the means to achieve and maintain the status of one of the four world powers of the twentieth century; with his belief that Germany should rely less on the landowners and the army as the future bases of economic power, and more upon industry, commerce and the navy; with his internal political calculations, the need to please the Kaiser and at the same time to erode all forms of Reichstag control over the fleet; and with the natural feelings of a patriot and a serving officer that having only a 'second best' navy was not good enough. Britain and her navy appeared to him to stand in the way of all these aims, to the extent that they posed a threat to the ever-upward trend of Germany's industry, shipping and trade and to the seemingly irresistible expansion of German power and influence into the outside world, which so impressed Tirpitz. As an avid disciple of both Treitschke and Mahan, he saw in a great battlefleet the only way to eliminate this threat; it was, he assured the Kaiser,

> an absolute necessity for Germany, without which it will face ruin. There are four World Powers: Russia, England, America and Germany. Since two of those World Powers can only be reached across the sea, so sea power must predominate. . . . Since Germany is particularly backward in sea power, it is a life-and-death question for her, as a World Power and great cultural state, to make up the lost ground. The development of Germany into an industrial and commercial nation is irreversible, like a law of nature. . . . Given such a commercial and industrial

development, collisions and conflict-points will grow with other nations, therefore power, sea power, is essential if Germany is not to go under swiftly.[92]

A great deal more evidence can be found in the archives and in the private papers of Tirpitz, Senden and others to indicate that they all firmly anticipated 'a new division of the globe', that they expected Germany to take the foremost part in this process but that she would continually encounter the rivalry of Britain and that 'a world-political freedom' would only be hers when she had built a vast fleet to neutralize such opposition. As early as 1895, Tirpitz had spoken of the need to have a large navy as 'a power factor, which Germany unquestionably requires in peace as well as war, if it is not to cede its place among the ranks of the Great Powers'. In 1903, the navy had felt 'that, if we wish to carry out a forceful overseas policy and gain valuable colonies for ourselves, we must be prepared in the first instance for a clash with England or America.'[93] It was clear that a second-class fleet would not be strong enough for these mighty political tasks, and the matter was too important to depend solely upon exploiting the split between Britain and the Dual Alliance to achieve Tirpitz's ends. It would be far safer to be independent of France and Russia when confronting Britain in some future affair; in other words, to have a fleet that could deal with the Royal Navy on any occasion. If this idea seems ridiculous, it must first of all be remembered that Tirpitz and Bülow were thinking in terms of a decade or two into the future, that they expected Britain to have been at war with Russia before that time, and that they were very optimistic about Germany's great rate of industrial and commercial progress. If she could exceed Britain in steel output, in the newer chemical and electrical industries, and in population, why not one day in warship production also? As Senden put it: 'Political constellations change unceasingly, and they can also change against England. . . .'[94]

As a final consideration, there are the hints we possess of the limitless nature of the fleet which Tirpitz and Wilhelm wished to build, despite the efforts to conceal them to the outside world. We know now that they sought to wrest control gradually from the Reichstag, and thus erase the hated '*Parlamentsflotte*', and to effect a building programme of three large and three small warships every year, automatically replaceable after twenty years, i.e. a constant force of sixty capital ships and sixty light cruisers, controlled in every respect by the monarch. However, Tirpitz gave no indication that these were his *maximum* aims, and the temptation to increase the *Bautempo* was always there; in fact, in 1905 he admitted that the permanent 'three-battleships-a-year' tempo was the aim 'in the first instance'; in 1907, that the 'four-a-year' tempo be adopted 'to begin with' for four years. Afterwards, though, one could always graft on (*aufpfropfen*) further increases; in 1905–7, there are clear references in the *Reichsmarineamt* records to future additions in excess of sixty capital ships.[95] Moreover, it is also unclear whether the many memoranda from 1903 onwards upon the possibility of a third double-squadron of battleships (in total, fifty-seven battle-ships) also contemplated retaining the twenty large cruisers, especially after the launching of the *Invincible*-class and Tirpitz's own reluctant decision to build battlecruisers; if so, this would imply that a fleet of seventy-seven capital ships was at one time under consideration, which is a staggering total. Yet since the admiral was hoping to take an ever-increasing share of the defence budget from the army, such a fleet cannot be regarded as pure fantasy. Tirpitz was not the man to announce his final aims in advance; to use his own words, 'If one wishes to achieve a great aim, one is not always in the position to disclose one's final thoughts.'[96]

There is, in any case, some evidence of this grander design, when Tirpitz occasionally expressed his future hopes in private conversations with political colleagues. As early as 1897, he told Monts that the dislike of conscription in Britain would prevent its government from maintaining the existing ratio between the two navies, while

We could in contrast provide a strong reserve of trained crews from the yearly intake of around 20,000 recruits into the Navy, in comparison to their annual reserve which was scarcely worth noting, and eventually with certainty provide the same number of ships as the English.[97]

A year later, he warned Hohenlohe that 'all policies hostile to

England must be put on ice, until we have a fleet which is as strong as the English one'.[98] The Empress Frederick, Holstein, Waldersee and Kühlmann all believed that this was what Tirpitz and the Kaiser hoped to achieve eventually.[99]

The final piece of evidence comes again from Tirpitz, in a paragraph of a letter to Lans at the beginning of the war which he later *deliberately omitted* from the version published in his *Politische Dokumente*, volume 2. Commenting somewhat jealously upon the army's successes in the field, he wrote:

> Had we in our case also performed, if not victoriously then at least with glory, things would be different, and then the opinion would break through that we must have *a fleet equally strong as England's*. This natural and single aim could not, however, be announced during the past two decades, it could only be kept in mind if Germany's trade and industry and colonies expanded further.[100]

If this, 'a fleet equally strong as England's', was Tirpitz's real aim, which he had been compelled to conceal for the past two decades, then it could only be achieved – if at all – at immense cost; it would strain the Reich's finances, infuriate the army, crystallize political opposition inside Germany, split the middle classes and Conservatives, and drive the British to desperate measures. But at least it had some strategical logic; if Germany had a fleet as powerful as the Royal Navy, then her strategic disadvantages would not be as great. This would also explain Tirpitz's unswerving, inflexible policy during the naval race with Britain, and why he was so dismayed when war broke out in 1914. Perhaps, if this interpretation is true, he was not such a poor strategist after all. But then, we should have to call his other qualities into question instead.

III

Strategy in a Global Context

6

The Western world has been engaged in an arms-race with the Soviet Union and its allies for nearly forty years, since the end of the Second World War. At certain times that 'race' has slackened off, and people have talked optimistically of *detente*; but the tensions and suspicions have never been eradicated for long and, at the time of writing this introduction, the monies allocated to armaments by both NATO and the Warsaw Pact are spiralling upwards. Because of the dreadful power of nuclear weapons this is, qualitatively, much more frightening in its implications than any previous arms-race, where man's capacity for destruction was more limited. But that seems all the greater reason to provide an historical perspective to the current debate, and to point to certain conclusions which can be drawn from arms-races of the preceding century.

This essay was first given as the introductory paper to an Oxford University seminar on 'Arms-races', and I am grateful to Professor Michael Howard for inviting me to deliver it and for his seminar's comments upon it. The King's College War Studies seminar of the University of London also offered valuable criticisms of this talk, and in so doing made it the more suitable for publication.

Arms-races and the
Causes of War, 1850–1945

Like most essays on very general topics, 'Arms-races and the Causes of War' needs defining, and needs certain limits set upon it, if it is to achieve any coherence at all. As the dates indicate, it covers the period from the 1850s, when industrialization was first beginning to make its sustained, variegated impact upon war, to the end of the Second World War, when the coming of nuclear weapons introduced a quite new element into the age-old Great Power rivalries.[1] What follows contains little upon arms-races between Balkan states, and nothing upon Latin American arms-races, but otherwise there are no obvious geographical restrictions. More positively, it proposes to include remarks upon the success or failure of arms limitations talks; the problem of bilateral as opposed to multilateral arms-races; the economic factor in arms-races; and the question of qualitative *versus* quantitative arms-races – before offering a general conclusion upon the relationship between arms-races and the causes of war.

The classic statement upon arms-races and war is that made by Sir Edward Grey in his memoirs, when he reflected upon the dark years before 1914:

The moral is obvious: it is that great armaments lead inevitably to war. If there are armaments on one side there must be armaments on other sides. While one nation arms, other nations cannot tempt it to aggression by remaining defenceless. . . . The enormous growth of armaments in Europe, the sense of insecurity and fear caused by them – it was these that made war inevitable.[2]

One can see why it is a classic statement: it is simple, sweeping and all-embracing. If it is used as a foil in this essay, it is not

165

because of total disagreement with Grey's assertion but because historical truth is – as usual – more complex than such generalizations suggest.

In the first place, even if Grey meant that all great arms-races lead inevitably to war, that statement does not necessarily mean that *all* wars are the consequences of arms-races. There are too many examples of where that simply was not so: the Russo-Turkish War of 1877, the two Boer Wars, the Sino-Japanese War of 1894, the Spanish-American War of 1898, the Italo-Abyssinian War of 1934–6, the Vietnam War. Political disagreements, territorial rivalries and ambitions, dislike of the other state's internal rule and ideology, were some of the chief causes here; and in many of those conflicts, for example the Russo-Turkish War and Spanish-American War, the contestants, far from having been feverishly engaged in an armaments spiral for years beforehand, were hard pressed to lay their hands upon the weapons and the trained men to do the fighting. The Falklands War of 1982 provides a very recent example to sustain this argument: for the evidence suggests that it was not a British arms build-up but the *reverse* – that is, the planned reduction in the Royal Navy's capacity to mount an extra-European operation – which tempted the Galtieri government to strike.

Secondly, there are many examples of arms-races which rose to a certain height and then, stabilizing, later began to fade away; and of arms-races which were somehow controlled, diplomatically, by a political decision, by a tacit or open concession.

The *first* example here was the Anglo-French arms-race of 1859–60, begun (in the British view) by France's construction of the armour-clad *La Gloire* and its announcement of a construction programme of sixteen ironclads. This would give the French a technological (and, therefore, a *battle*) advantage over the Royal Navy and, taken in association with the evident superiority of steam-driven vessels over sail, seemed to place the island kingdom in great danger. Steam, to use Palmerston's earlier phrase, had at last bridged the Channel. All this was linked to British concern at the unpredictable nature of Napoleon III's foreign policy, in Italy, Mexico, the Rhineland and the Mediterranean; in other words, the issue was *political* and not merely technological and strategical. This, in turn, produced a regular 'invasion scare', with the government not only compelled to increase the fleet (and to respond to *La Gloire* with HMS *Warrior*), but there was also felt a need to raise the Volunteers and to spend the then-enormous sum of £10 million upon fortifications.[3] Yet despite all the classic signs of international tension, and an accompanying arms spiral, this affair had blown over within a year or two. French naval construction fell away, and Napoleon III found that he had too much on his hands in Italy, in Mexico, and then in dealing with the rising power of Prussia inside Germany. The latter fact introduces the interesting role of *third* powers in influencing an arms-race – either by intensifying it, or ameliorating it if one of the contenders has to turn its attention and resources elsewhere.

The *second* example was the arms-race and concomitant tensions among the European powers in the late 1880s and early 1890s. With our eyes drawn irresistibly to the 1914 calamity and its causes, we tend to forget just how acute were the rivalries between the leading nations between (say) 1886 and 1893, with Boulanger leading a *revanchiste* campaign in France; with the Russians on the point of entering Bulgaria, which the Austrians were determined to oppose; with the elder Moltke and, after him, Waldersee at the Prussian General Staff pressing Bismarck and the Kaiser to permit a pre-emptive strike; with Salisbury perspiring at the awful twin prospect of the Russians in Constantinople and the Germans in Paris; and with, at various intervals, army bills and troop increases and new guns being announced by the war ministries.[4] There was not much difference, it can be argued, between those tense years and the period 1908–14; and yet the earlier crisis was surmounted. Bismarck, fighting off the generals, struggled to preserve links with Russia, control the Austrians, and keep everyone tied in diplomatic knots; the coming of the Franco-Russian alliance reduced the chronic feelings of insecurity of those two nations; many of the major powers turned to colonial and naval expansion, and Europe fell into a state of nervous stability.

Third, there was the prolonged *naval* arms-race between Britain on the one hand, and France and Russia on the other, from 1884 – the year of the *Pall Mall Gazette*'s agitation over 'The Truth about the Navy' – to 1904–5 – the year of the *entente cordiale* and the

Russo-Japanese War. In many ways, this was a more serious matter for British naval mastery than the much more famous 'race' with Tirpitz's fleet before 1914. Thanks to sustained building, the French fleet had come close to the size of the Royal Navy in the early 1880s; taken in conjunction with the rapidly growing Russian fleet, it threatened to be numerically superior to British naval forces and this remained the case even after the 1885 supplementary programme, the 1889 Naval Defence Act (with its proclaimed Two Power Standard), the Spencer Programme of 1893, and all the later annual increases in the naval budget. Not only did the Royal Navy lack clear superiority of numbers (cf. its 60 per cent lead over the German fleet later), but it was much more difficult *geographically* to mask the naval forces of the potential Franco-Russian foe than it was to contain the High Seas Fleet in the North Sea. The naval pressures in the Mediterranean were so great that many strategists advocated a 'scuttle' from that sea, and in the Far East the British battleship inferiority was an important factor in the Admiralty's case for an alliance with Japan. Nor were these two decades without acute diplomatic crises – Penjdeh, Siam, Fashoda, the Dogger Bank – which seemed to bring Britain to the brink of war with one or other member of the Franco-Russian alliance, with the Royal Navy's fleets steaming out to their battle stations.[5]

Yet after 1903, at the latest after 1905, this twenty-year-old arms-race began to fade away. This was not for financial or technological reasons but, in the main, for political ones. The steady rise of Imperial Germany, and in particular the flamboyant and aggressive nature of Kaiser Wilhelm II's *Weltpolitik*, started to alarm France, and Britain, and even Russia. The Anglo-French colonial *entente* of 1904 was cemented by the German intrusion in the Moroccan crisis of the following year. Russia's defeat in the war with Japan eliminated its navy, and had the additional bonus of allowing the British to withdraw their battleship squadron from the Far East – just in time to join those other vessels being stationed in the North Sea to counter Tirpitz's High Seas Fleet. Once again, the actions of a third power played a significant role in lessening the tension between two original rivals.[6]

It may be thought possible to offer, as a fourth example, the Anglo-German naval race itself since, despite all the excitement it generated, it was a 'controlled' process after 1912 and it was not a primary cause of the war in 1914. But the issue is more complicated than that – for it can be argued that the German naval challenge affected how the British would respond to the European crisis after the Sarajevo assassination[7] – and it is best to leave this example to one side.

There is, however, an excellent example in the naval field of an arms-race being brought to an end by diplomacy: namely, the Anglo-American battleship race at the beginning of the 1920s, and the incipient rivalry of both those powers with Japan – which were controlled, if not permanently eliminated, by the Washington Treaties of 1921–2. The clauses, and extent, of this naval limitations agreement were without historical precedent and have never really been repeated: there were restrictions on the overall size of the world's five largest battlefleets (Britain, USA, France, Italy, Japan) according to fixed ratios; restrictions upon the tonnage and gun-calibres of individual battleships; a virtual 'naval holiday' in capital ship construction for ten years; and a ban upon the construction of fortified bases in the Pacific and Far East (this being part of the larger political-cum-territorial package of measures for preserving the *status quo* in China and the Pacific and for quietly dissolving the Anglo-Japanese alliance).[8] The ban upon new capital ship construction was extended for another five years by the 1930 Treaty of London, and there were also restrictions upon cruiser numbers. That these agreements contained flaws – and, in particular, disadvantaged the Western democracies just before they had to face the threat from Fascism – is common knowledge, although everyone is wise in retrospect. What was significant at the time, and still seems so after the passage of sixty years, was the dominance of the political over the military arm of government. Despite the protests of admirals on all sides, the leading statesmen in Whitehall and Washington had decided that the economic and social costs of an arms spiral were not justified by the international situation, and would be unpopular domestically; while in Japan a quasi-liberal regime was not intent, in those years at least, in challenging the *status quo* by force.

If, on the evidence offered above, it is quite plausible to argue that open clashes between states arming against each other were avoided on numerous occasions by 'political' decisions – and by 'political' is meant here the totality of the reasoning used by the central decision-makers of a state, as distinct from some specific military pressure-group on the one hand or some general, imponderable force called an armaments spiral on the other: if 'political' decisions caused a drawing-back from the brink, a resort to diplomacy and to the control of arms spending, so also did they determine those cases of states going up, and *over*, the brink. This can be confirmed by brief reference to examples where the efforts to check an arms-race and reduce tensions failed.

The *first* example here was the attempt by the British Foreign Secretary, Lord Clarendon, to arrange a halt to the arms-race between France and Prussia in 1869–70. Although encouraged privately by the French, Clarendon's ideas were firmly checked by Bismarck. While employing the plausible political reason that King William I of Prussia would have a fit at the very notion of diplomats deciding the size and composition of his beloved army, Bismarck really rejected arms limitations for two deeper reasons. First, he was aware that in Prussia the economic costs of the short-service mass-army system could be borne more easily than in neighbouring states. A *general* limit on the overall size of armies, which Clarendon mooted, was therefore a *specific* aid to a country like France. Secondly, and more ominously, an arms freeze also implied a freezing of the *status quo*, which would have suited a nervous Napoleon III by then but in no way satisfied a Bismarck intent upon altering the European order.[9] This is but one of many examples of a 'dissatisfied' power refusing arms limitations because that might also restrict the chances of future territorial improvements: whereas nations at the top of the global wheel of fortune are usually very interested in measures to preserve the existing order (and thus their own favourable place in it).

The *second* example would be the efforts made, at the two Hague peace conferences of 1899 and 1907, to reduce armaments, restrict certain forms of warfare, and to have compulsory international arbitration of Great Power disputes. As has been shown in great detail by a recent study of these conferences,[10] the key determinant of a government's reaction to those various schemes was its perception of its own specific interests, and of its place in the international order. The original Russian proposal for a conference related to its difficulty in 1898 in both financing army and navy increases, *and* a strategic railway network; why not, therefore, suggest general arms reductions but exclude railway-building, which could be represented as a peaceful development? In consequence, it was not surprising that Germany, which could carry the burden of armaments more easily, opposed any restrictions on the size of armies and types of weapons – and also regarded the compulsory resort to arbitration over interstate disputes as a device to check the German army's capacity for mobilizing and going to war faster than anybody else. The French, for their part, although wishing to humour their Russian ally, were against the proclamation of permanent 'international peace' lest that imply recognition of German possession of Alsace-Lorraine for all time.

The same sort of self-centred objections occurred during the 1907 Hague Conference. Being engaged in building a navy so as to alter the existing maritime balance, the Germans violently opposed restrictions upon naval *construction*, for that would preserve the Royal Navy's numerical superiority; on the other hand, it was the British Admiralty which disliked restrictions on the *application* of naval force (for example, by commercial blockade), since that would remove its advantage over lesser maritime powers. Throughout all these discussions, there were the inevitable technical objections – about the actual verification of disarmament, and checking upon secret rearmament; or the contradiction of restricting war in one form (e.g. commercial blockade) but not in another (e.g. direct military invasion), and thereby encouraging the second form – problems which were just as contentious in the SALT talks more recently. But, above all, there was in the age of imperialism that strong objection – voiced most strenuously by the German delegates but tacitly accepted by all – to arms limitations *per se*, as being a slight upon the absolute sovereignty of the nation-state. Within a year of the second Hague Conference, the Anglo-German naval race was reaching a new intensity, and the Bosnian crisis was lighting that fuse in the Balkans which would soon erupt in the clashes of 1912, 1913 and 1914 itself. Preferring to trust in the sword rather than in the pen, the rival alliances lurched towards Armageddon, with their arms spending and troop increases rising higher year by year.

The *third* major example was the ultimate breakdown of the *land* disarmament talks of the late 1920s and early 1930s, which contrasted with the success of the Washington and London naval conferences – although even in the latter it is worth recalling that the British in 1921 could never get the submarine restricted, since second-class naval powers like France regarded such a ban as an artificial way of preserving the superiority of the first-class powers; and also that there was fierce disagreement on certain naval ratios between France and Italy, since the French could never agree to Italy being classed as their equal, whereas the Italians could never accept being classed as France's inferior. But that incompatibility was far less momentous than the clash between Berlin and Paris over land (and air) rearmament. To a French nation, scarred by the First World War and aware of its own population and industrial weaknesses *vis-à-vis* Germany, aware also from intelligence reports of secret German rearmament, it was national suicide to reduce the large, standing French army. To successive German governments, smarting from the Versailles Treaty, under attack from a demogogic Right, it was impossible to tolerate any longer that state of inferiority which the restrictions upon the size of the German army and upon the possession of tanks, aircraft and so on implied. The success of the aspirations of one country meant the ruination of the hopes of the other; each required the other side to make a political concession which was out of the question. All of the British and other efforts to produce a compromise foundered on this basic Franco-German incompatibility of views; and the final French gesture of September 1933, when Hitler was already consolidating his hold internally, that they would 'level down' their armaments but only on condition that the British bound themselves to automatic sanctions if Germany violated a treaty by secretly rearming, caused a prompt refusal in London. Britain would 'morally condemn' such a German violation but, for its own domestic-political reasons,

172

was determined to avoid any fixed pledges as to action.[11] From that time onwards, with the Geneva talks abandoned and Hitler pushing ahead with rearmament as fast as he dared, no international armaments treaty – except for the dubious and short-term Anglo-German naval pact of 1935 – could be concluded. The arms-race was on again, to the dismay and bewilderment of governments and public opinion in the democratic West, only two decades after that pre-1914 race from which everyone was supposed to have drawn the awful but correct lesson.

The examples provided above of arms-races which were controlled and of those which were not, have an obvious implication for that once-popular thesis about 'the merchants of death', that is, that armaments manufacturers pervert public policy, influence governments into excessive military expenditures, and are ultimately responsible for wars.[12] This does not seem to have been *at all* true for most of the arms-races and open conflicts dealt with here; and even for the three most notorious cases of the past century – the Second Boer War and the Chamberlain family's links with Kynochs armaments works; the Anglo-German naval race before 1914, and the influence of Krupps, Vickers and the shipyards; and the 'military-industrial complex' in the USA since 1945 – the argument is hardly proven. It is one thing to show that arms firms make profits out of increased orders, and therefore endeavour to get those orders increased; it would be perplexing if they didn't. But it is quite another to demonstrate that the armaments industry created, manipulated, and controlled an arms-race – with the implication that strategical fears, political decisions and nationalist emotions are all subordinate factors. Even the contemporary evidence suggests that the thesis about the influence of arms manufacturers does not fit the facts, either as to the timing, or the direction, or the meaning of the current armaments spiral.[13]

Yet to discount the crude 'hidden hand' theories is not to disprove *all* economic causes of wars and arms-races (just as, say, to destroy the vulgar 'surplus capital' theory of imperialism is not to undermine all economic interpretations of colonial annexations). Indeed, it is possible to go a long way in arguing that economic *tendencies*, with the shifts they cause in the balance of power, and economic *aspirations*, especially those of the 'have-not' countries for a greater share of the world's raw materials and territory, were at the bottom of the two great wars of this century. It seems true for an understanding of German policy before 1914;[14] and is even more the case for understanding German policy before 1939, Japanese policy before 1941 and, for that matter, a good part of Italian policy in the 1930s.[15] This is not, of course, an economic interpretation pure and simple. Rather, it stresses the vital importance which the élites in certain countries attached to the economic struggle for survival, which they regarded (literally) in Darwinian terms; and which, in their view, necessitated the creation or the expansion of armed force as the most likely means for gaining that greater share of the world's wealth; which, in its turn, provoked a nervous reaction on the part of the powers already enjoying large portions of that wealth. This, after all, is why arms limitations talks have so often failed in the past: because an agreement over reducing the number and size of weapons alone, without agreement over the non-military causes of the rivalry, has seemed to one side or the other – usually to the challenging, expanding power – to be pointless.

What, ultimately, this argument is saying is that arms increases – and arms-races – are the reflection of complex political/ideological/racial/economic/territorial differences rather than phenomena which exist, as it were, of themselves, uncaused causes, uncontrollable, unsteerable, unstoppable steamrollers of death. Such differences and tensions between states (or, at least, between the élites of states) have often produced feelings of insecurity, which are manifested in increased armaments, and *in some cases* eventually manifested in war. But it is logically false to see the sequence as arms-races *causing* war: what we should see, rather, is that antagonisms between nations often produce an arms-race and *may* also produce an armed conflict. Both of the latter phenomena are consequences of the former. The one consequence, the arms-race, *can* be controlled from merging into the other consequence, the armed conflict – and there are enough instances given above of where that has occurred. But there must be the political will to exert that control, there must be a decision that the economic/social/strategical costs of going to war are not

174

worth bearing, and that the arms-race must somehow be reduced. And it is fair to admit – here Grey was on far safer ground in his remarks – that an arms increase by one side is more likely to produce increased alarm and insecurity on the other side, rather than a conscious, open effort to defuse whatever antagonisms are separating the two nations. An arms-race will, then, all too easily contribute to the upward spiral of fears and hatreds and suspicions which were themselves the cause of the original armaments increases.

If the preceding argument is accepted, then it is now easy to deal with the interesting but subordinate issue of quantitative and qualitative arms-races. Perhaps the best example of a *quantitative* arms-race was the rise in the military establishments of the Great Powers in the three years before 1914; each alliance was seeking to improve itself qualitatively as well, of course, but at the centre of attraction was the French three-year-service bill, the 1913 army bill in Germany, the announced Russian increases, all of which were providing *far more of the same*, troops, divisions, cavalry, field-guns. A similar concern with numbers can be glimpsed in all the mathematical ratios offered to solve the Anglo-German naval race before 1914 and, more successfully, in the Washington Treaty talks of 1921; it is there again in the British concern about 'air parity' with Germany in the 1930s; and reappeared recently in the morbid counting of missiles and warheads in the SALT talks.

In general, however, attention has focused much more upon the *qualitative* upward spiral of the armaments-race, particularly in this modern age of near-constant technological innovation. An armour-covered ship like *La Gloire*, the needle-gun, the Dreadnought, the submarine, the tank, aircraft, the V-2 missiles and later ICBMs, were all seen to be significant because they vastly increased the deadliness and, usually, the costs of war. But if the *invention* of such weapons is a reflection of what David Landes termed the 'unbound Prometheus', that unstoppable interaction between scientific invention and industrial development which has taken place since the time of the spinning jenny (at least),[16] their *application* can only be seen as part of – and not separate from – the overall structure of antagonisms between nations. It is difficult to think of any new weapons, from *La Gloire* to today's particle-beam ray-guns, which were developed *outside* of an existing arms-race. To make a distinction, as some people have, between an increase in the size of armed forces (which is regarded as being deliberate and 'rational' and controllable) and the introduction of new weapons of war (which is seen as an autotelic, irresistible process) is misleading. Both quantitative and qualitative arms-races have involved decisions to go a step ahead of, or to catch up with, a rival; both have involved the spending of increased sums of money, justified in terms of national security, *not* scientific curiosity; and both have a political impact upon other states, and their public opinions.

To draw all the above points together into one neat conclusion would be impossible, but at least the overall *approach* of this essay ought to be summarized. What has actuated the handling of this topic has been the belief that arms-races are human things, arising out of specific social circumstances and determined by human perceptions. This essay does not accept, as Adam Smith, Cobden and Schumpeter did, that arms-races and wars are intrinsic to the feudal, precapitalist, warrior age and will melt away before the bright sun of *laissez-faire* rationality; it does not accept, as certain Marxists hold, that they are a product of a particularly competitive phase of Western capitalism, and will therefore wither away in a socialist world-order; and it does not believe that they are inevitable, necessary concomitants of rapidly changing technology. It asserts, more simply, that arms-races and wars are the reflection and the consequence of the fears, suspicions and ambitions within specific societies as they assess their relationship with certain other societies on this planet; that they *are* controllable, and can peter out as well as escalate, depending upon the political will existing.

If historians have a message for contemporary strategists and, more importantly, for today's politicians, it is precisely that: that despite some evidence to the contrary, the upward spiral is not inevitable even if it may be likely; and that the race need not end in an Armageddon. But it takes political willpower, percipience, a certain freedom from dogma, an ability to see other viewpoints and to make some allowance for them, in order to turn the spiral downwards and to reduce the arms-race. It is those *political* features which are nearly always in short supply, compared with the ample stocks of weapons that nations usually find it more comforting to possess, both in the past, and at this very moment.

7

This is the most strictly military of the contributions in the present collection, in that it concerns itself with decisions taken in wartime. But it conforms with the rest of the essays, since it tries to deal with grand strategy, with national policy and aspirations as a whole. It also seeks to illustrate the interaction between the larger, 'objective' factors like geography and economic production, and the more personalized decision-making process.

This article was written at the invitation of Barrie Pitt for the Purnell part-work *History of the Second World War*. At that time, although still a postgraduate at St Antony's College, Oxford, I was spending two days a week researching for the 'Pacific War' chapters of Sir Basil Liddell Hart's *History of the Second World War*, which was to be published posthumously in 1970. This invitation therefore offered an opportunity to look at the broad sweep of Japanese policy in the Pacific and East Asia, and to attempt a summary of the chief turning-points in that war.

Japanese Strategic Decisions, 1939–45

The most striking feature about the war in the Pacific is its tidal nature. In 1941 Japan burst forth and in a swift wave of victory engulfed vast regions of South-East Asia and the Pacific: yet within seven months this flood-tide was checked at the Coral Sea and Midway and within fourteen months it had receded from Guadalcanal. Then, with ever-increasing strength and swiftness, the American current surged across the Pacific, sweeping without a check over all the regions in enemy possession until by 1945 it lapped the very shores of Japan.

The absolute character of both the Japanese advance and retreat, in contrast to the to-and-fro character of the North African campaign, tempts the historian into a beautifully clean-cut view of the struggle in the Far East. This states that the Japanese gained early victories because their well-equipped forces struck the ill-prepared Allies in a series of brilliantly executed attacks, but that by such a spectacular advance they over-extended themselves and were thus unable to resist the American onslaught once the US economy was put upon a full war footing. It is an attractive generalization with much truth in it, but far too oversimplified to survive close scrutiny. Its major omission is to ignore the strategic decisions of both sides, decisions which had a vital influence upon each battle and in its turn upon the whole trend of the war. In other words, this tide did not simply surge forward and then retreat solely because of the comparative economies, but also because of strategic and tactical errors made by the one side or the other; errors which, if rectified, could well have altered the course of the tide in the Pacific war. It is in this light that the Japanese strategic decisions should be viewed.

In the Japanese system of command the body chiefly concerned with the making of strategic decisions was Imperial General

Headquarters (that is, the General Staffs of the army and the navy under the supreme command of the Emperor), although often this body could be swayed by suggestions and objections from individual area or fleet commanders. This system was not perhaps in itself unusual but of far greater importance was the additional power of the military over the civilian government. The Cabinet, which was not responsible to the Diet but to the Emperor alone, was dominated by the Army and Navy Ministers, without whom this body could not exist. These two ministers themselves were chosen by the armed forces, whose opinions they reflected; and the Prime Minister himself was usually a military man. In any case, the Chiefs of Staff had direct access to the Emperor, decided matters concerning military and naval operations, and did not even need to disclose these to the Cabinet. Finally, as no responsibility for decision-making was to be borne by the Emperor, who was expected to sanction the decisions of the Cabinet and IGHQ, the military could virtually commit the government to any course of action and the country to war instead of being limited to strategic and operational matters only.

The aims of the Japanese government, reflecting those of the army and the navy, were decidedly ambitious and expansionist. As a militaristic nation never defeated in battle and as the only industrially advanced state in Asia, Japan was naturally tempted to follow the European powers in an imperial role. With her appetite whetted by her gains in the First World War and her people disillusioned by the economic crisis of the 1930s and the apparent 'cold-shouldering' by the Americans and the British, it was not a difficult matter for the fanatical young officers of the army to drag the nation into the pursuit of territorial gains on the continent of Asia. Having swallowed Manchuria and turned it into a puppet state, the expansion continued apace into China proper in 1937. And this campaign was but a part of their overall design, which was the creation of 'The Greater East Asia Co-Prosperity Sphere' – a zone of Japanese economic and political dominance extending from Korea to Burma and from the Yangtse to the mid-Pacific.

One alternative to this policy was a northward expansion; after all, Russia had been the prime enemy of the Japanese army since the beginning of the century. But there were good reasons against such a course. First of all, the *status quo* was desirable; Japan had little to gain (the Siberian steppe) and much to lose (Manchuria, Korea, North China) by engaging in a fierce battle with the Soviets. Secondly, the drubbing they had received in the Nomonhan 'incident' in 1939 made them wonder if they could win such a battle. And even if they could win, Siberia hardly compared with the riches of the Indies. Finally, only southward expansion could solve the stalemate in China. The Japanese therefore concluded a neutrality pact with Russia in April 1941. Secured by this on her northern flank and later by Hitler's onslaught against Russia, Japan could prepare for the drive to the south. But she never felt secure enough to remove her Manchurian garrison which was maintained at a strength of some thirteen to fifteen divisions, even when such troops were desperately needed in other regions during the Pacific campaigns. This was a fearful number of troops to tie down for a 'possible' war and one of Japan's early blunders.

Much to Japan's surprise, a complete victory in China proved impossible to achieve, and from 1937 onwards an ever-increasing number of her troops became tied down in the task of eliminating the Nationalist government. The greater the military entanglements and frustration, the greater the temptation to cut off China's supply lines from the south and correspondingly the greater the risk of conflict with the Western powers, especially America, who looked upon Japan's activities with evident unease. Thus the Japanese decision for war, when it came in 1941, was not a unique, surprise action by Tokyo but merely the most important of a series of military escalations.

Impetus from Europe

In July 1941 the Japanese occupation of Indo-China, a great step forward in their encirclement of China, provoked a terrible retaliatory blow from the Americans, British, and Dutch. By freezing all Japanese assets, these powers cut off her vital oil supplies without which her campaign in China would soon splutter to a halt. The only answer, apart from the immense humiliation of abandoning her national policy, was the seizure of the rich oilfields of the East Indies. Already an Imperial Conference (consisting of the Emperor, the armed forces and the leading members of the government) had on 2 July decided to pursue their southward expansion, whether or not it involved war with the Western powers. At a later conference in early September the decision was taken for war if Japan's minimum aims could not be achieved by talks with the USA and Britain. But with these negotiations proving fruitless and the army and navy Chiefs of Staff (General Sugiyama and Admiral Nagano) becoming increasingly restive at their shrinking supplies of war materials, War Minister Tojo forced the resignation of Prince Konoye and became premier himself. The generals now had full control and at an Imperial Conference in early November took the decision for war, which was confirmed at the final meeting of 1 December.

The Japanese war plans were thrashed out during this time. As these strategic discussions proceeded, the areas of attack widened considerably by a process of military logic. Basically, Japan needed the oilfields of Java, Borneo, and Sumatra, and a stranglehold upon the Burma Road if the conquest of China was to be completed. Since the US forces in the Philippines and the British in Malaya would disrupt such moves – it could hardly be expected that the powers who imposed the embargo would consent to its being forcibly lifted – these areas too had to be eliminated. But could the US Pacific Fleet at Pearl Harbor be guaranteed not to intervene? The Commander-in-Chief Combined Fleet, Yamamoto, thought not and insisted that this danger should also be crushed.

The success of their strategy depended upon speed and timing to obtain surprise, and upon the use of air power, rather than large numbers of troops. For this vast complex operation, the Japanese were content to allocate only eleven divisions (in contrast to the thirteen in Manchuria and the twenty-two in China), 1200 aircraft, and most of their navy. The three main stages were:

(i) While the US Pacific Fleet was being neutralized at Pearl Harbor, attacks would be launched on Thailand, Malaya, and Hong Kong, followed by air-raids on the Philippines, Guam, and

Wake. These would precede landings in the Philippines and Borneo;

(ii) With these regions captured, Japanese troops would then proceed to take all of Malaya and Singapore, the South Burma airfields, the Bismarck Archipelago, and strategic points in the Dutch East Indies;

(iii) Occupying Java and Sumatra, they would then swing towards India, seizing Burma together with the Andaman and Nicobar Islands in the Bay of Bengal. They expected their task would be achieved within approximately six months.

In the midst of all this detailed planning little time was given by the Japanese to the problem of what would follow such a victory. Generally speaking, they contented themselves with the idea of what Admiral Morison has termed '*Festung Nippona*' – that is, a concentric defensive ring from the Aleutians to Burma which would defy US attempts at a breakthrough and thus force that country to accept Japan's gains. But few long-term preparations were made to strengthen such a defensive ring, and few people in Tokyo really queried whether or not the USA could be forced to accept a vast extension of Japanese control and the humiliation of defeat. In fact, apart from Yamamoto and several others, few really queried the value of their most important strategic decision – going to war with the US at all. Was it worthwhile to arouse the fury of a power whose immensely greater war economy would probably see her victorious in a long war? Immersed in the search for military glory, in the struggle for China, and in the cutting-off of their oil supplies, the Japanese leaders ignored all this and plunged headlong into battle.

An Irresistible Onslaught

The Japanese onslaught, when it struck, was an amazingly successful one. Within the six months prescribed they had taken all their objectives at a minimum cost to themselves, isolated China, and devastated the armed forces of the Allies in the process. Never before had such a comparatively large area been conquered in such a short time. It was a remarkable tribute not only to the superiority of the Japanese armour and the Japanese soldier, but also to the excellence of their planners.

The Japanese leaders themselves were perhaps surprised at the extent of their successes. In the full flush of victory, the idea of consolidating their gains was rejected in favour of a further advance. But advance to where? Various bodies argued for advances in different directions and it was at this confused point that the high standard of Japanese strategic planning began to slip, that mistakes were made, and that tremendous opportunities were lost.

Basically, the real fault was the army's, which was always the senior partner in important strategic decisions. The General Staff, orientated for years towards the war in China and the defence of Manchuria, was somewhat bemused by the possession of exotic territories such as Singapore and Rabaul and began to fear that further expansion would be a drain upon their continental war. The suggestion of the Navy General Staff for the seizure of Ceylon was rejected by the army who did not want to release more troops. At this stage in the war, with the British still reeling from an attack upon Ceylon and South India by Japanese carriers which had ruthlessly exposed their weak air and naval defences, such a move could have been tremendously decisive. The Japanese carrier fleet, based upon Ceylon, would not only have cut off India but also have dislocated the shipping route to the Persian Gulf and Egypt (and prevented the British build-up for Alamein). A German-Japanese link-up in the Middle East was not so impossible at this stage in the war, but the Japanese army rejected such a prospect.

The navy had other plans which were also frowned upon, namely operations against Australia and Hawaii, the two possible bases for an Allied comeback. An invasion of either place involved too many troops as far as the army was concerned, but under prodding from the Navy General Staff and the Combined Fleet, in April and May 1942 IGHQ sanctioned the following operations: an advance to Tulagi in the Solomons and Port Moresby in Papua; the occupation of Midway Island and the Aleutians, together with the neutralization of the US Pacific Fleet, which had just launched Doolittle's raid upon Tokyo; further operations in the direction of the New Hebrides and Samoa, in order to cut the American-Australasian line of communications.

The first operation led to the battle of the Coral Sea, the second operation to the battle of Midway, and the third operation to the battles for Guadalcanal. All three were failures, the latter two being so disastrous that Japan lost the initiative in the Pacific war and never again regained it. All three battles were lost because of faulty strategic planning by IGHQ and faulty tactical moves by the Japanese commanders of which the Americans took full advantage. The basic Japanese error was overconfidence, a result of their earlier overwhelming victories which had been gained with comparatively small forces. To ensure the success of the Coral Sea battle, for example, they should have thrown in all six of their fleet carriers, not two only, even at the risk of delaying the thrust against Midway. When victory is essential, it is safer to use a sledgehammer rather than a nutcracker. The fruits of such a victory, control of New Guinea and the Solomons, would have been well worth it.

Why the Tide Turned

In the battle for Midway the Japanese made a terrifying number of errors. The first black mark goes to the army for being so niggardly about the invasion of Hawaii. Had they plunged straight towards Pearl Harbor with all their fleet and about five divisions, they would have dealt their most devastating blow against an American comeback in the Pacific. Not only would they have cut the connection to Australia and seized a great fleet base but they would have pushed the American line of defence back to the Californian coast, a further 3000 miles away. Even if the US carriers had survived the battle, they would have had to retire. The Japanese Navy General Staff and the Combined Fleet also erred by devising a most elaborate plan and by tying the movements of all their various fleets to the slow-moving Midway invasion force. Thus the major objective, the destruction of the US carriers, was sacrificed for a small island and as a result

187

neither aim was achieved. Tactically the operation was bungled from beginning to end, and even Yamamoto could not retrieve the situation since he had isolated himself from the main carrier force. For the petty gains of two Aleutian islands, Japan lost four of her fleet carriers and with them, the greater part of her striking power.

In the south-west Pacific after Midway the Japanese erred, as in the battle of the Coral Sea, not so much in their planning but in their failure to act quickly and with sufficient force. Sending troops to Guadalcanal and Papua in such small numbers that they could be overcome by the Americans and Australians was no way to gain their objectives. As it was, the Allies were always able to keep one step ahead and after steady and increasing losses for six months the Japanese were forced to pull back.

The first stage of the Pacific war had seen the Japanese gain all their original targets with ease. The second had seen them attempt to expand further and be decisively rebuffed. Clearly the third was now going to see the Japanese revert to their prewar concept of firmly holding on to a strongly fortified defensive ring of island bases in the hope of beating off the American attacks. In November 1942 IGHQ ordered the retention and (optimistically) the securing of strategic points in New Guinea and the Solomons. To further this aim, the regional command structures were altered and troops and aircraft ordered to the area.

There were indications, even at this stage in the war, that the attempt to 'hold the ring' would fail. The IGHQ, or at least the Army General Staff, were still orientated towards continental Asia, and the reinforcements ordered to the south and west Pacific were still insufficient. By early 1943 MacArthur's land and air forces were already superior to General Imamura's and the gap was widening weekly. Naval reinforcements from the American shipyards were not only flowing to the south-west Pacific but also to Pearl Harbor where the Central Pacific forces were being built up. Japanese carriers and aircrews could not compare in either numbers or quality with their American counterparts. In the face of such rapidly growing odds, it is difficult to conceive of any local strategic or tactical decision which could have halted the American advance for long.

Thus, despite tenacious fighting by the Japanese, MacArthur and Halsey were able to move up the Solomons, break the Bismarck barrier, and advance along the New Guinea coast by 1944. Even before this, IGHQ had seen how things were going and in September 1943 prepared a new Operational Strategy in which a line from Burma through the Malay barrier and western New Guinea to the Carolines and the Marshalls, and thence to the Kuriles, was declared to be their 'absolute national defence sphere'. This impregnable barrier was to be created and Japan's war economy and armed forces were to be built up behind it during a period in which her troops slowly withdrew from inessential areas. The flow of troops from Manchuria and China to the Pacific islands and the East Indies was to be accelerated. (Even at this stage, there were fifteen divisions in Manchuria and twenty-six divisions in China.)

These Japanese strategic moves were correct but her forces were just too weak. The Americans, with control of the air and the sea, could choose when and where to strike and thus overwhelm the isolated Japanese garrisons, just as the Japanese themselves had done in the first six months of the war. In November 1943 the US Central Pacific forces moved into the Gilbert Islands; three months later, they had seized the Marshalls and delivered a devastating blow upon the naval base at Truk in the Carolines. Already the 'absolute national defence sphere' was being broken into, and with MacArthur's forces also pushing ever forward the Japanese were reeling under a two-pronged blow.

Since their early defeats in the Solomons the Japanese navy had been attempting to conserve its strength for the vital counter-attack battle which would halt the American onrush. The chance for such a victory appeared in June 1944 when an American invasion fleet approached the Marianas, an essential part of the Japanese defence system. The strategy of Admiral Toyada, Commander-in-Chief Combined Fleet, in attempting to catch the Americans by a pincer movement between the I Mobile Fleet and the aircraft operating from bases in the mandated islands, was basically a good one but the opposition was far too strong. In the battle of the Philippine Sea, Mitscher's force of fifteen carriers broke one arm of this pincer by paralysing the island airbases;

then, standing on the defensive, they devastated the attacking Japanese carrier aircraft; finally, they in their turn struck severe blows at the I Mobile Fleet. After this defeat the Marianas fell; so too did Tojo's government.

Without sufficient carriers or aircraft the Japanese could not adequately defend the Philippines, the next target for the American advance. Revising its strategy, the Japanese navy produced the astonishingly new plan of using the carriers as the bait and the battleships as the striking force, a complete reversal of their earlier method. What was more, the plan itself worked and Halsey's covering fleet for the Leyte Gulf landings was drawn completely out of the way. The Japanese, however, did not benefit, since their two-pronged attack on the US invasion forces failed miserably, one battleship group running into an over-whelming American force and the other suffering from the indecision of its commander. Moreover, the carriers paid a heavy penalty for being the decoy. The Japanese army also erred in deciding, on hearing exaggerated reports of US fleet losses, to fight for Leyte Island instead of concentrating their defence upon the main island of Luzon. Four divisions were wasted upon Leyte, and the defence of Luzon was correspondingly weakened. With the Japanese navy in ruins and their troops in the Philippines being steadily driven into the mountains, this great island group was lost and Japan's connection to her southern empire broken.

The loss only confirmed what the earlier loss of the Marianas had indicated – that Japan faced defeat. Such a fact could not be entertained by her *samurai*-minded war leaders, who hastened to order the strengthening of Iwo Jima, which they correctly divined as America's next target. The fight for this island was immensely fierce with Japanese troops in well-fortified positions defending every yard, but as the Americans possessed aerial and naval control plus superiority in troops and artillery the issue was never in doubt – the only question was the number of casualties. By the time of the US attack upon Okinawa, Japan had pinned her faith upon her deadly new weapon, the Kamikazes. But although the suicide planes wreaked immense havoc upon the Allied navies, they were insufficient to affect the campaign. Japan, who had gambled everything upon a quick victory and a negotiated peace, had thrown her last trump and it was plainly not powerful enough. An appropriate symbol of their scraping of the barrel was the one-way suicidal trip of the battleship *Yamato*. It was an empty gesture, nothing more.

Developments in Asia

What was happening during this period on the continent of Asia, the area which appeared to mesmerize the mind of the Japanese army? One must conclude that the strategic decision to keep a strong force in Manchuria was one of the most dismal ever made by the warlords of Tokyo. During the vital first years of the Pacific war approximately 700,000 Japanese troops were stationed there with nothing to do, while the despatch of one-tenth of that force to New Guinea and the Solomons in 1942 might well have swung the balance in Japan's favour. In 1944 and 1945 when it became obvious that the American onslaught was the main danger to Japan's empire, troops from Manchuria were hastily despatched to the mandated islands, to the Philippines, and to the homeland. Ironically, when the quality of the Manchurian army had declined to its lowest level, the Russians finally struck and cut it into pieces.

Throughout the war China remained an ever-increasing entanglement. Various offensives by hundreds of thousands of Japanese troops resulted in large gains of territory in 1942 and 1943 but the Nationalist army and government, supported from India by the Allies, always held on. In the summer of 1944 the Japanese 'China Expeditionary Force' launched its greatest offensive, driving fiercely towards the US airbases in south-east China. By the end of the year they had established contact with Japanese forces in French Indo-China and had cut China in half. There were approximately 1,000,000 Japanese soldiers in China at the beginning of 1945, yet it was all to no avail. Already divisions were being withdrawn to guard the coastline against a US attack and later being transferred to strengthen the Manchurian border. Yet neither these 1,000,000 troops nor the 650,000 or so in Manchuria could have helped to defend the homeland against an Allied invasion, for they were cut off, the victims of a misguided strategy.

The strategy for Burma after May 1942, that of static defence along the Indian border, was the wisest possible since the bulk of the Japanese air force had been withdrawn and their troop strength was too low for a major offensive. In 1944, however, IGHQ allowed itself to be swayed by Lieutenant-General Mutagachi into sanctioning an advance by XV Army towards the Imphal plain. The motives for this operation were the need to forestall the expected British offensive and the desire to obtain a more secure defence line in order to keep out Chindit expeditions. Yet only wishful thinkers could expect that Mutagachi's three ill-provisioned divisions could, without command of the air, overwhelm a much larger and better equipped British-Indian force. The Japanese paid the penalty for their rashness at the fierce battles of Imphal and Kohima. Their hold over Burma was fatally weakened, and Slim took full advantage of this in 1945 by thrusting his troops through the disorganized enemy lines, opening the China Road and recapturing Rangoon.

Brief mention should also be made of the strategic 'sins of omission' by IGHQ, which were equally as important as any misguided operational strategy. Although the war was a total one, the Japanese leaders tended to concentrate their attention upon the battles in the field and at sea, and they ignored other aspects of the struggle until it was too late. They appear to have shown little concern towards economic matters, although this was Japan's Achilles heel. With regard to their merchant marine, they devoted little thought to convoy systems, anti-submarine techniques, escort carriers and hunter-killer groups, although Japan was even more dependent than Britain upon imported materials. They were tardy in giving directives for an organized air defence system; in ordering a replacement for their Zero fighter, or the building of a heavy bomber; and in realizing the true role of the battleship. In every case these omissions and delays were exploited to the full by the more forward-thinking Americans.

The situation facing Japan by the summer of 1945 was desperate. In South-East Asia the British had taken Burma and were preparing to seize Singapore and other strategic areas. The Australians had seized Borneo and were engaged in mopping up isolated segments of Japanese resistance elsewhere. In China the Japanese Expeditionary Force was steadily withdrawing from the areas just occupied in their 1944 offensive. Meanwhile, along the Manchurian border the Soviets were poised to strike whenever Stalin gave the order. America had taken Japan's important oceanic possessions, Okinawa, Iwo Jima, the Philippines, the Marianas, New Guinea, and the Solomons, and in doing so had devastated the Japanese navy. The strategic bombing campaign, although only half under way, was tearing the face and landscape of Japan to pieces, while the submarine and air-dropped mine campaigns had cut off the external supplies upon which she was completely dependent. Plans and preparations for a massive Allied invasion, which Japan's armed forces could not have effectively opposed, were already under way: her many remaining troops and aircraft would have been swept away in the devastation which the attacking forces could unleash.

In the face of all this, the only sensible strategic decision that could have been made was to surrender. Moreover, in Admiral Suzuki Japan possessed, since April 1945, a Prime Minister who inclined to peace. This also was true of the Foreign and Navy Ministers – and the Emperor. Their only worry was the Allies' failure to give guarantees regarding the Imperial dynasty.

Opposing this view was the army which, true to the *samurai* tradition, showed no inclination to surrender. How could Japan, which had never before tasted defeat, ignominiously surrender while the homeland contained millions of troops and thousands of kamikazes?

Led by War Minister Anami and the Chiefs of Staff (General Umezu and Admiral Toyada), they had an alternative strategy which, ironically enough, depended upon an Allied invasion. Only when that came could they deal a heavy blow at the power whose bombers were systematically tearing their country to pieces. Japanese casualties in this fight would be enormous, but they hoped the Allies would also be badly hurt and thus Japan would be able to obtain a negotiated surrender. These war leaders not only sought a continuance of the Imperial dynasty but also the preservation of the status of the military in Japan and the prevention of an Allied army of occupation. Wishful thinking still prevailed at IGHQ even during the bleak days of 1945.

Refusal to Admit Defeat

Astonishingly, the devastation of Hiroshima did not shake these views. The 'hawks' of the Supreme War Council, despite the Emperor's wishes, avoided a meeting on 8 August. By the time they did meet on the following day, the Russians had declared war and the Red Army was moving through Manchuria. Even at this stage the War Minister and the Chiefs of Staff were insisting that they would not accept an army of occupation, nor disarm their own troops, nor try their war criminals. They did not recede from this position even at the news of the dropping of the second atomic bomb, and late that evening carried the argument before the Emperor in a special session of the Imperial Conference. Breaking tradition, he for once assumed responsibility for a strategic decision by declaring that he wanted an end to the war. Even as terms were negotiated with the Allies and they learned that the Imperial dynasty could be preserved, there was dissent by IGHQ, until on 14 August the Emperor had to say once again that he wished the Supreme War Council to accept the conditions offered. Thus the final strategic decision was his, for his military commanders preferred oblivion for the nation to facing the facts and admitting their absolute defeat. The wisdom of this decision can never be questioned: one can only be thankful that the Emperor had not the mentality of Hitler or of War Minister Anami, who committed suicide on 15 August.

One suspects that however fiercely and cleverly the Japanese fought, they would ultimately be defeated by their incredibly powerful American adversary. But one can also see that they themselves hastened their own defeat by a long series of erroneous strategic decisions. Two great blunders stand out above all others. The first was the army's overwhelming interest in the continent of Asia, which caused them to ignore their weakest flank until it was too late to recover. The second was that series of strategic blunders immediately after their first glorious campaign, the failures of the Coral Sea, Midway, and Guadalcanal. When Japan lost all three battles, the balance, so decisively tilted in her favour during the early months of the war, then steadied. The Americans gained their much-needed breathing space and their mighty economy came on to a war footing. From that time onwards the Japanese became increasingly outnumbered on land, at sea, and in the air. Frantic countermeasures were always too little and too late. From then on the possibility of a Japanese victory faded gradually away. By 1945 all that remained was to surrender; and even in this IGHQ acted too late and thus brought upon themselves the tragedies of Hiroshima and Nagasaki.

8

The following (previously unpublished) essay began life as the 1982 Cust Foundation Lecture at the University of Nottingham, and I should like to acknowledge my thanks to Professor William Doyle and his colleagues of the History Department for inviting me to deliver it. Since the Cust lecturers are asked to address some broad theme in imperial history, it seemed to me that this might be a good opportunity to raise questions about the increasing tendency among historians – including myself, on previous occasions – to antedate the beginnings of the decline of the British Empire and to emphasize its vulnerability and fragility. The recent historiography of what might be termed the 'weary Titan syndrome' is covered in the early part of the essay, and the main part considers objections to it. This has also been given as a lecture at the universities of Warwick, Cambridge, London and Oxford, and benefited greatly from the critical comments of the historians there. Although we are still too close to the demise of the British Empire to be able objectively to measure its overall impact and meaning, nonetheless historians of the 1980s *ought* to be at least sufficiently distant from feelings of imperial nostalgia or postcolonial guilt to start the process of reassessment. This particular contribution reflects my own growing interest in the comparative study of the rise and fall of great military powers.

Why Did the British Empire
Last So Long?

When Henry Cust, imperial enthusiast, editor of the *Pall Mall Gazette*, and Chairman of the Central Committee for National Patriotic Societies, died in March 1917, the British Empire was engaged in the most terrible struggle for survival which it had ever known – at sea, on land, and in economic terms. Unlike the contemporary Russian, Austro-Hungarian and German empires, however, it survived that crisis and went on to take a, if not *the* leading part in the ending of the First World War and in the peace settlement which followed.

In 1921, therefore – the year in which the first Cust Foundation lecture was delivered at the University of Nottingham – the British Empire was, territorially, at its widest extent: the recent acquisitions in East, West and South-West Africa, in the Middle East, in New Guinea and the Pacific, had brought an additional million square miles to the existing 13 million square miles of Imperial/Commonwealth lands. In this system there lived some 450 million people, over one-quarter of the human race. No contemporary empire, no previous empire, no subsequent empire could compare with this. At the close of the war which had just been won, the British Empire had raised over 8,500,000 men for the armed forces; the Royal Air Force, with 22,000 aircraft in 1918, had been the largest in the world; the Royal Navy, with 61 battleships and 9 battlecruisers, was by far the most powerful fleet. In foodstuffs and raw materials, in shipping and industrial products and financial expertise the Empire was well endowed, indeed graced with an embarrassment of riches. Britain's greatest recent foe, Imperial Germany, had been defeated in the war, its navy was now sunk, its army disbanded; the more ancient rival, Russia, had collapsed in a welter of internal dissensions. The other Great Powers of the time, France, Italy, Japan, the United

199

States, were recent allies and, with the exception of the last-named, were leading members of a new League of Nations designed to ensure lasting peace and stability in world affairs.

In such circumstances, it was not at all surprising that the titles of the early Cust Foundation lectures contain frequent references to the further 'development' of the Empire – in the tropics, in 'Our East African Territories', in an imperial airways system, in 'Empire Migration', in the expansion of 'The Food of the Empire', and so on. It is true that some other titles contain that equally intriguing word, the 'problem' – as in 'The Constitutional Problem in Kenya' and 'The Problem of the Mandate in Palestine'; but then, in running extensive empires one was bound to encounter problems, and the very ethos of the white man's burden was that these should be met squarely, wrestled with, and overcome. A reference to imperial problems revealed, therefore, neither an apprehension of weakness nor, necessarily, an intimation of decline. Even thirty years later, in the Cust Foundation lectures of the 1950s and 1960s, the titles still convey a sense of purpose and development: 'The Future of the African Colonies'; 'Agricultural Developments in the Colonies'; 'Canada as a World Power'; 'African Development – the Challenge to Ourselves', and so on. Only, in fact, in the last two Cust lectures of all (before the present one) – by Sir Kenneth Roberts-Wray on 'The Rise and Fall of the British Empire' in 1969, and Professor Robin Winks on 'Failed Federations: Decolonization and the British Empire' in 1970 – was there a recognition that the show was over, that the Empire was finally at one with Nineveh and Tyre.[1]

It is interesting to contrast, then, those earlier attitudes, and those spoken and unspoken assumptions about the purpose and the future of the British Empire, with the historiography of that body which has emerged during the past ten to twenty years. Even in 1959, in his magisterial survey *The Imperial Idea and Its Enemies*, A. P. Thornton had traced the challenges to the exercise of British power posed by indigenous nationalists, left-wing critics at home and internationalists abroad, from at least the Second Boer War onwards.[2] In 1961, in their seminal work *Africa and the Victorians*, Robinson and Gallagher painted a picture of the late-Victorian ship of state, buffeted by global forces unknown to their forebears, and compelled to run before the tempests of the 'New Imperialism', tacking and adjusting their course as circumstances permitted: compromising with this imperial rival in order to stand rather more firmly against another; reluctantly converting their 'informal rule' in various regions to formal annexations lest foreign powers annexed before them; and discovering ever more frontiers of insecurity.[3] The African acquisitions of the late nineteenth century, like those of the First World War in the Middle East, were not evidence of growth, it was suggested, but preventative actions by a power in decline. Indeed, Bernard Porter in his brilliant book *The Lion's Share*, published in 1975, has put it even more bluntly:

> . . . the real significance of the empire for Britain was that it had cushioned her fall in the world. From 1870 to 1970 the history of Britain was one of steady and almost unbroken decline, economically, militarily and politically, relative to other nations, from the peak of prosperity and power which her industrial revolution had achieved for her in the middle of the nineteenth century. The empire which she had accumulated towards the end of that century, and then lost, was an incident in the course of that decline. It was acquired originally as a result of that decline, to stave it off. It was retained largely in spite of that decline. And it was eventually surrendered as a final confirmation of that decline.[4]

This tale, which might well be termed 'downhill all the way', has been told again and again in a whole variety of recent works, the titles of which give ample indication of their contents: *The Fall of the British Empire*; *The Collapse of British Power*; *Imperial Sunset*; *Who Killed the British Empire?*; *The Troubled Giant*; *The Crisis of Imperialism*; *Retreat from Power*.[5] By now, it was not imperial historians alone, but also those interested in diplomacy, in economic trends, in power-politics, in the measurement of comparative military strengths, who had joined the team of morphologists seeking to trace the first signs of decay in the body politic of the British Empire. The official records of the ministries in London,

and the private letters and diaries of the decision-makers, were
explored in order to determine when it was that British governments sensed that the world was no longer their oyster, that
Britain was a *status quo* and not an expanding power, and that the
central political issue of all was to find an efficacious way of
preserving that *status quo*.

Having himself been one of those morphologists of Empire, the
present writer cannot now be strongly critical of such scholarly
activity. But it seems proper to remark that this recent historiography runs the risk of becoming a curious variant of (or, perhaps
better, the imperial converse of) 'the Whig interpretation of history'. That is to say, instead of assuming the inexorable rise of
constitutional freedom and parliamentary democracy, and
categorizing historical events and personalities as they fitted that
teleology, as the Whig writers did, one was assuming here the
inevitable decline of the British Empire and then searching out
the evidence of weakness, the early habits of practising 'appeasement', the intimations of cultural and world-political Angst, the
ominous references to strategical overextension and fiscal strain.
The notion that the Empire was at its height in 1921 was, in
consequence, soon pushed back to 1897, the year of Queen Victoria's Diamond Jubilee; and then pushed further back, to the
1860s, that is, before the rise of German power in Europe, before
the 'New Imperialism', before that succession of late-Victorian
naval races and invasion scares which had so swiftly followed the
self-confident era of Palmerston and Cobden. It may be appropriate to note here that certain more recent writings have now begun
to focus upon the early nineteenth-century period as offering
manifest signs of strain and stress in the imperial system.[6]

Before this tendency goes any further, therefore, and before the
beginnings of the decline of the British Empire are identified as
occurring in the age of Marlborough or Cromwell, it seems worthwhile to ask the question: 'Why did the Empire last so long?' If
the late-Victorian Empire resembled, in Joseph Chamberlain's
words, a weary Titan, staggering under the too-vast orb of its own
fate; if, following the early disasters of the Boer War, proconsuls
like Milner despaired of being able (as he put it) 'to save the
Empire', and planners in the Prussian General Staff talked of the

coming 'war of British Succession'; if the rise of democracy and the pressures for social reform and the evidence of the relative industrial decline of Britain were troubling politicians in Westminster, and the stirrings of nationalist ideas in the Dominions, India and the colonies were adding to that concern, how on earth did the British Empire survive the storms of the First World War? If in 1921 it was, in the choice language of Correlli Barnett, '. . . a polyglot empire; a rummage-bag of an empire, united by neither common purpose in its creation, nor by language, race, religion, nor by strategic and economic design . . . a vast, vulnerable sprawl across the globe . . .'[7] then how was it still in one piece when the next world war threatened, and only gradually dissolved after that conflict?

For the purposes of simplicity, the attempted answer to these questions will be divided into three broad areas: domestic politics and opinion; the handling of nationalist movements within the Empire; and relations with other powers. All three had given the imperialists cause for concern, and had been identified by them as weakening factors, potentially capable of bringing the imperial edifice crashing to the ground.

I

The first of these can be dealt with fairly rapidly: for, despite all the fears of the Milnerites that the British people refused to 'think imperially', that they were 'such fools',[8] interested only in parish-pump politics and too easily seduced by Labour and radical-Liberal calls for internal reform and external entrenchment, the fact remains that there was no broad-based demand at home to 'dump' the Empire; no equivalent, say, to the domestic protests which eventually forced the United States government to abandon the Vietnam War.

This lack of a domestic disintegrator can be explained by a number of reasons, some selfish, some idealistic. In the first place, for the greater part of the nineteenth and twentieth centuries, the running and preserving of the British Empire did not, like the Vietnam War or even France's Algerian War, cost a great deal in men and money. The one imperial conflict which did, the Second Boer War, is noticeable for the amount of domestic criticism which it provoked, and for the anxious wringing of hands at Westminster, Whitehall and in the City at how it was to be paid for. But most of the smaller 'gentleman's wars' (as Bismarck dismissively termed them) were relatively cheap – and often financed by the Indian rather than the British taxpayer. Moreover, it was not easy to show that the burden of defence expenditures, which rose rapidly from the 1880s onwards, was due to the existence of the Empire. After all, the size of the Royal Navy, whose budget was doubling every ten years even in peacetime, was determined chiefly by the expansion of rival battlefleets in *European* waters, which seemed to threaten the British Isles itself and its overseas food supplies.[9] Of course, in maintaining maritime superiority against other navies, the safety of the sea routes to the colonies would normally be ensured as well, but the point is that the large British battlefleet could not be represented as a burden caused by the existence of an empire. Even the enormous array of cruisers in distant waters could be, and was, justified in terms of trade protection rather than imperial defence *per se*. The army was a different matter, but perhaps precisely because it was kept down to an absolute minimum by all British governments, because it was chiefly out of sight, and because conscription was not required, its function as an imperial *gendarmerie* was not seriously questioned. The post-1919 determination, shown by politicians and public alike, to end conscription and drastically reduce the colossal wartime expenditures did not, in any significant way, imply hostility to the army's imperial role. It was the so-called 'continental commitment' and the slaughter in Flanders – plus the use of troops against the Irish, the Bolsheviks, and strikers nearer home – which was so disliked. This suggests, therefore, that the decision of both Tory and Liberal governments to refuse the demands of Lord Roberts' National Service League and all later pressures for conscription was, paradoxically, a good way of keeping the Empire going – and keeping it reasonably popular at home.

Secondly, and following on from that last remark, it could be argued that there always existed, in broad sections of British society, a considerable feeling of pride in the Empire and of attachment to it, from the late nineteenth century almost to the day of its dissolution. Whether one argues that the imperialist propagandists had succeeded only too well in getting their message across, through the popular press, boys' comics, school history and geography lessons, the Scouts and other youth movements; and that, as left-wing critics complained, the working classes of Britain were more likely to learn from the *Boys' Own Paper*, the adventures of Biggles, and the *Daily Mail* leaders rather than from the writings of Lenin, is not for examination here. But it seems clear that there existed little hostility to the Empire. Even in those circles where, in theory, it ought to have been prominent, that is, among the radical-Liberals of the pre-1914 period or the Labour Party later, there were very few who sought to dissolve the Empire overnight. In an ironic way, they, too, had swallowed the notion of the white man's burden: at least, they argued that, whatever the rights and wrongs of the original colonial annexations, Britain now had a responsibility, a trust, a mandate, to care for less developed peoples and to ensure that they advanced steadily towards self-government. It is interesting to note, in this connection, the indignant reaction of Labour ministers during and after the Second World War to what they regarded as ignorant American attacks on the purpose of the British Empire.[10]

Thirdly, and more cynically, it could be argued that in the twentieth century the British nation had become well aware of how important the possession of the Empire was to their own economic well-being. Was not George Orwell correct, in writing in *The Road to Wigan Pier*, that:

at the bottom of his heart no Englishman . . . does want it to disintegrate. For, apart from any other consideration, the high standard of life we enjoy in England depends upon our keeping a tight hold on the Empire, particularly the tropical portions of it such as India and Africa. . . . The alternative is to throw the Empire overboard and reduce England to a cold and unimportant little island where we should all have to work very hard and live mainly on herrings and potatoes.[11]

One need not put it that strongly, but had not the average Briton been frequently and correctly told, from his schooldays on, of the importance of the Empire as a source of raw materials and foodstuffs, and as a market for British manufactures: an economic importance which, ironically, was proportionately greater in the interwar years than it had been in Victorian and Edwardian times, and greater still after 1945 than it was in the interwar years.[12]

There is little need to explore this aspect further. For there rarely have been in history examples of an empire collapsing because of domestic disenchantment and opposition. The Spanish Empire did not disintegrate because of a change of mood at home, nor were Ottoman controls removed because of rising Turkish sympathies for the peoples of the Balkans, North Africa and Arabia. And if the present Soviet-Russian Empire ever contracts, it is unlikely to be prompted chiefly by the average Russian being pervaded by a new spirit of enlightenment. No, empires have usually been terminated because the colonized peoples have managed to throw off the external yoke, or at least to make it too costly and impractical for the imperial power to maintain that yoke; or because rival Great Powers, usually by means of war, have compelled territorial retrenchment or surrender, or even overwhelmed the imperial power itself.

II

If we turn to examine this second broad area, fissiparous tendencies within the Empire, then there is no doubt that sufficient ideas and movements for independence existed to give the imperialists cause for concern. Leaving aside the Irish issue as a half-domestic, half-imperial problem – although, of course, British governments could not divorce it from Empire policy simply because Ireland was a precedent for other national independence movements – there were still enough potential flashpoints elsewhere to require constant delicate handling by the Colonial and Dominions Office. Hardline Afrikaners, after the Boer War as well as before it, always strained to see how far they could reduce the ties which bound their land to Westminster and Whitehall. French-Canadians, too, disliked any emphasis upon relations with Britain, which in turn forced governments in Ottawa to play down the imperial connection in order to paper over internal disunity. It was a curious combination of Canadians, Afrikaners and Irish Free-Staters who forced ever looser definitions of Dominion status upon the British (and also upon the Australians and New Zealanders) during the famous Imperial conferences of the interwar years. By that time, too, London was facing the almost intractable problem of how to handle the broad-based nationalist movement in India, of how to pacify a rather similar movement in Eygpt, and how to deal with the unique Zionist nationalism in Palestine; while, in the background, there were stirrings in West and East Africa, in the West Indies, in Ceylon and Burma and other tropical possessions.[13] With the British Empire showing so many apparent signs of coming apart, how did it stay together so long?

The first, almost brutal explanation must be that, so far as the dependent empire was concerned, the British always enjoyed a superiority of military and naval and, increasingly, air power which could be used to crush indigenous revolts. No doubt the Committee of Imperial Defence and the planners in the Imperial General Staff constantly worried about how thinly stretched across the globe their garrisons were; but, to many of the colonial peoples of the Empire, a squadron of cruisers, a battery or two of field-guns, a regiment of Gurkhas, were very real and very powerful. The military and technological gap between the Western nations and their dependencies was at this time probably greater than ever before. Even in India, whose population and size tested the imperial system more than any other area, the degree of military control was very real, as Indian nationalists discovered on numerous occasions from Amritsar to the massive round-up of the Congress Party in 1942–3. (By comparison, *non-violent* protest was more difficult for British troops to contain.)

Furthermore, the mere coincidence of these nationalist challenges to imperial rule did not mean that they were all of the same intensity and seriousness, still less that there was any coordination between the rebel movements. As many historians have pointed out, the British Empire was in reality a *cluster* of empires, a congeries of different parts moving at different speeds. While some of those parts (e.g. the Dominions) were close to full independence by the 1920s, others (e.g. African colonies) were being drawn more tightly into a nexus of economic, administrative and other links with the metropolitan power. Between these two extremes, there was a whole variety of circumstances in which, for local reasons (Arab-Jewish rivalry, tribal disputes, strikes by Rhodesian copper miners), unrest would occur and 'imperial policing' actions follow. But such a deployment of the military was a normal rather than abnormal event in the peacetime history of the British Empire and did not imply that the latter was, like Imperial Rome, now facing the massed hordes of barbarians poised to overrun the entire system.

Even where the use of force was impossible – Canada, for example – or where its application would have been regarded as unnecessary or counterproductive, there were still various alternative forms of control, and a whole variety of inducements to persuade subject-peoples to respect their imperial overlords. It is worth remarking here that it is a further variant of 'the Whig interpretation of history' when scholars anticipate and exaggerate the size and appeal of indigenous pressures for colonial independence before the post-1945 period. On the whole, the British rule was not essentially brutal or prone to provoke resistance; the application of military force, although (as noted above) not remarkable, was usually regarded as a last resort; and millions of subjects of the King-Emperor rarely came into contact with district officers, still less with colonial governors and garrison troops and gun-boats. The British practice of 'indirect rule' not only cushioned indigenous societies from the impact of Western man, but also provided, in the African chiefs and elders and Malayan sultans and Indian princes, an array of what Professor Ronald Robinson would term 'collaborators' in imperial rule. The tribal and religious and ethnic divisions within a colonial territory, the presence of minorities like the Muslims in the Indian sub-continent, or the Indians in Fiji and East Africa, were each in their way brakes upon any impulses towards independence: they may not all have been invented by the British, but they played a certain role, negatively as it were, in the maintenance of the imperial system.

Even the evolution of Dominion self-government, lovingly traced by earlier generations of constitutional historians of the Empire-Commonwealth, was hardly the inexorable process of disintegration which it sometimes appeared to be. On the contrary, it could be argued – and was argued – that the steady redefinitions of Dominion status and the slow metamorphosis from Empire into Commonwealth was a *progressive* development. As Smuts, in his famous speech of May 1917, declared:

> The British Empire is much more than a State. . . . We are a system of states, and not a stationary system, but a dynamic and evolving system, always going forward to new destinies . . .

and followed that up by his reference to

> the so-called Dominions, independent in their government, which have been evolved on the principles of the free constitutional system into almost independent States, which all belong to this community of nations, and which I prefer to call 'The Commonwealth of Nations'.[14]

It may well be said that Smuts was always too optimistic in his assumption that the sovereignty claims of the Dominions were reconcilable with the unity of the Empire; and that such codifications as the Balfour Declaration of 1926 and the Statute of Westminster of 1931 were merely a sham, a figleaf to disguise the awful fact that the widely dispersed, self-governing regions of the Empire had irretrievably broken into their separate parts. But if it *was* such a fiction, it did not appear in that light to many people at the time. The theory of Dominion status which could be redefined as circumstances changed, and the concept of a metamorphosis from Empire into Commonwealth, stayed the hand of nationalists who otherwise would have pressed for outright independence – Hertzog, the South African Prime Minister, for example; for a while, it even bemused de Valera and the more extreme Irish nationalists. Conversely, it strengthened the position of those Dominion politicians like Mackenzie King, who needed to mollify French-Canadian suspicions. There is also evidence that the notion of Dominion status checked for a while the Indian Congress Party's demand for complete independence, and redirected people like Nehru towards the aim of self-government *within* the Empire-Commonwealth framework; and that, in rather the same way, the seductive idea of evolution undercut those nationalists who argued that only armed revolution would bring independence.

While this 'liberal' British tendency to compromise with indigenous nationalist movements reduced the prospects of a violent break, it can be argued that the British political culture also offered a *positive* 'pull'. Although there may not have been a proclaimed policy of cultural assimilation on the French lines, nevertheless the British way of life attracted admiration from many within the Empire. It was not merely in such loyal Dominions as (say) New Zealand that the emphasis upon the rule of law, reasoned parliamentary debate, the 'gentlemanly code' and so on, had their imitators; the educated élites in India and Africa – from Smuts to Gandhi to Nyerere – were all, in their way, drawn to respect the political culture of the imperial power. A legal education in particular, one suspects, produced many ambivalences: it provided the erudition and skills of advocacy and the ability to spot the weaknesses in an opponent's case, all of which stood an aspiring nationalist politician in good stead and made him much more dangerous to continued British rule than a border rebel; but it simultaneously drew such men to imbibe, consciously or unconsciously, the legal and cultural assumptions of the country whose sovereignty they sought to end.

But it was not merely in terms of politics, law and culture that British overlordship offered positive attractions; it was also true, in some respects, at the *economic* level. For the gatherers, growers and producers of cocoa, coffee, vegetable products, rubber, cotton and groundnuts, Britain was the main (sometimes the only) market. During the interwar Depression, the Colonial Office intervened in a number of ways – with commodity-control programmes and cartel schemes, by acting as financial broker, and by persuading the Dominions to make tariff concessions on primary imports from the colonial territories. To be sure, this benefited the British firms (and their shareholders) who also grew and marketed such products, but it was nevertheless true that many natives had a material interest in preserving ties with the imperial power. This interest was even greater *after* 1945, ironically enough, when the Colonial Development and Welfare Acts really began to have effect. Such 'modernization' schemes, with their open implications about preparing a territory for future independence, were at the same time creating new economic links between Britain and the tropical colonies. Only when 'development' implied new taxes (as in India), import restrictions or other economic burdens did the system show signs of strain.[15]

Last but by no means least was the fact that, as external circumstances became more threatening to a weakened British power, so, ironically, were the most developed and independent parts of the Empire compelled to stay close to the motherland. This trend had already been in evidence in the late nineteenth and early twentieth centuries, as the Dominions entered into military staff arrangements with Britain and agreed to contribute warships – support which had not been necessary in the happier days of Palmerston. If the 1920s saw the slackening of such bonds, the alarming international scene in the 1930s halted these centrifugal tendencies.[16] In the first place, the Great Depression and the division of the globe into trading blocks caused Commonwealth farmers in particular to become ever more dependent upon the metropolitan market – a dependency, and economic complementarity, which the Ottawa Conference of 1932, setting up imperial tariffs, could only intensify. Above all, despite their earlier desire for a separate foreign policy and their distrust of schemes of imperial defence, the Dominions soon took alarm at the rise of the dictator-states. While warmly supporting London's 'appeasement' policy, therefore, the governments in Ottawa and Cape Town reluctantly, and in Canberra and Wellington much more enthusiastically, joined the old country in a rearmament programme and planned for combined military cooperation. When 'appeasement' failed, they, too – except Eire – entered the Second World War. The Commonwealth alliance was still holding together, cemented as much by shared fears as by ideals of imperial unity. And, for the second time within a generation, the British in their struggle against Germany were going to benefit from the sizeable reinforcements of manpower, and the massive supplies of raw materials, munitions and hard cash provided by those distant Dominions.

III

The third, and perhaps the most important aspect of all was the attitude of other powers. If, as we know, successive British governments from the 1880s onwards were coming under pressure right across the globe; if, as historians have argued,[17] the objective indices of power (that is, population size, industrial capacity, steel production) were swinging from the island-state to these large, land-based empires well before the end of Queen Victoria's reign, why did it take so long before the territorial and political transformation came 'into line' with these economic and strategical realities?

The first, and perhaps very obvious remark to make here is that British strategic planners, whose vast output of memoranda and minutes are now available in the Public Record Office and elsewhere, usually made 'worst case' assumptions. They knew that all of their requests for additional men and materials would encounter resistance in the Treasury, the Cabinet and parliament; and that to make a convincing argument they had to focus upon the Empire's military weaknesses and deficiencies rather than its strengths, whereas it was always felt prudent to assume that a potential enemy would strike at the optimal moment, when *his* forces were at their peak but one's own defences might not be so. It was also assumed, when making budgetary bids, that a foe would be arming to his maximum capacity: one sees this in the Admiralty calculations during the great 'naval scare' of 1909, and in some of the gloomy assessments of German air strength in the 1930s. By contrast, the British planners rarely summoned up the imagination, and often didn't have the details, to see things from the other side. Did the British Empire seem so vulnerable and weak to the *German* Admiralty staff before 1914, whose planners were acutely aware of the geographical and firepower disadvantages under which the High Seas Fleet would operate? Did not

Whitehall's gloomy assessments in the 1930s of a Japan, poised to 'gobble up' the British Empire in the Far East, fail to see Tokyo's anxieties about Russia and the USA, its intractable military difficulties in the China War, its acute dependence upon overseas oil supplies? With the wisdom of retrospect, knowing that Britain did eventually decline as a world power, do we not sometimes fall into the habit of *anticipating* that collapse by overinterpreting the gloomy forecasts of the strategic planners?

As a related point, did not the rhetoric about 'splendid isolation' and 'the weary Titan', or the contemporary propaganda of the National Service League and Navy League about defying the four corners of the earth to come in arms, obscure the fact that Britain's rivals were usually very divided among themselves? Between the War of American Independence and June 1940, there was no time when Britain was fighting alone against two or more Great Powers. No doubt there were many occasions when English arrogance, and its possession of a disproportionate share of the world's trade and colonies, caused other states to seek to undermine that preeminence; but a full-scale and *combined* onslaught was out of the question, for practical reasons. Charles II's observation to his tactless brother, that 'they will not kill me, to make thee King', is apposite here. The French might bitterly resent Britain's occupation of Egypt during the 1880s but were hardly likely to go to war while a malevolent Bismarck was watching across the Rhine. The Germans, for their part, grew increasingly resentful of British policies in the following decade, but usually admitted that they could not permit a Franco-Russian combination to destroy the British Empire, for that would leave Germany isolated and at the mercy of its neighbours. When, at the height of the Boer War, the European powers secretly discussed a league against Britain, those talks ultimately foundered because none of the participants was keen to be pushed forward first to confront the perfidious islanders. And, within a few years of that event, France and Russia felt that they had more to fear from a resurgent Germany inside Europe than from a static British Empire in Africa and Asia.

The period following the First World War – during which conflict, it must be remembered, Britain fought with between two and four Great Powers on its side – produced a rather similar

213

situation. The British Empire might be vulnerable, and uniquely dispersed across the globe; but France, Italy and Germany all feared and hated each other so much that a European combination against Britain was impossible; Russia was in chaos, and then in its self-imposed socialist isolation; and in the Far East Japan and the United States were more worried about the other's intentions than about Britain.

But all this is very negative: it is also possible to argue that the British Empire performed certain useful functions, especially in economic terms, for some of the other powers at least some of the time, which mollified (as it were) their jealousy and antagonism. In that classic statement on British foreign policy, Sir Eyre Crowe's Memorandum on Relations with France and Germany of January 1907, Crowe had observed that the supreme naval power could only avoid provoking a global coalition against itself by having a national policy which (in his words) harmonized 'with the general desires and ideals common to mankind, and more particularly . . . is closely identified with the primary and vital interests of the majority . . . of the other nations'.[18] In a curious and ironic way, the British adherence to free trade, which many of the arch-imperialists denounced as a weakness, and the structural shift in Britain's economy from being the world's workshop to being its banker, investor and commodity-dealer, which alarmed tariff-reformers and strategists alike, helped to ameliorate Britain's relations with other Great Powers – or, at least, with influential interest-groups within those powers. For example, American jingos were delighted at Cleveland's Venezuela message of 1895, with its threats of war against Britain to defend the Monroe Doctrine; but to Wall Street, through which Britain's massive investments in the USA were channelled and which collapsed overnight at Cleveland's message, and to the midwestern farmers and southern cotton-growers, to whom Britain was their major market, a war would have been a disaster. The pressures by German bankers, shippers and merchants of Hamburg and Frankfurt before 1914 to head off an Anglo-German war is another good example of how Britain's cosmopolitan trading role, its open markets and supplies of colonial produce made it in the interest of many foreign nationals to strive to preserve peace.

Conversely, and without subscribing totally to the view that business interests manoeuvred the United States into the First World War on Britain's side, one can observe how the enormous expansion in American munitions exports and war loans prior to 1917 tied vital sectors of the United States economy to the success of the Allied war effort – as happened, albeit to a lesser degree, in the years before 1941 as well.

In other words, one is bound to wonder what the international consequences would have been if the ideas of Joseph Chamberlain and Milner – that is, of an autarkic, self-sufficient, fortress-Empire, protected by high tariff walls – had been realized. It can be noted, as a partial response to such a hypothetical question, that: first, the tariff reform campaign in Edwardian England greatly alarmed many otherwise friendly Germans, and strengthened the claims of those anglophobes, like Tirpitz, who claimed that an Anglo-German war was inevitable;[19] and secondly, that nothing so alienated influential sections of the American business community, the United States Treasury, and especially the Secretary of State Cordell Hull, as the 1932 Ottawa decision to adopt imperial preference. A fully blown 'Milnerite' British Empire would have quite ruined Anglo-American relations, as the Foreign Office was careful to point out.[20] More moderate and modest policies were required instead.

This finally brings us to a theme which has been discussed elsewhere in this book (see essay 1): the British political habit, at least once Palmerston and Disraeli were deceased, of trying to remain on good terms with as many foreign nations as possible, that 'tradition of appeasement', which was not originally a negative but a *positive* concept, which some years ago was defined as:

a policy of settling international quarrels by admitting and satisfying grievances through rational negotiation and compromise, thereby avoiding the resort to armed conflict which would be expensive, bloody, and possibly very dangerous.[21]

It is possible to see this policy in action in the many attempts to improve Anglo-American relations in the late nineteenth century, by concessions over the Venezuela dispute, the isthmian canal, the Alaska boundary and the seal fisheries; by the persistent efforts of British Foreign Secretaries from Salisbury to Grey to settle the 'great game' in Asia by diplomacy if possible, rather than by war with Russia; and, even during the tensions of the Anglo-German antagonism, by talks with Berlin over arms control, colonial concessions in the Middle East and Africa, the Haldane Mission, and so on. 'The interest of this country is now *and always* – peace,' Balfour told the King in 1903, a sentiment echoed twenty years later when Baldwin – another Tory leader – asserted that peace was 'the greatest British interest'.[22]

It was not meant by this to represent British appeasement policy simply in rosy terms, as a positive, idealistic, purely Gladstonian set of attitudes; clearly, there were other aspects to it as well. Indeed, the cynic could say that the British sought to 'buy off' and appease a major challenger whenever they could, simply out of self-interest, because they had so much to lose if a great war occurred that small-scale, regional concessions were nearly always going to be preferable; and further, that the British could afford to concede quite a lot, especially in their spheres of so-called 'informal empire', because their own earlier pretensions and claims to influence had been so enormous. Even if the British Empire *was* under challenge from the 1880s onwards, it had lots of buffer-zones, lots of less-than-vital areas of interest, lots of room for compromise. When, in contrast, its back was right against the wall in 1940, it made no concessions.

This more cynical interpretation is perfectly plausible; yet it does not obviate the equally valid observation that the political culture of most of the British élite – the dislike of extremes, the appeal to reasoned argument, the belief in the rationality of politics and the necessity of compromise[23] – may form a very important part in explaining why the British Empire lasted so long. The rulers of that Empire had many faults, to be sure. But they did not usually try to crush their domestic-political opponents by sending in the troopers, as was the Czarist habit; they did not usually respond to pressures for self-government, in the Dominions and later in India and Ireland, with a completely negative, diehard policy, at least not for long – the violence of Amritsar, and of the 'Black and Tans', frightened British ministers into further consideration of *political* solutions. Furthermore, in their relations with foreign countries, they did not pull up the drawbridge, engage in tariff wars, refuse to compromise in colonial disputes, and assume the worst in other powers' intentions. And because they did not do those things, because they did not pursue what one might term the false *Realpolitik* of the diehard arch-imperialists, in some way they may well have given the Empire a longer lease of life than otherwise. They certainly ensured that its decline and fall was a reasonably gentle process, at times slightly inglorious and involving a certain loss of face, but also avoiding the cataclysm and chaos and domestic fissures which attended the fall of the Roman Empire, the collapse of the Third Reich, or, on a lesser scale, the end of the Portuguese Empire a few years ago.

The final irony, then, is this – and perhaps Mr Reagan and Mr Andropov, now presiding over their own declining empires, may take note. A century ago, alarmed by what they sensed as new threats to their country's world position, a significant segment of British opinion called – and thereafter never ceased calling – for hard-nosed policies to check foreign rivals, to protect British industry and markets, to turn their Empire into a self-contained armed camp. At the same time, they never ceased complaining of the weak, compromising, appeasing policies of Mr Gladstone, of the flaccid stance of Salisbury and the languid reactions of Balfour, of Asquith's refusal to face the facts and Baldwin's unwillingness to take hard but necessary decisions.

In certain respects, of course, the imperialists and the anti-appeasers were correct: on specific issues, British governments made wrong decisions, indulged in wishful thinking, failed to take full advantage of a given situation. But in the longer-term perspective – on the fundamental issue of how to preserve a worldwide Empire for as long as possible once the economic and strategical tides had turned – was not this flexible, reasonable, compromise-seeking policy preferable to the assertive 'no surrender' one? Mr Gladstone in Bismarck's day, Mr Baldwin in Hitler's, did not look very prepossessing members in the select club of great world leaders; but, even when Bismarck's Reich had foundered and Hitler's had collapsed in flames, British statesmen

217

muddled through with their far larger, Heath-Robinson Empire until it had converted itself into that equally puzzling, equally remarkable structure known as the British Commonwealth of Nations. It was not a bad performance on the whole, not a bad diplomatic juggling-act. If those who, a century ago, were beginning to despair of 'saving the Empire', were brought back to life and given our wisdom of retrospect, one wonders whether they might not moderate their criticisms. After all, keeping a declining British imperial omnibus going along the road for such a long time is a fair art, and not one that should be entrusted to persons who are liable to shoot the passengers, who don't know how to service and oil the machine, and who have the nasty habit of trying to crash into oncoming vehicles.

Notes

Notes

1. The Tradition of Appeasement in British Foreign Policy, 1865–1939

Originally published in the *British Journal of International Studies*, volume 2, no.3 (1976), pp.195–215.

1. M. Gilbert, *The Roots of Appeasement* (London, 1966), p.9.
2. W. N. Medlicott, review of A. Furnia's *Diplomacy of Appeasement*, *International Affairs*, 38 (1962), pp.84–5.
3. See especially the strong criticism of this feature in C. Barnett, *The Collapse of British Power* (London, 1972), pp.20ff.
4. On the influence of economic and strategical factors upon Britain's world position after 1815, see P. M. Kennedy, *The Rise and Fall of British Naval Mastery* (London & New York, 1976), pp.149ff.
5. G. Niedhart, 'Friede als nationales Interesse: Grossbritannien in der Vorgeschichte des Zweiten Weltkriegs', *Neue Politische Literatur*, 17 (1972), pp.451–70.
6. A. J. P. Taylor, *The Trouble Makers. Dissent over Foreign Policy, 1792–1939* (London, 1969 edition); P. M. Kennedy, 'Idealists and Realists: British Views of Germany 1864–1939', *Transactions of the Royal Historical Society*, 5th series, 25 (1975), pp.137–56.
7. Ibid.; and J. R. Jones, 'England', in H. Rogger and E. Weber (eds), *The European Right. A Historical Profile* (Berkeley/Los Angeles, 1965), pp.29ff.
8. See especially K. Hildebrand, '"British Interests" als Staatsräson', *Mitteilungen der Gesellschaft der Freunde der Universitat Mannheim e.V.*, Jahrgang 22, Heft 2 (1973); idem, 'Von der Reichseinigung zur "Krieg-in-Sicht" Krise. Preussen-Deutschland als Faktor der britischen Aussenpolitik 1866–75', in M. Stürmer (ed.), *Das kaiserliche Deutschland. Politik und Gesellschaft 1870–1918* (Düsseldorf, 1970).
9. W. E. Mosse, 'Public Opinion and Foreign Policy: the British Public and the War-Scare of November 1870', *Historical Journal*, vi (1963), pp.38ff; and C. C. Eldridge, *England's Mission. The Imperial Idea in the Age of Gladstone and Disraeli 1868–1880* (London, 1973).
10. J. Roach, 'Liberalism and the Victorian Intelligentsia', *Cambridge Historical Journal*, xiii (1957), pp.58–81; P. Marshall, 'The Imperial Factor in the Liberal Decline, 1880–1885', in J. E. Flint and G. Williams (eds), *Perspectives of Empire. Essays presented to Gerald S. Graham* (London, 1973), pp.136–47.

Notes

11. G. W. Monger, *The End of Isolation. British Foreign Policy 1900–1907* (London, 1963), pp.8–14; H. V. Emy, 'The Impact of Financial Policy on English Party Politics before 1914', *Historical Journal*, xv (1972), pp.103ff.
12. Kennedy, *British Naval Mastery*, p.220 and passim.
13. See B. Perkins, *The Great Rapprochement* (London, 1969).
14. K. Robbins, *Sir Edward Grey* (London, 1971), pp.125ff.
15. Taylor, *The Trouble Makers*, chapter 4; A. J. A. Morris, *Radicalism against War, 1906–1914. The Advocacy of Peace and Retrenchment* (London, 1972).
16. B. Semmel, *Imperialism and Social Reform* (London, 1960); Kennedy, 'Idealists and Realists', pp.142–7.
17. Ibid., pp.149–50; J. M. Blum, *Woodrow Wilson and the Politics of Morality* (Boston, 1956).
18. M. C. Pugh, *British Public Opinion and Collective Security 1926–1936* (PhD thesis, University of East Anglia, 1975); Barnett, *Collapse of British Power*, pp.237ff.
19. Ibid., especially pp.420–35; Taylor, *The Trouble Makers*, chapter 4; P. M. Kennedy, 'The Decline of Nationalistic History in the West 1900–1970', *Journal of Contemporary History*, 8 (1973), pp.92–3.
20. E. Hobsbawm, *Industry and Empire* (Harmondsworth, 1969), p.207.
21. Barnett, *Collapse of British Power*, especially pp.12–14, 564; M. Howard, *The Continental Commitment* (Harmondsworth, 1974), pp.97ff.
22. Cited in W. N. Medlicott, *British Foreign Policy since Versailles 1919–1963* (London, 1968 edition), p.xvi.
23. Barnett's details, in *Collapse of British Power*, pp.342ff, are very informative here.
24. H. Pelling, *Britain and the Second World War* (London, 1970), pp.22–3; Howard, *The Continental Commitment*, pp.118–20.
25. Ibid., p.121.
26. Kennedy, *British Naval Mastery*, pp.271ff.
27. M. Cowling, *The Impact of Labour* (Cambridge, 1971).
28. Cited in Howard, *The Continental Commitment*, p.79.
29. See especially the thesis by Pugh, cited in note 18 above.
30. C. Thorne, *The Limits of Foreign Policy* (London, 1972); B. A. Lee, *Britain and the Sino-Japanese War 1937–1939* (Stanford, 1973).
31. A. J. Marder, 'The Royal Navy and the Ethiopian Crisis of 1935–6', *American Historical Review*, xxv, no.5 (1970); R. A. C. Parker, 'Great Britain, France and the Ethiopian Crisis, 1935–1936', *English Historical Review*, lxxxiv, no.351 (1974); F. Hardie, *The Abyssinian Crisis* (London, 1974).
32. Gilbert, *The Roots of Appeasement*; W. M. Jordan, *Great Britain, France and the German Problem 1918–1939* (London, 1943).

33. Apart from the brief synopses in Jones, 'England', pp.57–69, and Kennedy, 'Idealists and Realists', pp.153ff, see N. Thompson, *The Anti-Appeasers* (Oxford, 1971); and fresh but scattered details in M. Cowling, *The Impact of Hitler* (Cambridge, 1975).
34. See Kipling's poem in the *Daily Telegraph* of 3 November 1930, and the leader of that day, as an illustration of this sentiment.
35. Cowling, *The Impact of Hitler*, p.122.
36. Cowling's new book confirms the findings of Thompson's *The Anti-Appeasers* in this respect.
37. See especially J. F. Naylor, *Labour's International Policy* (London, 1969).
38. *The Impact of Hitler*, passim.
39. Kennedy, 'Idealists and Realists', pp.154ff.
40. A. J. P. Taylor, *The Origins of the Second World War* (Harmondsworth, 1964), pp.250–4.
41. British policy in 1939 is covered in Taylor, op.cit., pp.244ff; M. Gilbert and R. Gott, *The Appeasers* (London, 1969 edition), pp.199ff; I. Colvin, *The Chamberlain Cabinet* (London, 1972), pp.177–259; R. Parkinson, *Peace for Our Time* (London, 1971), pp.89–226; S. Aster, *1939: the Making of the Second World War* (London, 1973), passim.
42. Gilbert and Gott, *The Appeasers*, pp.301–26.
43. Kennedy, *British Naval Mastery*, pp.295–8.
44. Gilbert, *The Roots of Appeasement*, pp.165–8, 179–88, covers this change of attitude well.
45. There is, unfortunately, no 'politico-semantic' analysis of this word as detailed by R. Koebner and H. Schmidt, *Imperialism: the Story and Significance of a Political Word 1840–1960* (Cambridge, 1964), but a glance at the *Oxford English Dictionary*'s definitions of appeasement – all before 1933, when vol.1 of the *OED* appeared – suggests traditionally that the word implied a natural satisfaction or conciliation of desires, e.g. 'appeasement of one's appetite'. No doubt it was in this sense that C. P. Scott argued for a 'peace of appeasement' (see Gilbert, *The Roots of Appeasement*, p.54). Only in the post-1945 dictionaries is there the added meaning of a craven surrender to threats.

2. Mahan *versus* Mackinder: Two Interpretations of British Sea Power

Originally published in *Militärgeschichtliche Mitteilungen*, no.2 (1974), pp.39–66.

1. Standard treatments of Mahan are W. E. Livezey, *Mahan on Sea Power* (Norman, Oklahoma, 1947); W. D. Puleston, *The Life and Work of Captain Alfred Thayer Mahan* (New York, 1940); M. T.

Sprout, 'Mahan: Evangelist of Sea Power', in E. M. Earle (ed.), *Makers of Modern Strategy* (Princeton, 1952).

2. A. J. Marder (ed.), *Fear God and Dread Nought. The Correspondence of Admiral of the Fleet Lord Fisher of Kilverstone*, 3 vols (London, 1952–9), iii, p.439.

3. Livezey, op.cit., p.274.

4. H. J. Mackinder, 'The Geographical Pivot of History', *Geographical Journal*, XXIII, no.4 (April 1904), pp.421–44. Livezey, op.cit., pp.286–92, and G. S. Graham, *The Politics of Naval Supremacy* (Cambridge, 1965), pp.29–30, also point out the significance of Mackinder's doctrines for an understanding of the development of sea power in this past hundred years.

5. Mackinder, 'The Geographical Pivot of History', p.433.

6. Ibid., p.441 (my stress).

7. J. R. Seeley, *The Expansion of England* (London, 1884), p.301.

8. Mackinder, *Britain and the British Seas* (Oxford, 1925 edition), p.358.

9. This section is taken from E. J. Hobsbawm, *Industry and Empire* (Harmondsworth, 1969), pp.134–53, 172–85; P. Mathias, *The First Industrial Nation* (London, 1971), pp.243–53, 306–34, 345–426; C. Barnett, *The Collapse of British Power* (London & New York, 1972), pp.71–120.

10. C. Barnett, *Britain and her Army 1509–1970: a Military, Political and Social Survey* (London, 1970), pp.295–303.

11. Quoted in G. Barraclough, *An Introduction to Contemporary History* (Harmondsworth, 1967), p.51.

12. Mackinder, *Democratic Ideals and Reality* (New York, 1962 edition), p.115.

13. The *Naval and Military Record* (London), 26 December 1901.

14. D. Owen, 'Capture at Sea: Modern Conditions and the Ancient Prize Laws', given at the United Services Institute on 6 April 1905, *printed for private use*. A copy of this interesting paper came into the hands of the German naval attaché and is to be found in the Bundesarchiv-Militärarchiv, Freiburg i.Br., F. 5145, *II.Jap.11b*, vol.2, Coerper to Reichsmarineamt, no.246 of 7 April 1905.

15. P. M. Kennedy, 'Maritime Strategieprobleme der deutsch-englischen Flottenrivalität', in H. Schottelius and W. Deist (eds), *Marine und Marinepolitik im kaiserlichen Deutschland 1871–1914* (Düsseldorf, 1972), p.198.

16. *The Times* (London), 5 June 1914; A. J. Marder, *From the Dreadnought to Scapa Flow*, 5 vols (London, 1961–70), i, p.373.

17. Cited in I. F. Clarke, *Voices Prophesying War 1783–1984* (London, 1970 edition), p.134.

18. B. H. Liddell Hart, *The British Way of Warfare* (London, 1932), pp.7–41.

Notes

19. A. J. P. Taylor, *The Struggle for Mastery in Europe 1848–1918* (Oxford, 1954), pp.xix–xxvi; F. Fischer, *Germany's Aims in the First World War* (London, 1967), pp.3–49.
20. Cited in Marder, *From the Dreadnought*, i, p.289.
21. Lord Hankey, *The Supreme Command 1914–1918*, 2 vols (London, 1961), i, p.82.
22. S. R. Williamson, *The Politics of Grand Strategy: Britain and France prepare for War, 1904–1914* (Cambridge, Mass., 1969), p.367.
23. Marder, *From the Dreadnought*, ii, p.4.
24. W. Baumgart, *Deutschland im Zeitalter des Imperialismus (1890–1914)* (Frankfurt, 1972), pp.79–81; D. K. Fieldhouse, *The Colonial Empires* (London, 1966), pp.370–1; M. Balfour, *The Kaiser and his Times* (New York, 1972 edition), pp.437–47.
25. Marder, *From the Dreadnought*, ii, p.123.
26. Balfour, op.cit., pp.442–4.
27. H. W. Richmond, *National Policy and Naval Strength and Other Essays* (London, 1928), p.142.
28. Ibid., p.71.
29. M. Howard, *The Continental Commitment* (London, 1972), pp.68–70.
30. Richmond, op.cit., p.25.
31. Cited in Marder, *From the Dreadnought*, i, p.391.
32. Ibid., ii, p.175.
33. Sir Sydney Fremantle, *My Naval Career, 1880–1928* (London, 1949), pp.245–6.
34. Mathias, op.cit., pp.431ff; S. Pollard, *The Development of the British Economy 1914–1967* (London, 1969 edition), pp.49–92; Barnett, *The Collapse of British Power*, pp.424–8.
35. D. Dignan, 'New Perspectives on British Far Eastern Policy 1913–1919', *University of Queensland Papers*, vol.1, no.5.
36. Marder, *From the Dreadnought*, v, p.225. See also W. R. Braisted, *The United States Navy in the Pacific 1909–1922* (Austin, Texas, 1971), pp.153–208, 289ff.
37. Ibid., pp.437, 440.
38. J. Terraine, 'History and the "Indirect Approach"', *Journal of the Royal United Services Institute for Defence Studies*, CXVI, no.662 (June 1971), pp.44–9.
39. F. S. Northedge, *The Troubled Giant. Britain among the Great Powers* (London, 1966), p.623.
40. Mackinder, *Democratic Ideals and Reality*, p.170.
41. Howard, *The Continental Commitment*, pp.112–33; Barnett, *The Collapse of British Power*, pp.438–575.
42. J. R. M. Butler, *Grand Strategy*, vol.II (London, 1957), pp.10–11.
43. S. W. Roskill, *The Navy at War 1939–1945* (London, 1960), p.448.
44. M. M. Postan, *British War Production* (London, 1952), p.289.

45. Cited in Marder, *Winston is Back: Churchill at the Admiralty 1939–1940* (the *English Historical Review*, Supplement 5, London 1972), p.11.
46. K. Feiling, *The Life of Neville Chamberlain* (London, 1957), p.426; W. K. Hancock and M. Gowing, *British War Economy* (London, 1949), p.72.
47. This section upon the German war economy is based upon A. S. Milward, *The German Economy at War* (London, 1965); R. Wagenführ, *Die deutsche Industrie im Kriege 1939–1945* (Berlin, 2nd edition, 1963); Berenice A. Carroll, *Design for Total War. Arms and Economics in the Third Reich* (The Hague, 1968); Burton H. Klein, *Germany's Economic Preparations for War* (Cambridge, Mass., 1959); W. N. Medlicott, *The Economic Blockade*, 2 vols (London, 1952 & 1959).
48. Ibid., i, p.43.
49. See Marder, *Winston is Back*, pp.31–3.
50. Carroll, op.cit., p.104.
51. Klein, op.cit., p.211.
52. H. U. Faulkner, *American Economic History* (New York, 1960 edition), p.701; A. Russell Buchanan, *The United States and World War II*, 2 vols (New York, 1964), i, p.140.
53. Milward, op.cit., p.115.
54. Medlicott, op.cit., i, pp.631, 640.
55. B. H. Liddell Hart, *History of the Second World War* (London, 1970), p.547.
56. M. Howard, *Grand Strategy*, vol.IV (London, 1972), p.3. The raw material shortage is described in Postan, op.cit., pp.211–17.
57. Ibid., p.244.
58. Barnett, *Collapse of British Power*, p.592.
59. H. Pelling, *Britain and the Second World War* (London, 1970), p.273.
60. M. Gowing, *Britain and Atomic Energy* (London, 1964).
61. M. Howard, *The Continental Commitment*, pp.142–3.
62. F. P. King, *The New Internationalism: Allied Policy and the European Peace 1939–1945* (Newton Abbot, 1973).
63. Hancock and Gowing, op.cit., p.555.
64. Cited in M. Matloff, *Strategic Planning for Coalition Warfare 1943–1944* (Washington, DC, 1959), pp.523–4.

3. Strategy *versus* Finance in Twentieth-century Britain

Originally published in the *International History Review*, volume III, no.1 (1981), pp.45–61.

1. This article began as a seminar paper, presented to (and much

improved by the comments of) various audiences; and was then produced in limited numbers by the Woodrow Wilson Center, Washington, DC, under the title of 'The Contradiction between British Strategic Planning and Economic Requirements in the Era of Two World Wars' (International Security Studies Program, Working Paper no.11, Washington, DC, 1980). Since then it has been further amended, especially in its introductory paragraphs and in the footnotes.

2. See the analysis of contemporary theories about the mercantilist state in E. Schulin, *Handelsstaat England. Das politische Interesse der Nation am Aussenhandel vom 16. bis ins frühe 18. Jahrhundert* (Wiesbaden, 1969); and also the discussion in C. Hill, *Reformation to Industrial Revolution* (Harmondsworth, 1969), pp.72–81, 155–68, 226–39.

3. A. H. John, 'War and the English Economy, 1700–1763', *Economic History Review*, 2nd series, vol. vii, no.3 (1955), pp.329–44; E. J. Hobsbawm, *Industry and Empire* (Harmondsworth, 1969), pp.48ff; P. M. Kennedy, *The Rise and Fall of British Naval Mastery* (London & New York, 1976), chapters 2–5; J. R. Jones, *Britain and the World 1649–1815* (London, 1980), passim.

4. P. G. M. Dickson, *The Financial Revolution in England. A Study in the Development of Public Credit 1688–1756* (London, 1967); and, more narrowly, N. J. Silberling, 'Financial and Monetary Policy of Great Britain during the Napoleonic Wars', *Quarterly Journal of Economics*, vol.xxxviii (1923–4), pp.214–33.

5. Selborne's remark is quoted in C. J. Lowe, *The Reluctant Imperialists: British Foreign Policy 1878–1902*, 2 vols. (London, 1967), i, p.5.

6. The disruptive influences of prolonged war have been most recently detailed in C. Emsley, *British Society and the French Wars 1793–1815* (London, 1979). On the question of Britain's greater richness in absolute terms, see T. S. Ashton, *Economic Fluctuations in England 1700–1800* (Oxford, 1959), and P. Deane, 'War and Industrialization', in J. M. Winter (ed.), *War and Economic Development* (Cambridge, 1975), pp.91–102. For the *relative* decline of Britain's rivals, see F. Crouzet, 'Wars, Blockade and Economic Change in Europe, 1792–1815', *Journal of Economic History*, vol.24, no.2 (1964), pp.567–88.

7. On this development, see P. Mathias, *The First Industrial Nation* (London, 1969), pp.395ff; Hobsbawm, *Industry and Empire*, chapter 9; Kennedy, *The Rise and Fall of British Naval Mastery*, chapter 7; B. Murphy, *A History of the British Economy 1086–1970* (London, 1973), pp.660ff; D. H. Aldcroft (ed.), *The Development of British Industry and Foreign Competition 1875–1914* (London, 1968), passim.

8. Mathias, op.cit., p.255. The argument in pre-1914 Britain over the

significance of *relative* decline, but *absolute* rises in productivity and wealth, is analysed in P. M. Kennedy, *The Rise of the Anglo-German Antagonism 1860–1914* (London & Boston, 1980), chapters 15–16.

9. P. M. Kennedy, 'Mahan *versus* Mackinder: Two Interpretations of British Sea Power', essay 2 in this book. A rather similar analysis to this has recently appeared in M. Wight's *Power Politics*, edited by H. Bull and C. Holbraad (Harmondsworth, 1979), chapter 6, 'Sea Power and Land Power'.

10. See the statistics on the British balance of payments in Mathias, *First Industrial Nation*, p.305; and the more detailed analysis in A. H. Imlah, *Economic Elements in the 'Pax Britannica'* (Cambridge, Mass., 1958). Also important here are S. B. Saul, *Studies in British Overseas Trade 1870–1914* (Liverpool, 1960), and M. de Cecco, *Money and Empire. The International Gold Standard, 1890–1914* (Oxford, 1974).

11. Mathias, op.cit., pp.332–3. I have attempted to explore some of the implications of this argument in my paper on Britain's pre-1914 war planning, presented to the conference on 'Potential Enemies' at Harvard University, July 1980.

12. Public Record Office, London, Cab.(inet Records) 16/18A, 'Trading with the Enemy'.

13. Idem; and see also Cab.17/81, 'Finance of War', Sir George Clarke to Asquith, 7 November 1906, and the ensuing correspondence. These CID papers can be read in conjunction with de Cecco's *Money and Empire*, but a new analysis of Britain's prewar political economy and the tentative steps towards planning for war will soon supplant the existing literature: see D. French, *British Economic and Strategic Planning 1905–1915* (London & Boston, 1982).

14. Cab.16/18A, 'Trading with the Enemy', p.140. After prolonged persuasion by the authorities, the Lloyds' underwriters agreed discreetly to alter the terms of their shipping-insurance contracts to exclude compensation for captures by the Royal Navy.

15. G. P. Gooch and H. Temperley (eds), *British Documents on the Origins of the War*, 11 vols (London, 1926–38), xi, p.369.

16. S. Pollard, *The Development of the British Economy 1914–1967* (London, 2nd edition, 1969), chapter II; C. Barnett, *The Collapse of British Power* (London & New York, 1972), pp.71ff; Kennedy, *The Rise and Fall of British Naval Mastery*, chapter 9.

17. Hobsbawm, *Industry and Empire*, p.207. See also Pollard, *The Development of the British Economy*, pp.92–241; W. E. Alford, *Depression and Recovery? British Growth 1919–1939* (London, 1972); D. H. Aldcroft, *The Inter-War Economy: Britain 1919–1939* (London, 1970); A. J. Youngson, *Britain's Economic Growth 1920–1966* (London, 1967).

Notes

18. A. T. Peacock and J. Wiseman, *The Growth of Public Expenditure in the United Kingdom* (London, 1967 edition), pp.184–7. Explanations of the manner of calculating these figures are given in this book.
19. The defence aspects of appeasement are well covered in Barnett, *The Collapse of British Power*, passim; M. Howard, *The Continental Commitment* (London, 1972), chapters 4–5; N. H. Gibbs, *Grand Strategy*, vol.1 (London, 1976), passim; R. Meyers, *Britische Sicherheitspolitik 1934–1938* (Düsseldorf, 1976), passim. There is in addition a host of new studies about the individual services, and specific regional defence aspects of appeasement, which cannot be listed here for reasons of space.
20. Cited in Howard, *The Continental Commitment*, p.98.
21. Ibid., p.138. See also R. A. C. Parker, 'Economics, Rearmament, and Foreign Policy: the United Kingdom before 1939 – A Preliminary Study', *Journal of Contemporary History*, vol.10, no.4 (1975), pp.637–47.
22. See the analysis of their report early in 1939, in Gibbs, *Grand Strategy*, i, pp.658ff.
23. Cited in Barnett, *The Collapse of British Power*, p.564.
24. Cited in R. P. Shay, Jr, *British Rearmament in the Thirties. Politics and Profits* (Princeton, 1977), p.243. Also very important on this matter is G. C. Peden, *British Rearmament and the Treasury 1932–1939* (Edinburgh, 1979).
25. See the detailed coverage in B.-J. Wendt, *Economic Appeasement. Handel und Finanz in der britischen Deutschlandpolitik 1933–1939* (Düsseldorf, 1971); and M. Gilbert and R. Gott, *The Appeasers* (London, 2nd edition, 1967), pp.189ff.
26. Barnett, *The Collapse of British Power*, p.564. See also Shay, op.cit., pp.233ff; Peden, op.cit., pp.64ff.
27. Apart from Wendt's massive study on this subject, see also C. A. MacDonald, 'Economic Appeasement and the German "Moderates", 1937–1939: an Introductory Essay', *Past and Present*, no.56 (1972), pp.105–36.
28. Ibid., p.121.
29. British economic interests in the Far East are detailed in S. L. Endicott, *Diplomacy and Enterprise: British China Policy 1933–1937* (Vancouver, 1975); W. R. Louis, *British Strategy in the Far East 1919–1939* (Oxford, 1971), chapter VII; A. Trotter, *Britain and East Asia 1933–1937* (Cambridge, 1975); B. A. Lee, *Britain and the Sino-Japanese War 1937–1939* (Stanford, 1973); and in the preliminary chapters of C. Thorne, *Allies of a Kind* (London, 1978).
30. British economic interests in eastern Europe are covered in A. Teichova, *An Economic Background to Munich* (Cambridge, 1974); B.-J. Wendt, 'England und der deutsche "Drang nach Südosten".

Kapitalbeziehungen und Warenverkehr in Südosteuropa zwischen den Kriegen', in I. Geiss and B.-J. Wendt (eds), *Deutschland in der Weltpolitik des 19. und 20. Jahrhunderts* (Düsseldorf, 1973), pp.483–512; S. Newman, *March 1939. The British Guarantee to Poland* (Oxford, 1976); and W. D. Gruner, ' "British Interest" in der Zwischenkriegszeit. Aspekte britischer Europa-Politik 1918–1938', in K. Bosl (ed.), *Gleichgewicht – Revision – Restauration* (Munich, 1976), pp.85–151.
31. See especially the arguments of Endicott (for China) and Newman (for eastern Europe).

4. Fisher and Tirpitz Compared

Originally published as 'Fisher and Tirpitz: Political Admirals in the Age of Imperialism', in G. Jordan (ed.), *Naval Warfare in the Twentieth Century 1900–1945. Essays in Honour of Arthur Marder* (London & New York, 1977), pp.45–59.

1. A. J. Marder (ed.), *Fear God and Dread Nought. The Correspondence of Admiral of the Fleet Lord Fisher of Kilverstone*, 3 vols (London, 1952–9), iii, p.334.
2. The early life of Fisher has been well covered in Sir Reginald Bacon, *The Life of the Lord Fisher of Kilverstone*, 2 vols (London, 1929); R. Hough, *First Sea Lord* (London, 1969); R. F. Mackay, *Fisher of Kilverstone* (Oxford, 1973), the latter in particular being an excellent study. There is no modern, detailed biography of Tirpitz and one must perforce rely upon the earlier and mainly hagiographical works such as U. von Hassell, *Tirpitz* (Stuttgart, 1920); and A. von Trotha, *Grossadmiral von Tirpitz* (Breslau, 1932).
3. On which developments generally, see A. J. Marder, *The Anatomy of British Sea Power. A History of British Naval Policy in the Pre-Dreadnought Era, 1880–1905* (Hamden, Conn., reprint, 1964), pp.3–9, 355–71, 483–545; P. Padfield, *The Battleship Era* (London, 1972), passim.
4. See P. K. Kemp (ed.), *The Papers of Admiral Sir John Fisher*, 2 vols (London, Navy Records Society, 1960 & 1964), as well as the reference in note 1 above.
5. V. R. Berghahn, *Der Tirpitz-Plan: Genesis und Verfall einer innenpolitischen Krisenstrategie unter Wilhelm II* (Düsseldorf, 1971); J. Steinberg, *Yesterday's Deterrent: Tirpitz and the Birth of the German Battle Fleet* (London, 1965).
6. Hough, *First Sea Lord*, p.155; and for the other controversies, see especially Mackay, *Fisher of Kilverstone*, passim.
7. Tirpitz's quarrels are well documented in Berghahn, *Der Tirpitz-*

Plan; C.-A. Gemzell, *Organization, Conflict and Innovation. A Study of German Naval Strategic Planning 1888–1940* (Lund, 1973); P. J. Kelly, *The Naval Policy of Imperial Germany, 1900–1914* (PhD thesis, Georgetown University, 1970).

8. For this, and further interesting observations by Tirpitz, see Naval Library, Ministry of Defence, Ca.2053, reports of the British naval attachés to Berlin (1906–13). They have been well used in P. Padfield, *The Great Naval Race* (London, 1974).

9. Hough, *First Sea Lord*, p.309.

10. Mackay, *Fisher of Kilverstone*, p.243.

11. W. Deist, *Flottenpolitik und Flottenpropaganda. Das Nachrichten-bureau des Reichsmarineamtes 1897–1914* (Stuttgart, 1976).

12. Tirpitz to Trotha, 2 August 1917, Trotha Papers, Niedersächsisches Staatsarchiv, Bückeburg, A362/no.31.

13. C. Graham, *The Politics of Naval Supremacy* (Cambridge, 1965), p.124.

14. Mackay, *Fisher of Kilverstone*, pp.327–34, 366–422; P. Haggie, 'The Royal Navy and War Planning in the Fisher Era', *Journal of Contemporary History*, vol.8 (1973).

15. Gemzell, *Organization, Conflict and Innovation*, pp.50–91; P. M. Kennedy, 'The Development of German Naval Operations Plans against England, 1896–1914', *English Historical Review*, lxxxix, no.350 (1974), p.72.

16. P. M. Kennedy, 'Maritime Strategieprobleme der deutsch-englischen Flottenrivalität', in H. Schottelius and W. Deist (eds), *Marine und Marinepolitik im kaiserlichen Deutschland 1871–1914* (Düsseldorf, 1972), passim.

17. *Fear God and Dread Nought*, ii, p.485.

18. Mackay, *Fisher of Kilverstone*, pp.426–7.

19. Ibid., p.514.

20. V. R. Berghahn, *Germany and the Approach of War in 1914* (London, 1973), pp.29–30.

21. This aspect of Tirpitz's politics has never been thoroughly explored, but the deterministic and Social-Darwinistic flavour of his September 1899 audience with the Kaiser (see P. M. Kennedy, 'Tirpitz, England and the Second Navy Law of 1900: a Strategical Critique', *Militärgeschichtliche Mitteilungen*, no.2 (1970), pp.38–41) and of his *Politische Dokumente*, 2 vols (Berlin, 1924 & 1926) is more than confirmed by the contents of the Tirpitz Papers in the Bundesarchiv-Militärarchiv, Freiburg, and the letters to Trotha in the Niedersächsisches Staatsarchiv, Bückeburg.

22. Tirpitz to Hess, 13 November 1922, Tirpitz Papers, Bundesarchiv-Militärarchiv, Freiburg, N253/296.

23. I should not like to close this paper without acknowledging the great

help afforded to me by the comments of Professor V. R. Berghahn, Professor J. R. Jones and Dr R. F. Mackay.

5. Strategic Aspects of the Anglo-German Naval Race*

Originally published in H. Schottelius and W. Deist (eds), *Marine und Marinepolitik im kaiserlichen Deutschland 1871–1914* (Düsseldorf: Droste Verlag, 1972), pp.178–210.

*I should like to acknowledge the kind help given to me in preparing this article by Professor A. J. Marder, Professor J. R. Jones, Dr. J. Steinberg, Professor V. R. Berghahn and Professor P. J. Kelly; and to the German Academic Exchange Service, which supported my research trip to Freiburg in summer 1971. The abbreviations BA and BA-MA used in the footnotes below refer to the Bundesarchiv (Koblenz) and the Bundesarchiv-Militärarchiv (Freiburg) respectively.

1. *The Times*, 25 June 1897. There is also a brief description of the Spithead review in A. J. Marder, *The Anatomy of British Sea Power. A History of British Naval Policy in the Pre-Dreadnought Era, 1880–1905* (Hamden, Conn., reprint, 1964), pp.281–2.
2. 'Another proof', he added, 'that we belong to the ten lost tribes of Israel!' Quoted in A. J. Marder, *The Road to War 1904–1914: From the Dreadnought to Scapa Flow*, vol.1 (London, 1961), p.41.
3. P. M. Kennedy, 'Imperial Cable Communications and Strategy 1870–1914', *English Historical Review*, lxxxvi (October 1971), pp.728–52.
4. As Mahan put it, 'if a nation be so situated that it is neither forced to defend itself by land nor induced to seek extension of its territory by way of the land, it has, by the very unity of its aim directed upon the sea, an advantage as compared with a people one of whose boundaries is continental'. A. T. Mahan, *The Influence of Sea Power upon History 1660–1783* (London, 1965 edition), p.29.
5. Quoted in Marder, *From the Dreadnought*, i, p.431.
6. This memorandum is reproduced fully in J. Steinberg, *Yesterday's Deterrent: Tirpitz and the Birth of the German Battle Fleet* (London, 1965), pp.208–21.
7. The line taken generally by W. Hubatsch, *Die Aera Tirpitz* (Göttingen, 1955); idem, 'Realität und Illusion in Tirpitz' Flottenbau', in W. Hubatsch (ed.), *Schicksalwege Deutscher Vergangenheit* (Düsseldorf, 1950).
8. Steinberg, passim; R. Stadelman, 'Die Epoche der deutsch-englischen Flottenrivalität', in *Deutschland und Westeuropa* (Schloss-Laupheim, 1948); P. M. Kennedy, 'Tirpitz, England and the

Notes

Second Naval Law of 1900: a Strategical Critique', *Militärgeschichtliche Mitteilungen*, no.2 (1970); P. J. Kelly, *The Naval Policy of Imperial Germany, 1900–1914* (PhD thesis, Georgetown University, 1970); V. R. Berghahn, *Der Tirpitz-Plan: Genesis und Verfall einer innenpolitischen Krisenstrategie unter Wilhelm II* (Düsseldorf, 1971).

9. Kelly, *The Naval Policy*, passim.
10. Berghahn, *Der Tirpitz-Plan*, passim; idem, 'Zu den Zielen des deutschen Flottenbaues unter Wilhelm II', *Historische Zeitschrift*, vol.210, no.1 (1970); idem, 'Flottenrüstung und Machtgefüge', in M. Stürmer (ed.), *Das kaiserliche Deutschland. Politik und Gesellschaft 1870–1918* (Düsseldorf, 1970).
11. In my opinion, a point well worth investigating, in view of his known devotion to Treitschke; his later role in the Vaterlandspartei; the arguments he used in the September 1899 Immediatvortrag (see Kennedy, 'Tirpitz', pp.38–41); and the tone of his *Politische Dokumente: Der Aufbau der deutschen Weltmacht*, vol.1 (Stuttgart & Berlin, 1924), pp.1–5, passim.
12. *Brassey's Naval Annual* (London, 1898).
13. Tirpitz, *Politische Dokumente*, i, p.7.
14. Idem, *Erinnerungen* (Leipzig, 1919), p.101.
15. For details of the Second Navy Law, see Berghahn, *Der Tirpitz-Plan*, pp.205–48.
16. BA-MA, F 2044, PG66074, Tirpitz Denkschrift zum Immediatvortrag, 28 September 1899.
17. BA-MA, F 2045, PG66080, Tirpitz memo, 9 March 1907, with accompanying table; Kelly, op.cit., pp.212–17; Berghahn, 'Zu den Zielen', passim.
18. Tables in Berghahn, *Der Tirpitz-Plan*, pp.607–17; Tirpitz, *Politsche Dokumente*, i, appendices.
19. BA, Bülow N1, Bd.24, Rede zum BudgetCommission (Entwurf), 27 March 1900.
20. BA, Richthofen N1, Bd.5, Bülow to Richthofen, Geheim, 26 July 1899. For further details of Bülow's role in the early part of the danger zone, see Berghahn, *Der Tirpitz-Plan*, 380–415; and P. M. Kennedy, 'German Weltpolitik and the Alliance Negotiations with England, 1897–1900', *Journal of Modern History*, xlv, no.4 (1973).
21. On the latter, see BA-MA, F 2044, PG66077, Tirpitz to Richthofen, 1 November 1904.
22. For Tirpitz's elaboration of this theory in the Reichstag, see *SBR*, X. Legislaturperiode, 1.Session (1898/1900), vol.iv, 119. Sitzung, 11 December 1899, pp.3295–6.
23. Steinberg, *Yesterday's Deterrent*, pp.208–9.
24. Tirpitz, *Politische Dokumente*, i, p.346.
25. BA-MA, Büchsel N1, Bd.11, Tirpitz to Büchsel, 29 July 1899.

26. BA-MA, F 5656, VI.1.–3, Bd.1, Grapow's draft memo, 19 January 1900. (There is a more polished version, entitled 'Betrachtungen über die Kriegführung Deutschlands zur See gegen England in den Jahren 1904 und 1920', in BA-MA, F 2036, PG66040.)

27. BA-MA, F 5587, III.1.–10, Bd.1, Immediatvortrag betreffend Grundzüge für einen Operationsplan Deutschlands allein gegen England allein, 31 May 1897, which summarizes much of the early discussion in that particular volume on planning against England; cf. BA-MA, F 7639, Bd.3, Bendemann Denkschrift zum Immediatvortrag, 'Die Defensive gegen England', 12 December 1899. German naval operations plans against England were surveyed by Captain Weniger, 'Die Entwicklung des Operationsplanes für die deutsche Schlachtflotte', *Marine Rundschau* (1930), pp.1–10, 51–9; but the article lacks references and avoids certain delicate political points.

28. BA-MA, F 5656, VI.1.–3, Bd.1, Grapow's draft memo, 19 January 1900.

29. Marder, *Dreadnought* i, p.431.

30. BA-MA, F 2044, PG66074, Tirpitz Denkschrift zum Immediatvortrag, 28 September 1899.

31. For a succinct survey of the two navies by 1914, see Marder, *Dreadnought*, i, pp.413–28.

32. BA, Bülow N1, Bd.24, Rede zum BudgetCommission (Entwurf), 27 March 1900. Bülow was of course trying to sway the political parties into supporting the Second Navy Law here (see Kennedy, 'Tirpitz', pp.35–6), but it was clear to all that without a stronger navy Germany's prospects in a war with Britain would be hopeless.

33. The question of a German invasion of England, much discussed by the British popular press, did not reach a very serious stage of planning in Berlin; but it was contemplated for a while in the very early *Oberkommando* drafts of operations plans in the years 1897–8. The more realistic assessments of what could be achieved in the near future, together with Schlieffen's demand that communications across the North Sea with the invasion army be maintained for at least seven days, caused the postponement of further planning. See the correspondence in BA-MA, F 5587, III.1.–10, Bd.1; and in Friedrich-Christian Stahl, 'Armee und Marine im kaiserlichen Deutschland', in *Die Entwicklung des Flottenkommandos*, pp.40–2 (vol.iv, *Beiträge zur Wehrforschung*). This topic was not seriously resumed, probably because of Germany's worsening position after 1905; but had things gone the way Tirpitz had originally planned, interest in it might well have revived. (The Kaiser's vapourings in December 1912 about 'eine Invasion grossen Stiles nach England' – see J. C. G. Röhl, 'Admiral von Müller and the Approach of War, 1911–1914', *Historical Journal*, xiii, no.4 (1969), p.663 – do not seem to have led to anything.)

Notes

34. Marder, *Anatomy*, pp.456–514; idem, *Dreadnought* i, pp.105ff; G. W. Monger, *The End of Isolation: British Foreign Policy 1900–1907* (London, 1963), pp.63, 68–9, 82–3.

35. On which see Marder, *Dreadnought*, vols.ii–v; and my articles on the surface war in Purnell's *History of the First World War* (London, 1969ff), vol.2, no.7; vol.4, no.14; vol.6, no.12; vol.8, no.14. The confusion and political incoherence in German government circles in the years 1904–5, when Tirpitz's strategical and foreign policy calculations began to fall apart, have been cleverly illustrated in Dr Steinberg's article, 'Germany and the Russo-Japanese War', *American Historical Review*, lxxxv, no.7 (1970).

36. Tirpitz, *Erinnerungen*, pp.57, 164.

37. Ibid., pp.129–30; idem, *Politische Dokumente*, i, p.7.

38. Marder, *Anatomy*, pp.456–9; E. L. Woodward, *Great Britain and the German Navy* (London, 1964 reprint), p.48.

39. Quoted in Monger, *The End of Isolation*, p.163.

40. Marder, *Anatomy*, pp.290–1.

41. BA-MA, F 2044, PG66074, Tirpitz Denkschrift zum Immediatvortrag, 28 September 1899.

42. Tirpitz, *Erinnerungen*, pp.54–60, 104–9, 167–72; idem, *Politische Dokumente*, i, pp.1–8.

43. BA-MA, Büchsel N1, Bd.11, Tirpitz to Büchsel, 29 July 1899.

44. *Brassey's Naval Annual* (1898).

45. Mahan, *The Influence of Sea Power*, p.539, footnote.

46. Selborne memo, 4 September 1901, quoted in C. J. Lowe, *The Reluctant Imperialists*, 2 vols (London, 1967), ii, p.130.

47. Marder, *Anatomy*, pp.209–33, 396–414.

48. Admiralty (Admiralty Records, Public Record Office, London) 116/900B, Confidential Memorandum on the Strategic Conditions governing the Coast Defences of the United Kingdom in war as affected by naval considerations, March 1902.

49. BA-MA, Levetzow N1, Bd.100, Ausarbeitung Levetzows, 'Operationen zur Erkämpfung der Seeherrschaft' (1902?).

50. Admiralty 116/940B, Arnold-Forster memo on Observations on a visit to Germany, 15 September 1902.

51. 'A Statement of Admiralty Policy', 1905 (Cd.2791), p.6; copy in BA-MA, F 5521, III.1.–E.28, Bd.1.

52. Quoted partly in Marder, *Dreadnought*, i, p.125; and Monger, p.310.

53. Admiralty 116/942, Fisher to Prince of Wales, 23 October 1906.

54. Naval Library, Earls Court, Pre-War Despatches from the Naval Attaché, Berlin (1903–14), Captain Watson to Goschen, 9 October 1913.

55. BA-MA, F 5587, III.1.–10, Bd.1, AIII (Scheder?) minute of 11 March 1896 on Diederichs memo, 'Gesichtspunkte für einen Oper-

ationsplan der feindischen Streitkräfte bei einem Kriege Deutschlands allein gegen England allein', 3 March 1896. See also the comment of AVII of 9 March 1896 that, if the British attacked, it would be with large numbers. (*Admiralstab* officers rarely placed their signature under a minute, preferring to give their staff number instead, as above.)

56. Ibid., Anlage I zu Knorr's Immediatvortrag betreffend Grundzüge für einen Operationsplan Deutschlands allein gegen England allein, 31 May 1897; ibid., AIII^b memo, 16 December 1897; ibid., AIII^a (Scheder) memo, 5 January 1898.

57. BA-MA, F 5587, III.1.N.10, Bd.1, Souchon memo, 'Krieg mit England', 22 November 1902.

58. BA-MA, F 5588, III.1.–10^a, Bd.1, Souchon marginal comment on Grapow's memo, 'Welche Aussichten bietet für uns die Führung eines Kreuzerkrieges gegen England?', 20 September 1902.

59. Ibid., Abeken memo, 'Die Kriegführung gegen England', summer 1902.

60. BA-MA, F 5587, III.1.N.10, Bd.2, Büchsel Denkschrift zum Immediatvortrag über den Aufmarsch und der Verwendung E. M. Flotte im Kriege gegen England im Ms. Jahre 1905, 20 March 1905.

61. Quoted by W. C. B. Tunstall, 'Imperial Defence, 1897–1914', in E. A. Benians, J. Butler and C. E. Carrington (eds), *The Cambridge History of the British Empire*, vol.iii (Cambridge, 1959), p.571.

62. Marder, *Dreadnought*, i, p.367.

63. On which theme, see D. C. Gordon, 'The Admiralty and Dominion Navies, 1902–1914', *Journal of Modern History*, xxxiii, no.4 (1961).

64. Mahan, *The Influence of Sea Power*, p.138.

65. Ibid., pp.507, 511.

66. The meaning of 'command of the sea' is most brilliantly explained in an introduction (by Corbett) to a 1907 British war plan, now reproduced in *The Papers of Admiral Sir John Fisher*, vol.ii, edited by P. K. Kemp (London, 1964), pp.320–3. (Navy Records Society, vol. CVI.)

67. Admiralty 116/866B, 'The Protection of Ocean Trade in Time of War', memo of secret Admiralty conference of 31 April 1905. (The very title of this memo suggests again that discussion about offensive British naval actions related to a *guerre de course* situation.)

68. Admiralty 116/1036B, Captain Slade memo, 'War with Germany', 1 September 1906; the final draft is reproduced in *Fisher Papers*, ii, pp.346ff.

69. The most thorough appraisal of British planning is contained in the study by Neil W. Summerton, *The Development of British Military Planning for a War against Germany, 1904–1914*, 2 vols (unpublished PhD thesis, London, 1970). Dr Summerton shows conclusively that

both the Admiralty and War Office held that it would be useless to assault the German coast or offshore islands in a purely Anglo-German war. If the British government decided to support France in the event of German aggression, then Fisher and A. K. Wilson held that such amphibious operations should be carried out, whatever the cost; but the War Office consistently criticized such wild schemes and preferred to send direct military assistance to France or Belgium. See pp.34–49, 59, 220–97, 320–41, 451–71, 622–8.

70. Mahan, *The Influence of Sea Power*, pp.85, 138.

71. Marder, *Anatomy*, pp.109–15; idem, *Dreadnought*, i, pp.367–83; W. E. Livezey, *Mahan on Sea Power* (Norman, Oklahoma, 1947), pp.280–1.

72. Admiralty 116/1043B. 'W.1. War Plan against Germany, 1908'; Marder, *Dreadnought*, i, pp.369–77.

73. H. Hallmann, *Der Weg zum deutschen Schlachtflottenbau* (Stuttgart, 1933), pp.240–1.

74. BA-MA, F 5587, III.1.N.10, Bd.1, Büchsel minute on November 1899 Bendemann memo, 'Die Defensive gegen England'.

75. Ibid., Bd.2, Boedecker memo, 'Kriegführung gegen England', 15 March 1904.

76. BA-MA, F 5588, III.1.–10ᵃ, Bd.1, Heeringen Denkschrift betreffend Krieg zwischen Deutschland und England, 12 April 1902.

77. Ibid., Bd.2, Büchsel memo of 8 January 1904.

78. BA-MA, F 5587, III.1.N.10, Bd.2, Büchsel Denkschrift über Kriegführung gegen England, 1906.

79. 'Dann werden unsere U-Boote es schaffen müssen!' he added prophetically. Quoted in K. Assmann, *Deutsche Seestrategie in zwei Weltkriege* (Heidelberg, 1957), p.30. For Pohl's view, see his minute on Müller to RMA (copy), no.689 of 30 July 1914, in BA-MA, F 5522, II.–E.30, Bd.3. For a short resumé of the operations plans against England in the years 1906–14, see Weniger, pp.3–7.

80. These criticisms are summarized in Kennedy, 'Tirpitz', pp.48–52; and Berghahn, *Der Tirpitz-Plan*, passim.

81. As the British Foreign and Colonial Offices were well aware: see their protests in 1907 against the Royal Navy's abandonment of its worldwide 'police' role in: CO (Colonial Office Records, Public Record Office, London) 537/348, paper 5520 Secret, 'Distribution of the Navy'.

82. This conclusion is also reached by Livezey, *Mahan*, pp.69, 273–4; and M. T. Sprout, 'Mahan: Evangelist of Sea Power', in E. M. Earle (ed.), *Makers of Modern Strategy: Military Thought from Machiavelli to Hitler* (Princeton, 1943), p.443.

83. W. Wegener, *Die Seestrategie des Weltkrieges* (Berlin, 1929), passim.

84. BA-MA, F 5587, III.1.N.10, Bd.3, Auszug aus einem vorläufigen

Exposé über Blockadewirkungen bei einem Kriege England-Deutschland, 13 March 1906.

85. BA-MA, F 737, PG69174, Behncke memo, Ganz Geheim, 22 August 1914, 'Ausnutzung der belgisch-französischen Küste für die Kriegführung gegen England'; ibid., Pohl to Behncke, Ganz Geheim, 18 September 1914, and reply of 10 October 1914; ibid., Behncke memo, 24 October 1914, 'Kriegführung gegen England von belgisch-französischen Häfen und der Schelde aus'; BA-MA, Tirpitz N1, Bd.262, Tirpitz to Landrat a.D. Winckler, vertraulich, 24 December 1914 (copy); ibid., Bd.104, Tirpitz Denkschrift, 16 January 1915.

86. Ibid., Bd.141, Tirpitz memo, 'Die Bedeutung Belgiens und seinen Häfen für unsere Seegeltung', October 1915.

87. Ibid.; see also Hans W. Gatzke, *Germany's Drive to the West: a Study of Germany's Western War Aims during the First World War* (Baltimore, 1950), pp.49, 60–2, 80, 159–60, 208–9, 213.

88. Quoted in Berghahn, 'Zu den Zielen', p.67.

89. Marder, *Anatomy*, p.65; idem, *Dreadnought*, i, pp.3, 273.

90. Ibid., p.432.

91. A. T. Mahan, *Retrospect and Prospect: Studies in International Relations Naval and Political* (London, 1902), pp.165–6. The quotation is from an article called 'Considerations Governing the Dispositions of Navies', published also in the *National Review* (1902).

92. BA-MA, F 2044, PG66074, Tirpitz Denkschrift zum Immediatvortrag, 28 September 1899.

93. Berghahn, 'Zu den Zielen', pp.63–70.

94. Ibid., p.63.

95. Idem, *Der Tirpitz-Plan*, pp.170, 506–8, 557.

96. Tirpitz, *Erinnerungen*, p.110.

97. K. F. Nowak and F. Thimme (eds), *Erinnerungen und Gedanken des Botschafters Anton Graf Monts* (Berlin, 1922), p.194.

98. Fürst Chlodwig zu Hohenlohe-Schillingsfürst, *Denkwürdigkeiten der Reichskanzlerzeit*, edited by K. A. von Müller (Stuttgart, 1931), p.464.

99. Kennedy, 'Tirpitz', p.54.

100. BA-MA, Tirpitz N1. Bd.100 Tirpitz to Lans, 31 August 1914 (my stress), and compare with the version in *Politische Dokumente*, ii, pp.81–3. Important here is not so much the date but the clause beginning 'This natural and single aim . . .' which indicates that it was not solely the outset of war which caused a sudden increase in Tirpitz's final aims, but that these had been secretly held for the previous two decades.

6. Arms-races and the Causes of War, 1850–1945

Not previously published.

Notes

1. For general background, the following are useful: J. F. C. Fuller, *The Conduct of War 1789–1961* (London, 1961); M. Pearton, *The Knowledgeable State: Diplomacy, War and Technology since 1830* (London, 1982); W. McElwee, *The Art of War, Waterloo to Mons* (London, 1974); W. H. McNeill, *The Pursuit of Power: Technology, Armed Force and Society since 1000 A.D.* (London, 1983); E. B. Potter (ed.), *Sea Power* (Annapolis, 2nd edition, 1981).

2. Viscount Grey, *Twenty-Five Years*, 2 vols (London & New York, 1925), i, pp.89–90.

3. P. M. Kennedy, *The Rise and Fall of British Naval Mastery* (London & New York, 1976), pp.172–4; A. J. Marder, *The Anatomy of British Sea Power* (Hamden, Conn., reprint, 1964), pp.66–8. I. F. Clarke, *Voices Prophesying War 1763–1984* (London, paperback edition, 1970), pp.25–9, sets this in the broader context of nineteenth-century invasion scares.

4. For details, see G. F. Kennan, *The Decline of Bismarck's European Order* (Princeton, 1979), passim; P. M. Kennedy, *The Rise of the Anglo-German Antagonism, 1860–1914* (London & Boston, 1980), pp.186ff.

5. Marder, *The Anatomy of British Sea Power*, is still the best treatment here. Also very useful is J. J. Sumida, *Financial Limitation, Technological Innovation, and British Naval Policy, 1904–1910* (PhD thesis, University of Chicago, 1982), chapter 1.

6. Kennedy, *The Rise of the Anglo-German Antagonism*, chapter 14.

7. Ibid., pp.415–31.

8. Full details are in S. W. Roskill, *Naval Policy between the Wars*, vol.1 (London, 1968).

9. J. L. Herkless, 'Lord Clarendon's attempt at Franco-Prussian disarmament, January to March 1870', *Historical Journal*, vol.xv (1972), pp.455–70; K. Hildebrand, 'Lord Clarendon, Bismarck und das Problem der europäischen Abrüstung 1870', in L. Kettenacker, M. Schlenke and H. Seier (eds), *Studien zur Geschichte Englands und der deutsch-britischen Beziehungen* (Munich, 1981), pp.130–52.

10. For what follows, see J. Dülffer, *Regeln gegen den Krieg? Die Haager Friedenskonferenzen 1899 und 1907 in der internationalen Politik* (Frankfurt, 1981).

11. E. W. Bennett, *German Rearmament and the West, 1932–33* (Princeton, 1979), is excellent here.

12. For some flavour of that controversy, see J. T. Walton Newbold, *How Europe Armed for War* (London, 1916); P. Noel-Baker, *The Private Manufacture of Armaments*, vol.1 (London, 1936); Marder, *The Anatomy of British Sea Power*, chapter III; A. J. P. Taylor, *The Trouble Makers* (London, 1969 edition), chapters IV–VI; C. Trebilcock, 'Legends of the British Armaments Industry, 1890–1914: a Revision', *Journal of Contemporary History*, vol.v (1970).

13. Again, this does not mean that (for example) the US arms lobby does not seek an increase in armaments spending; but simply that it does not *control* the process. See J. S. Gansler, *The Defense Industry* (Cambridge, Mass., 1980), for a convincing analysis of the large-scale post-Vietnam War reductions in defence spending and the impact upon the armaments industry – which left it ill-equipped to produce the required weaponry when Reagan followed Carter, with *political* views on the international order quite different from those of his predecessor.
14. Kennedy, *The Rise of the Anglo-German Antagonism*, chapters 15, 16 and Conclusion; F. Fischer, *Germany's Aims in the First World War* (London, 1967), chapter 1; L. L. Farrar; *Arrogance and Anxiety. The Ambivalence of German Power, 1848–1914* (Iowa City, Iowa, 1981), passim.
15. Offering a full booklist here would be pointless. Interested readers could begin with: W. Carr, *Arms, Autarky And Aggression: a Study in German Foreign Policy 1933–1939* (London, 1972); B. Carroll, *Total War. Arms and Economics in the Third Reich* (The Hague, 1968); J. B. Crowley, *Japan's Quest for Autonomy* (Princeton, 1966); M. A. Barnhart, 'Japan's Economic Security and the Origins of the Pacific War', *Journal of Strategic Studies*, vol.4 (1981), pp.105–24; D. Mack Smith, *Mussolini's Roman Empire* (London, 1977 edition).
16. At least, since Professor McNeill would put the beginning of the process much earlier: see again, *The Pursuit of Power*, passim.

7. Japanese Strategic Decisions, 1939–45

(Originally published in Purnell's *History of the Second World War*, volume 8, no.3 (London, 1968), pp.3216–20.

8. Why Did the British Empire Last So Long?

Not previously published.

1. University of Nottingham, Cust Foundation lectures list, 1921–70. (The present essay is the first revived Cust lecture, following a twelve-year gap.)
2. A. P. Thornton, *The Imperial Idea and Its Enemies* (London, 1959).
3. R. Robinson and J. Gallagher, with A. Denny, *Africa and the Victorians* (London, 1961).
4. B. Porter, *The Lion's Share: a Short History of British Imperialism 1850–1970* (London, 1975), pp.353–4.
5. C. Cross, *The Fall of the British Empire 1918–1968* (London, 1968);

Notes

C. Barnett, *The Collapse of British Power* (London, 1972); M. Beloff, *Imperial Sunset*, vol.1, *Britain's Liberal Empire 1897–1921* (London, 1969); G. Woodcock, *Who Killed the British Empire?* (London, 1974); F. S. Northedge, *The Troubled Giant* (London, 1966); R. Shannon, *The Crisis of Imperialism, 1865–1915* (London, 1974); D. Dilks (ed.), *Retreat from Power*, 2 vols (London, 1981).

6. W. D. Gruner, 'The British Political, Social and Economic System and the Decision for Peace and War: Reflections on Anglo-German Relations 1800–1939', *British Journal of International Studies*, vol.6, no.3 (1980), p.194, fn.5; E. Ingram, *Commitment to Empire: Prophecies of the Great Game in Asia 1797–1800* (Oxford, 1981), especially Introduction; E. L. Presseisen, *Amiens and Munich: Comparisons in Appeasement* (The Hague, 1978).

7. Barnett, *The Collapse of British Power*, pp.74, 120.

8. P. M. Kennedy, *The Rise of the Anglo-German Antagonism, 1860–1914* (London & Boston, 1980), chapters 15–18, covers those prewar attitudes.

9. P. M. Kennedy, *The Rise and Fall of British Naval Mastery* (London & New York, 1976), chapters 7 and 8.

10. W. R. Louis, *Imperialism at Bay* (Oxford, 1978); C. Thorne, *Allies of a Kind* (London, 1978).

11. G. Orwell, *The Road to Wigan Pier* (Harmondsworth, 1962 edition), pp.139–40.

12. For the figures, see Porter, *The Lion's Share*, pp.121, 260–1, 320–1.

13. Ibid., chapter VIII; Barnett, *The Collapse of British Power*, chapters IV and V.

14. Cross, *The Fall of the British Empire*, p.181.

15. I. M. Drummond, *British Economic Policy and the Empire 1919–1939* (London, 1972), chapter 3; W. K. Hancock, *Survey of British Commonwealth Affairs*, vol.II, *Problems of Economic Policy 1918–1939*, part 2 (London, 1942), chapter II; J. M. Lee and M. Petter, *The Colonial Office, War and Development Policy* (London, 1982). The Indian difficulties are well covered in B. R. Tomlinson, *The Political Economy of the Raj 1914–1947* (Cambridge, 1979), who also offers more general ideas in 'The Contraction of England: National Decline and the Loss of Empire', *Journal of Imperial and Commonwealth History*, vol.xi (October 1982), pp.58–72.

16. R. F. Holland, *Britain and the Commonwealth Alliance 1918–39* (London, 1981), chapter 10.

17. G. Barraclough, *An Introduction to Contemporary History* (Harmondsworth, 1967), chapter III; Kennedy, *The Rise and Fall of British Naval Mastery*, chapter 7.

18. Cited in ibid., p.158.
19. For details, see Kennedy, *The Rise of the Anglo-German Antagonism*, chapters 15 and 16.
20. C. A. MacDonald, *The United States, Britain and Appeasement 1937–1939* (London, 1981).
21. P. M. Kennedy, 'The Tradition of Appeasement in British Foreign Policy, 1865–1939', essay 1 in this book, p.16 above.
22. Quotations from P. Kennedy, *The Realities behind Diplomacy: Background Influences on British External Policy, 1865–1980* (London, 1981), pp.27, 229.
23. Ibid., pp.58–73, 253ff.

Index

Index

(of people, places, events and institutions)

Index